The G

MANCHESTER
UNIVERSITY PRESS

TEXTS · IN · CULTURE

This series offers specially commissioned, cross-disciplinary essays on texts of seminal importance to Western culture. Each text has had an impact on the way we think, write and live beyond the confines of its original discipline, and it is only through an understanding of its multiple meanings that we can fully appreciate its importance.

TEXTS · IN · CULTURE

THE
GREAT EXHIBITION
OF 1851
New interdisciplinary essays

LOUISE PURBRICK
editor

Manchester University Press
Manchester and New York
distributed exclusively in the USA by Palgrave

Published by Manchester University Press
Oxford Road, Manchester M13 9NR, UK
and Room 400, 175 Fifth Avenue, New York, NY 10010, USA
http://www.manchesteruniversitypress.co.uk

Distributed exclusively in the USA by
Palgrave, 175 Fifth Avenue, New York, NY 10010, USA

Distributed exclusively in Canada by
UBC Press, University of British Columbia, 2029 West Mall, Vancouver, BC, Canada v6T 1Z2

British Library Cataloguing-in-Publication Data
A catalogue record is available from the British Library

Library of Congress Cataloging-in-Publication Data applied for

ISBN 0 7190 5591 1 *hardback*
  0 7190 5592 x *paperback*

First published 2001

08 07 06 05 04 03 02 01   10 9 8 7 6 5 4 3 2 1

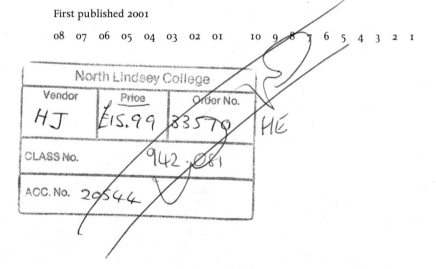

Typeset in Apollo by Koinonia, Manchester
Printed in Great Britain
by Bookcraft (Bath) Ltd, Midsomer Norton

Contents

List of figures

Figures 2.1, 2.2, 2.3 and 2.4 are reproduced with the permission of the
Manchester Metropolitan University Library; 4.1 and 4.2 are reproduced with the permission of the University of Sussex Library; all
other illustrations are reproduced with the permission of the University
of Brighton, Special Collection, Faculty of Arts and Architecture
Library at St Peter's House.

Series introduction

Texts are produced in particular cultures and in particular historical circumstances. In turn, they shape and are shaped by those cultures as they are read and re-read in changing circumstances by different groups with different commitments, engagements and interests. Such readings are themselves then re-absorbed into the ideological frameworks within which the cultures develop. The seminal works drawn on by cultures thus have multiple existences within them, exerting their influence in distinct and perhaps contradictory ways. As these texts have been 'claimed' by particular academic disciplines, however, their larger cultural significance has often been obscured.

Recent work in cultural history and textual theory has stimulated critical awareness of the complex relations between texts and cultures, highlighting the limits of current academic formations and opening the possibility of new approaches to interdisciplinarity. At the same time, however, the difficulties of interdisciplinary work have become increasingly apparent at all levels of research and teaching. On the one hand the abandonment of disciplinary specialisms may lead to amorphousness rather than challenging interdisciplinarity; on the other, interdisciplinary approaches may in the end simply create new specialisms or sub-specialisms, with their own well guarded boundaries. In these circumstances, yesterday's ground-breaking interdisciplinary study may become today's autonomous (and so potentially circumscribed) discipline, as has happened, it might be argued, in the case of some forms of History of Ideas.

The volumes in this series highlight the advantages of interdisciplinary work while at the same time encouraging a critical reflexiveness about its limits and possibilities; they seek to stimulate consideration both of the distinctiveness and integrity of individual disciplines, and of the transgressive potential of interdisciplinarity. Each volume offers a collection of new essays on a text of seminal intellectual and cultural importance, displaying the insights to be gained from the juxtaposition of disciplinary perspectives and from the negotiation of disciplinary boundaries. The volumes represent a challenge to the conception of authorship which locates the significance of the text in the individual act of creation; but we assume that no issues (including those of interdisciplinarity and authorship) are foreclosed, and that individual volumes drawing contributions from a broad range of disciplinary standpoints, will raise questions about the texts they examine more by the perceived disparities of approach that they encompass than by any interpretative consensus that they demonstrate.

All essays are specially commissioned for the series and are designed to be approachable to non-specialist as well as specialist readers: substantial editorial introductions provide a framework for the debates conducted in each volume, and highlight the issues involved.

We would, finally, like to dedicate the series to the memory of our colleague Stephen Copley, whose insight and energy started it all.

Jeff Wallace, University of Glamorgan
John Whale, University of Leeds
SERIES EDITORS

Acknowledgements

I want to thank Brian Maidment; he helped develop this collection of essays in its early stages and his consideration of mid-nineteeth century literature and the Great Exhibition significantly shaped its content.

I would like to thank Monica Brewis for her assistance with the illustrations. Rafael Cardoso Denis wishes to acknowledge the support of the Brazilian Ministry of Education (CAPES) in funding the research upon which his essay, included in this volume, was based. Sara Peacock copy-edited the whole work with consideration as well as accuracy and she deserves special thanks here.

Chronology

Introduction

LOUISE PURBRICK

1851 and the problem of periodisation

The Great Exhibition of the Works of Industry of All Nations held in Hyde Park, London, in 1851, opens nineteenth-century histories as if it was a revolution, a coronation, the last year of a war or the first of a parliament. Although, of course, it was none of these things, the year in which it took place provides a point of departure for historical accounts of European design and art, French and American literature, English society, British politics, British imperialism, Victorian culture and patterns of consumption.[1] The Great Exhibition has been used to provide nineteenth-century origins for various historical phenomena. It would appear that after 1851 the principles of modern design are accepted, shopping becomes dreaming, empire is popularised and the working class no longer presents a revolutionary threat since its representatives visited Crystal Palace and learnt how to behave in public. A series of different things, which tend only to be occasionally connected and not closely related, seem to have occurred for the first time in the same place.

Not all histories which begin in 1851 claim the Great Exhibition is a place of origins. Sometimes it is just somewhere to summarise from: 'a perfect vantage point for a survey of nineteenth-century England', according to Asa Briggs,[2] while Nikolas Pevsner called Crystal Palace 'the mid-nineteenth century touchstone' which not only revealed 'what belongs wholly to the nineteenth century', but also indicated features of the following century, 'what points forward into the twentieth'.[3] There is a

tendency to introduce the Great Exhibition in order to summarise the future rather than assess the past. Thus, even when it
is inserted for periodisation purposes only and is a fairly
arbitrary historical beginning, it appears as an inaugural event,
an announcement of a new regime. The assumption that any
collection of objects contained in a building has the capacity to
signal a change of historical time, or even to instigate that change,
as it is sometimes implied about the Great Exhibition, is an
important historical manoeuvre and deserves careful consideration.

The assumed historical effect of the Great Exhibition is
usually based upon its identification as an early example of
modernist form. Crystal Palace was actually and aesthetically
functional. Quickly constructed from industrial materials, prefabri-
cated glass and iron, it was architecturally completely modern.[4]
For one famous visitor, Crystal Palace simply 'stands for modernity'.[5] Its collection of industrial objects have either been characterised as mechanical or referred to as commodified, both of which
express the technological materialism of modernity. Accounts of
the exhibits, both official and popular, also delivered a modern
political version of imperial relationships in which British superiority over Africa and Asia was represented as an effect of
industrial skill rather than the result of military conquest or
commercial subjugation. And, to visit the Great Exhibition, enter
its building and see its collection, was to participate voluntarily in
an officially sanctioned display of things; visitors thus inhabited
the modern political subjectivities associated with consenting and
consuming.

These instances of architectural, economic and political
modernism derived from the systematic industrial vision of the
Great Exhibition. It presented an ideal industrial world. The
enormous quantities of exhibited manufactures, regardless of how
they were actually produced, seemed to owe their existence to the
benevolence of the machines, while these exhibits, displayed
without the demands of actual production, illustrated the achievement of industrial technology without reference to conditions of
industrial labour. Visitors were positioned as the recipients of
industrial plenty produced by mechanical means. Six million
visits were made to the Great Exhibition during the entire period
when it was open, from 1 May to 31 October, and most were on

the Shilling Days: Mondays to Thursdays from 26 May. Each of these days repeated a performance of rational recreation where industrial workers learnt in their own time about the benefits of a technological regime. There would not have been enough time on any day to study each of the hundred thousand exhibits, but all visitors were witnesses to the demonstration of industrial quantity.

Thus the Great Exhibition suggested the significance of industry. But Sylvi Johansen has argued that rather than register-ing agreed industrial achievements, the Exhibition was an attempt to universalise their importance, equating industrial develop-ment with that of the state and nation. Johansen presents a political landscape before the Exhibition, at 'the beginning of 1850, or even later', that was largely undetermined; 'there was no clear and concise discourse that defined the nature of Britain' she states, maintaining that the relative importance of agriculture and industry was not agreed.[6] While a political settlement between a landed order and industrial capital has been linked to dates earlier in the nineteenth century than 1851, associated with the Reform Act of 1832 and the repeal of the Corn Laws in 1846, Johansen implies that such a settlement, which relates to the periodisation of bourgeois ascendancy, was not finalised until the Great Exhibition. According to her, the Exhibition 'was intended to remedy the tendency to marginalise industry', and did so successfully, 'showing that industrial production was not a strictly sectoral activity, but was beneficial to everyone not only in Britain but in the whole world'.[7]

The use of industrial production to represent industrial interests has been recognised as a remarkable historical moment. 'At one stage in the history of industry, it displayed a culture for itself', Molly Nesbitt writes of nineteenth-century international exhibitions, 'rather than as came to be the case, using another kind of culture to represent its interests'.[8] Marshall Berman has made a similar point about the Great Exhibition of 1851. Its direct style of class representation did not last. 'The bourgeoisie enjoyed the Exhibition, but rejected the building and went back to building Arthurian railroad stations and Hellenistic banks.' Berman concludes that 'no more genuinely modern buildings would be built in England for another fifty years'.[9] The unequivocal

industrialism of 1851 and its obvious class associations made it a
unique nineteenth-century event. Both Nesbitt and Berman have
reflected upon the mediated representation of industrial culture
that followed the Great Exhibition. Its expression of modernism
was indeed early, and only eventually influential rather than
quickly effective. If it was an announcement of a new regime, it
was of one which did not begin immediately; it was a false start.
Berman describes 'the unwillingness of the British bourgeoisie to
accept and live with such a brilliant expression of its own
modernity' as a strategic error caused by a failure of imagination.
'In retrospect', he suggests, '1851 appears as its zenith and the
beginning of its gradual decline'.[10] He inserts the Crystal Palace
into an account of a bourgeois cultural authority which waned
from almost the very moment that it was accomplished.

It is possible, without entirely accepting the cultural decline
of the bourgeoisie thesis, to consider the atypicality of the Great
Exhibition and question why a one-off nineteenth-century modern
form has become such an important tool of periodisation. There is
a convenient chronology: the Exhibition happened about half
way through the nineteenth century. The same could apply to
the 10 April Chartist demonstration, but 1848 is a much less
preferred mid-century marker. John Saville has suggested a
relationship between these two dates, or rather these two events,
the first a mass political assembly and the second a huge
exhibition, both of which took place in Hyde Park and are often
simply referred to by their dates, 1848 and 1851. In his book
entitled *1848* (1987), Saville argues that 1851 contributed a state
of amnesia about the political significance of Chartism and the
extent of its state suppression. '[T]he strength that continued in
Chartism in the months that followed the events of 10 April, and
even the memory of the mass arrests and jailings were wiped
from public memory'. The Great Exhibition of 1851, with other
high-profile national events, 'much assisted the processes of
indifference and forgetfulness'.[11]

Histories which begin by using 1851 to summarise the mid-
nineteenth century cannot help but continue to diminish the
significance of 1848. However, work which focuses on the Great
Exhibition itself does not necessarily demonstrate a preference
for exhibitions over revolutions and tends to be interested in the

historical management of class confrontation, how a 'problem of order' became 'one of culture'.[12] Cultural institutions formed around the mid-nineteenth century combined education with entertainment and developed strategies of incorporation of oppositional subjects into the hierarchies of the state. Visiting displays of material splendour of various kinds shown in national museums or at international exhibitions enforced, for instance, the adoption of acceptable codes of public conduct. Thus, the Great Exhibition of 1851 continued the project of state management of class affairs by concluding a phase of open warfare with cultural domination. That is to say, it was not a beginning but an ending. It demonstrated the completion, as Philip Corrigan and Derek Sayer have suggested in *The Great Arch* (1985), of English state formation. 'What else was the Great Exhibition of 1851 unveiling to the world?'[13]

Historical interest in the Exhibition has not, then, attempted to avoid a discussion of state power and class structure, but using 1851 rather than 1848 to address the issues of the mid-nineteenth century has reflected a significant shift in the disciplines of history about what counts as a key historical event. The importance placed on the interpretation of culture within social history and the development of cultural history as discipline or distinct subject area, in particular, has focused scholarly attention upon the undeclared politics of cultural expression rather than upon the cultural practices of the formally political. The investigation of worlds not already marked out as politically significant, the study of cultures which appear peripheral or seem routine because they are removed from national-scale decision-making, is now a recognised method of historical work which has produced new periodisations and new understandings of what is significant. Despite its display of routinely consumed objects from colonial peripheries and some overlap between industrial exhibits and everyday things, the Great Exhibition did not occur within an everyday world. It was a popular event, but exhibitions are, by definition, not of the everyday; they interrupt its cultural patterns. Visiting an exhibition distracts from the repetition of daily matters and looking around the exhibited collection encourages reflection upon objects by prohibiting their habitual use: suspending the practices of culture for its contemplation.[14]

Thus, the Great Exhibition was extraordinary and, as such, has been recorded within a traditionally elite historical canon of events comprising exceptional moments and great achievements. This Exhibition, and those that followed its international and industrial format, feature within established historical frameworks which trace the development of national and modern life. Great exhibitions punctuate and celebrate the movement of both through time. They have, Tony Bennett comments, 'aimed to overlap these two times – of nation and modernity – on to one another by projecting the host nation as among the foremost representatives of the time, and tasks, of modernity'. This, he argues, 'was the pattern established by the Great Exhibition of 1851'.[15] The attempts to recapture a leading nation identity by using rhetorical and structural references to 1851 at subsequent exhibitions, most notably at the Festival of Britain in 1951 and the Dome Experience of 2000, confirms a lasting influence. A Crystal Palace from the mid-nineteenth century is still appealing and, at least for the state sponsors of industrial displays, remains a desirable model to reproduce, because it held both representational power and popularity. It produced a picture of modern success in front of a mass audience; a great many people witnessed, and in doing so participated in, a representational event which was not of their own making. The Great Exhibition was, and is, a compelling historical form.

Great Exhibition histories

The significance of the Great Exhibition is sometimes related to its large scale, the quantity of objects it housed and the amount of people who visited it. Its historical record, however, is neither a collection of all the meanings of each of the objects nor the sum of the visitors' responses to their display, far from it. Layers of meaning about the Great Exhibition have been produced in published contemporary assessments and in subsequent historical writing. Simultaneously an aesthetic and industrial, cultural and commercial, popular and imperial event, the understanding of its effect also has been revised with almost every academic trend and new disciplinary concern. It has been used to demonstrate how, in mid- to late nineteenth-century England, stability was established in society by increased prosperity or was secured with state power. It has exemplified the class politics of commodity culture and then the nationalism of imperial display. These are simplifications; the lines of historical interpretation of the Great Exhibition are more messy. Histories of 1851 overlap at some points, then diverge at others. Points of difference, precisely where contrasting accounts conflict, are not always immediately apparent. The intention of this part of my introduction is to make some sense of the Exhibition's dense significance by tracing the shifting focus of historical inquiry. There are different types of Great Exhibition history and the first was written by its organisers.

The first official historical representation
The organisers of the Great Exhibition produced and published their own history of it. The Exhibition has been called 'the best documented event of the nineteenth century'[16] and the most widely consulted are the official records of the Royal Society of Arts and Royal Commissioners of 1851; their reports and lectures have been a first call for historical information. A historical framework was provided by Henry Cole, a central figure in both organisations. His introduction to the *Official Descriptive and Illustrated Catalogue of the Industry of All Nations* (1851) presents itself as a history of the Exhibition and has been used as such despite being in print before the Exhibition closed. Cole did not reflect upon the Exhibition and its content; he would not have had the time. Rather, he describes the events that led up to the display: the Society of Arts was founded; national industrial exhibitions were held in France and Dublin; Prince Albert expressed the idea of an international exhibition; the Royal Commission of 1851 was instituted, which promoted the Exhibition (and did so in Anti-Corn Law League style) then determined the classification system, adopted Joseph Paxton's building design, decided the floor-plan, agreed the entry prices, arranged for the publication of the catalogues, established the juries which evaluated the objects, and awarded prizes.[17]

It is hardly surprising that the subject of the organiser's history of the Great Exhibition is its organisation. The narrative space of Cole's 'Introduction' is taken up with administrative details. His account of the Great Exhibition is a history of how it happened, which has become its standard version. Histories published around the time of the Festival of Britain in 1951 follow the sequence of events set out by Cole, emphasise the achievement of arranging the Exhibition and thus find its meaning in its making.[18] This is the stuff of liberal narratives: precedents are shown to have been improved upon; set-backs contribute to eventual success; decision-making is the heroic endeavour of individuals.

When Cole did reflect upon the Great Exhibition, in a Royal Society of Arts lecture delivered after it closed, he claimed its most important effect was derived from the fact that it happened. The act of arranging a collection of industrial products from different nations instituted friendly international relationships and thus contributed to world peace. The lecture is another formulation of the making of the Great Exhibition as a narrative of achievement which demonstrates Cole's commitment to liberal politics rather than just his use of liberal historical conventions. He considered why, rather than how, it took place. He gave two reasons for its location: 'England, beyond any other nation, was prepared', he claimed, 'by the cosmopolitan character of its people and by its commercial policy, to be the first nation to carry out an International Exhibition of Industry'.[19] Cole had already suggested that 'an event like this Exhibition could not have taken place at any earlier period, and perhaps not among any other people than ourselves'.[20] For him, the background to the Exhibition was the historical development of international capitalism and that of the English race; but the decisive factor in the siting of the Great Exhibition in London rather than anywhere else, and especially rather than Paris, was free trade. 'In France, an International Exhibition was a philosophical theory, and must remain a bauble to be talked about until she alters her commercial tariff.'[21]

Free trade was not only an economic principle promoted by Cole and other Exhibition organisers; they believed it was the sign of political liberty and a condition of international peace. A projection of the world as a free market and at peace was produced by the Great Exhibition. Participating in it, sending exhibits which were both industrial products and national objects, was premised on a mix of co-operation and competition;

it was a performance of a liberal dream of international politics being based in commercial relationships, in friendly exchanges. Free trade was idealised as a form of international communication.[22]

In its first and official history, and without any appraisal of its specific contents, the Great Exhibition is conceived as a political event, and as a success. Details are given of only one of its material constituents: Crystal Palace. Matthew Digby Wyatt's 'The construction of the building' follows Henry Cole's 'Introduction' in the *Official Catalogue*. Digby Wyatt repeated and rephrased Cole's liberal themes, which become expressed in a condensed form in Crystal Palace:

> Had the circumstances determined that the present industrial position of England should have been represented by the building alone ... it is singular to remark how few elements, essential to her commercial success, would have been lost sight of.
>
> The happy condition of liberty of the subject would have been attested by the circumstance of its having been in the power of the people alone to will the existence of such a structure; while the fact that the whole expenses had been provided for without in any way trenching on the national resources, would have evidenced at once the wealth and the spirit of enterprise common to every class of society.[23]

Using Crystal Palace to summarise the Great Exhibition with the suggestion that it also symptomatic of something else is an early interpretative strategy subsequently often repeated. For Digby Wyatt, the building stood in for the English contribution to the Exhibition and English liberalism. In twentieth-century historical criticism, however, it has come to represent a conflicting variety of forms in urban and modern European life.

On the objects

The first substantial re-assessment of the Great Exhibition of 1851 is offered in Nikolas Pevsner's account of the historical development of modern design, initially titled *Pioneers of the Modern Movement* (1936). Pevsner contrasts Henry Cole's version of its political success with the appearance of the exhibits. 'The aesthetic quality of the products was abominable'; they were 'bulging'.[24]

Pevsner was not the first to condemn the types of decorative
order that prevailed at the Great Exhibition. Participants within
its organisation (Digby Wyatt, Richard Redgrave, Owen Jones
and, of course, Henry Cole) constituted a mid-nineteenth-
century design reform movement. They were concerned with too
much ornamentation on industrial objects and their publications
and commentaries on the Great Exhibition's objects are cited by
Pevsner with varying degrees of approval. Their approach to
design reform was ultimately limited, according to him, because
it did not go far enough in its assessment of the causes of
nineteenth-century over-decoration. The organisers of the Great
Exhibition are thus presented as the impoverished predecessors
of William Morris whose flatter, less fussy and more modern
designs are understood as an effect of his social and aesthetic
critique of industrial capitalism. *Pioneers* presents the basic
analysis that the dismantling of the medieval guilds and the use
of machines caused the substitution of art by decoration, an
argument which can be traced to Morris' writings. But Pevsner,
like Morris, also understood the machine as a symptom as well as
a cause of aesthetic deterioration and in fact lays the blame for
mid-nineteenth-century ugliness on the speed of industrialisation
and the pervasive economic philosophy of the bourgeoisie.
'[R]apid and impetuous industrial growth' left 'no time to refine
all those innumerable inventions' and '[l]iberalism ruled unchecked
in philosophy as in industry, and implied complete freedom for
the manufacturer to produce anything shoddy and hideous'.[25]

Many more details about the appearance of the 1851 exhibits
are provided by Pevsner fifteen years after the publication of the
Pioneers in *High Victorian Design* (1951). However, some of the
complexity of his analysis of industry, class and aesthetics is lost:

> The buoyancy and showiness of so much at the Crystal Palace thus
> marks the final flourish of a century of greatest commercial
> expansion ... A universal replacement of the straight line by the
> curve is one of the chief characteristics of mid-Victorian design ...
> the Victorian curve is generous, full or bulgy. It represents, and
> appealed to, a prospering, well-fed, self-confident class.[26]

A fat capitalist stereotype is at work here as is a human–object
analogy between complacent prosperity and unnecessary excess.

For Pevsner, both are forms of bad taste. He makes clear his dislike of decoration, both here and in *Pioneers*, which is a history of how it was pressed out of objects until they were properly modern. Despite disliking the contents of the Great Exhibition, he does discuss them in detail and the European manufactures dominate. This almost exclusive focus on manufactures rather than the other main categories of exhibit (raw materials, machinery, fine arts) is typical of most Great Exhibition histories, many much more recent than Pevsner's. His bias reflects a modernist preoccupation with the aesthetics of mass production. It is modernist ideals that determine his derision of the contents and preference for the building. He opens *High Victorian Design* with the contradiction between the inspirational building and its ugly contents. For him, Crystal Palace achieved something like abstraction, its standard industrial shapes produced so much 'uniformity' that it reached 'a scale of monumentality',[27] while the exhibits were always far too realistic. Certainty about the poor quality of the Great Exhibition's objects has made Pevsner's account difficult to appropriate in later twentieth-century design criticism which has moved towards cultural and aesthetic relativism.[28] But his key contribution to Great Exhibition historiography – the allocation of the building and contents to their different places in a modern history, is the result of the same certainty of judgement.

Circuses, class, crowds, Crystal Palace
In *Art and Industrial Revolution* (1948) F. D. Klingender catalogued the engineering and artistic achievements of industrialisation, its social contradictions and its human cost. He incorporated the Great Exhibition into a history which related industrial events, positioning it at the end of the railway boom, an example of the advance of industry and an illusion of its social success. Klingender gave details of the construction of Crystal Palace and commented: 'In its adulation for this symbolic achievement, and in the noise and colour of the great fair, England for a time forgot the agonies and struggles of the hungry 'forties.'[29] He cast the Great Exhibition as a technically wonderful circus which took attention away from poverty and politics and introduced another of its aspects: the visit. By considering the effect of going to the

Exhibition, he shifted the focus of historical inquiry from the intentions of the organisers and the over-decorated objects to the visitors within the building. An interest in visitors, particularly in those who paid the lowest ticket price of a shilling and represented the working class, has since informed much of the teaching of the Great Exhibition.

The Great Exhibition has been part of the Open University arts or humanities foundation courses since at least 1970. Editors of the source book *Industrialisation and Culture 1830–1914* (1970), Christopher Hardie, Graham Martin and Aaron Scharf, included official and popular accounts of the Exhibition within their compilation of technical, economic, social, religious, philosophical, artistic and literary documents. Their intention in this collection and in the course overall was to indicate the complexity within nineteenth-century society and suggest relationships between its usually separately analysed parts, or, as the editors put it, to account for 'the full nature of historical change'.[30]

The Great Exhibition has continued to feature in inclusive explanations of nineteenth-century formations. A later Open University Arts Foundation Course text, John Golby's *The Great Exhibition and Re-reading 'Hard Times'* (1986) developed the holistic historical approach characteristic of the Open University, which came to be called interdisciplinary. Golby's text was also shaped by the rise of a social history which privileged the interpretation of patterns of everyday life over that of political events. It deals with the Great Exhibition as a popular event rather than a political one: its significance derives from its high attendance, its visitors, and not, as Henry Cole would have it, from its contribution to liberal politics. High politics are not ignored here, but the issues of free trade and peace are refracted through an over-riding interest in the control of working-class culture. Golby's text drew upon and contributed to a debate, generated by Marxist scholarship, about how far culture was shaped by the expansion of the nineteenth-century state. The Great Exhibition as an official, if not state, institution which encouraged contemplation of the achievements of industry, could now be understood to demonstrate the desirable content for working-class culture, usefully filling unregulated time outside work. Golby summarises: 'So the Exhibition was seen as a wonderful occasion for fusing recreation with instruction and thereby improving the lot and the minds of the working classes.'[31] The assumption is that Crystal Palace could alter the state of the shilling visitors, could change the working class.

While the interest in the effect of going to the Great Exhibition can be traced to Klingender's work, he did not attribute to the visit any transformative powers. In *Art and the Industrial Revolution*, he noted a new working-class 'outlook' noticeable around mid-century, but he indicated that the change occurred within their collective organisations and interest.[32] This is not a side issue in Great Exhibition historiography, it is about how far it was historically effective. For Klingender, it is only momentary: a circus which closed. More recent studies, however, have invested the Exhibition, and particularly its building, with large powers, drawing out that which the Open University analysis implied was possible: it performed the regulatory work of the state.

In Tony Bennett's essay, 'The Exhibitionary Complex', first published in 1988, Crystal Palace is a counter-revolutionary measure, pacifying crowds, disciplining visitors as they take part in its display: 'one of the architectural innovations of the Crystal Palace consisted in the arrangement of relations between the public and exhibits so that, while everyone could see, there were vantage points from which everyone could be seen, thus combining the functions of spectacle and surveillance.'[33] Here a Foucauldian analysis of the containment of individual bodies through architectural entrapment has been adapted, by Bennett, to the ordering of a freely moving collective. Despite an obvious opposition between exhibition and incarceration, Foucault's account of the relationship between vision and knowledge has been considered particularly appropriate to an investigation of public display since it provides a systematic account of the effects of looking. For Foucault, the act of viewing is premised upon the assumption of power. Viewing presupposes unequal political arrangements. The purest expression of that inequality is the Panopticon, Jeremy Bentham's model prison.[34] A tower is at the centre and above a ring of cells. The occupant of the tower can view each cell while the occupant of the cell cannot see if the tower is occupied or when he is being viewed. He acts as if he is always seen, anticipating the effect of surveillance and thus accepting his individual place.

Bennett inverts some of this visual sequence. In Crystal Palace, the visitors are the viewer and the viewed, and the result is a controlled collective rather than an isolated and conforming body. The building formed 'a technology of vision which served not to atomise and disperse the crowd but to regulate it, and to do so by rendering it visible to itself, making the crowd itself the ultimate spectacle'.[35] Looking and being looked at actually produced a political subjectivity, as Bennett describes it, 'a voluntarily self-regulating citzenry',[36] which could be taken as a definition of a public, a respectable collective of the type preferred, produced and incorporated into the liberal state. Thus Crystal Palace is understood to operate internally only partly like a Panopticon, but its adaptation of the rules of power is as influential. The visual hierarchies and consequent political inequalities of the Panopticon pervade all modern institutional relationships. Foucault claimed it 'must be understood as a generalizable model of func-tioning' and a 'political technology that may and must be detached from any specific use'.[37] Similarly, the spatial and visual structure of Crystal Palace is not limited to its location in Hyde Park; its visual regime was reproduced in a series of urban spaces. It 'brought together an ensemble of disciplines and techniques of display,' Bennett argues, that 'were to have a profound and lasting influence on the development of museums, art galleries, expositions, and department stores.'[38]

All about consumption

The design influence of Crystal Palace on the first department stores has been quite widely remarked upon. Transparent walls suggest an architectural debt and the development of the same technique of display intended to attract attention to the objects behind the glass. Visitors were seduced in this Palace of Consump-tion scenario. They were not, we should note, surveyed and transformed into a citizenry; they appeared as consumers in another version of modern life.

The resemblance between Crystal Palace and mid-nineteenth-century department stores is striking, although it is not what allocates the Great Exhibition a place in the world of consumption.

For that, two theoretical propositions have to be in place: the exhibits must be defined as commodities, objects with representational rather than useful properties; and the consumption of commodities must be understood as a process of looking at representations rather than buying actual objects.[39] Walter Benjamin recognised Great Exhibitions as commodity worlds. A short section of *Paris – Capital of the Nineteenth Century* (completed in 1935) has been enormously influential on interpretations of 1851, but Benjamin barely mentioned this exhibition, nor did mid-nineteenth-century London feature in his evocation of urban modernity. The Expositions Universelles held in Paris in 1855 and 1867 are the subjects of the section and provide the point of departure for a few brief but powerful sentences on the Great Exhibitions generally:

> World exhibitions were places of pilgrimage to the fetish Commodity … World exhibitions glorified the exchange-value of commodities. They created a framework in which their use-value receded into the background. They opened up a phantasmagoria into which people entered in order to be distracted … The world exhibitions erected the universe of commodities. [40]

Fetish is the condition of the commodity. Historically, commodities have always assumed idol status and the Great Exhibitions which celebrated their various forms heightened their fetishistic character. Amassing commodities made them appear more powerful, extending their representational properties into illusion. The 'phantasmogoria', as Benjamin called it, is an effect of 'capitalist culture'.[41] The Great Exhibition of 1851 is currently differently categorised as exemplary of commodity culture, consumer culture or capitalist culture. These cultures overlap, of course, but are related in a particular way. The constitution of consumption as a separate sphere, a world apart from production, is the peculiar feature of capitalism. Commodification is the effect of separation which was also called spectacle by Guy Debord.[42]

Thomas Richards' *The Commodity Culture of Victorian England* (1990) is the most thorough account of the Great Exhibition as spectacle, although it is not the first. Rachel Bowlby opens her 1985 literary history of consumer culture with Benjamin, Debord and the Great Exhibitions. '[M]odern consumption is a matter not

of basic items bought for definite needs, but of visual fascination
and remarkable sights of things not found at home'. [43] She gives a
succinct definition of spectacle which Richards insists started in
1851. He announces: 'The era of spectacle had begun'[44] and
explains:

> during and after the Exhibition the commodity became the still
> center of the turning earth, the focal point of all gazing and the end
> point of all pilgrimages. The Great Exhibition of 1851 was the first
> outburst of the phantasmagoria of commodity culture. It inaugurated
> a way of seeing things that marked indelibly the cultural and
> commercial life of Victorian England.[45]

The particular concern of Richards' book is the impact of the
Great Exhibition on advertising practices, how the commodity
took over the image. More important to historians of the Exhibition itself is the larger claim that it spectacularised all visual
forms, instating a capitalist mode of representation. Inside Crystal
Palace, according to Richards, there was greater autonomy for
objects than ever before. He states: 'things now spoke for themselves ... using a language of their own.'[46] They were more
detached, separate and superficial. Richards does not use the
latter term although it is implied in his account of 'a way of
seeing things' at the Great Exhibition. Visitors were something like
flâneurs. 'Crystal Palace turned you into a dilettante, loitering
your way through'.[47] The amount of objects in the Exhibition
becomes the equivalent of the speed of city life. There is so much
to see that looking is no effort; impressions keep passing by.

Spectacle, as Don Slater points out, is only one key aspect of
consumer culture in the mid-nineteenth century; another was
'the construction of bourgeois domesticity'.[48] The Manufactures
section of the Great Exhibition did include, albeit in a 'high
key',[49] objects usually intended for middle-class homes, and if
the Great Exhibition was about domestic consumption it is difficult to maintain that it was, at the same time, a spectacular space.
The amount of decoration could contribute to the visual excess
associated with spectacle, although a history of ornamented
objects and one of visual seduction resist being easily moved
together. The account of the Great Exhibition as a spectacle does
not investigate the exhibits: objects are presented as it is assumed

they would have been seen; they are just glimpsed. The actual objects are not as significant as the way they were displayed. The 'wonder' of the Exhibition, Richards has argued elsewhere, was 'not in its contents but the special effects designed to illuminate them'.[50]

Ultimately imperial

From the 1990s, the Great Exhibition has been consistently characterised as imperialist. This interpretation does not, of course, belong exclusively to that decade. In his 1988 study of the historical and aesthetic forms of international exhibitions, Paul Greenhalgh described how '[i]mperial achievement was celebrated to the full at international exhibitions', and he warned: 'study of them that would exclude or underplay this aspect would run the risk of misrepresenting their overall flavour'.[51] Work by Bennett and Richards has paid proper attention to the Great Exhibition's contribution to the development of imperial representations, but this is different, slightly but significantly, from the consideration that the Great Exhibition was about imperialism above anything else.

There is no single text that makes this latter claim, but literature on imperial display either mentions or implicates the Exhibition within its historical trajectory. As Curtis M. Hinsley, in an article on the World's Colombian Exposition held in Chicago in 1893, states:

> The London Crystal Palace exhibition was classically imperialist in conception and construction; on display was the material culture of an industrial, commercial empire, with an emphasis on manufactured goods derived from colonial raw materials. The Paris Exposition of 1867 celebrated another form of colonial appropriation in featuring archaeological and ethnological materials. Virtually all subsequent fairs embodied these two aspects: displays of industrial achievement and promise for the regional or national metropolis, and exhibits of primitive 'others' collected from peripheral territories or colonies. As a collective phenomenon the industrial exposition celebrated the ascension of civilised power over nature and the primitives. Exhibition technologies tended to represent those peoples as raw materials; within the regnant progressivist ideology they occupied the same category.[52]

Initiating rather than completing the imperial form, the Great Exhibition of 1851 fairly straightforwardly reproduced the activity of colonial commercial conquest. Objects were taken from a periphery to a centre, from their original location to an artificial one, wherein their forms were appropriated and their meanings altered. Not for the first time, the Exhibition appears like a market; Hinsley recasts its industrial character as imperial, and without too much difficulty, because the contents have not had to be redefined. Industrialisation and imperialism were not separate processes; they did not have different objects. The 1851 exhibits have, therefore, maintained their status as commodities.

Commodification is always a process of decontextualisation, an eviction from a place of production, and this condition of being without context is exacerbated in objects when that place is geographically distant. By 1851, some forms of Eastern production for Western consumption were well established and European nations used the Great Exhibition precisely to display the commercial success of their colonial relationships. Two points should be made here. First, objects from the East might have became familiar in the West but were still out of context; decontextualisation is no less acute when it becomes a perpetual condition. And, second, objects from the East were part of the spectacle from its inception and gave it its defining characteristic of 'visual fascination and remarkable sights of things not found at home'.[53]

Analysis of the Great Exhibition's imperial character has drawn upon and developed the account of its spectacular nature. Pleasures of looking have been identified as processes of political definition, and 1851 has been interpreted through readings of Edward Said's *Orientalism* (1978). At least in part, this work can be understood as a geographical reworking of Foucault's architectural model of modern politics in which vision, knowledge and power depend upon position, as Said explains:

> In quite a constant way, Orientalism depends for its strategy on this flexible *positional* superiority, which puts the Westerner in a whole series of possible relationships with the Orient without ever losing him the relative upper hand ... The scientist, the scholar, the missionary, the trader, or the soldier was in, or thought about the orient because *he could be there*.[54]

Observing the Orient by being there, or by viewing the various Orientalist forms that were institutionalised in the West, reproduced the positions of ruler and ruled. The Great Exhibition, therefore, did not simply show imperial work which was carried on somewhere else; it performed that work. It is thus implicated in imperial history, although it may not be a typical Orientalist form. Said's analysis of the political relationships embodied in representation has tended to be applied to realist images, which display their origin in observation and have the authority of a record suitable for archiving.[55] The apparent realism of the archive contrasts with the illusory effects of the spectacle. This produces at later international exhibitions, if not at the Great Exhibition itself, a potent confusion of science and dream, realism and illusion, education and entertainment.[56]

This book is unlike much of the published work which describes or debates the Great Exhibition of 1851. It is not a celebration of the achievement of its collection or the ingenuity of Crystal Palace. It does not deliver another wholesale re-casting of 1851 with Crystal Palace re-incarnated in another new modernist form. Instead, it asks how the Great Exhibition has been historically produced, exploring the structures through which its meanings have been made, managed, preserved. The words and images which represented the Great Exhibition to its mid-nineteenth-century audience, who may or may not have actually visited it, and which have been employed as evidence, attributed with varying degrees of authority, in its subsequent histories, are re-examined here. Often cited sources are analysed in the context of the conditions in which they were produced and received. Texts are read for their complexities and contradictions and considered in their own terms rather than squeezed into existing formulations of the Great Exhibition. But its previous interpretations are not easily abandoned. *The Great Exhibition of 1851* does not offer any escape from the historical frameworks within which the event has already been understood. That would not be possible or, indeed, desirable. This book comprises six studies of specific components of the Great Exhibition experience and its aftermath which draw upon, debate and develop past scholarship, in particular that which has focused upon how class and empire as cultural and political formations have operated in and around 1851.

Chapters 1 to 4 (by Steve Edwards, Rafael Cardoso Denis, Brian Maidment and Peter Gurney respectively) are concerned with the formation and representation of class subjectivities. Edwards, in his analysis of the 1851 *Punch* cartoon 'The Pound and the Shilling' in Chapter 1, discusses who are the expected and unexpected visitors to the Great Exhibition. The cartoon is a fragment in an argument about the nature of knowledge produced at the Exhibition and the class position of those who produced it. He draws out the politics of Lyon Playfair's intellectual work of classification system and William Whewell's philosophical interpretation. The relationship between knowledge and class is the underlying theme of Chapter 2. Here, Denis traces the expansion of drawing instruction and its dissemination to industrial workers after the Great Exhibition. He considers technical drawing as a form of industrial knowledge and interprets the programme of improving its practice as a 'process of inculcating an industrial vision' (p. 55). He documents in detail how a pattern of looking has been historically produced.

Chapter 3 by Maidment and Chapter 4 by Gurney shift the focus of the book from what could be termed official projects of the Great Exhibition to sites, one literary and one geographical, where its meanings were appropriated. Maidment examines *The Illustrated Exhibitor*'s re-interpretation of the Exhibition for an artisan audience. He argues that the periodical's approval of the Exhibition resisted objectification by re-inscribing the process of labour on to exhibits which had been viewed in isolation as well as through humanist rather than imperialist representations of national difference. Maidment explores the progressive potential of a productivist working-class culture shaped by the Great Exhibition while Gurney examines the possibilities of collective consumption. He details the working people's organised celebrations which took place in Crystal Palace after it moved to Sydenham and provides an alternative ending to the Great Exhibition's histories. Most accounts project the Great Exhibition idea into the middle-class spaces of the museum or the department store[57] whereas Gurney explores the moments in the second half of the nineteenth century when the 'highly significant recreational space' (p. 118) of Crystal Palace was commanded by temperance organisations and the Co-operative Movement. Thus he presents an independent working-class identity which was not dismantled at the Great Exhibition or through participation in consumer culture. Gurney's work, like that of Maidment, is a useful corrective to histories which have assumed that official control over the Great Exhibition's meanings was always maintained.

The representation of colonial relationships is the theme of Chapters 5 and 6 by Lara Kriegel and Richard Pearson respectively. Kriegel examines strategies of domestication. India, she suggests, was feminised and miniaturised at the Great Exhibition. Her chapter provides a detailed account of the textual and visual production of India, arguing that the collection was not simply seen in 1851, it was *narrated*. She traces 'the work these stories performed in defining Britain's imperial project' but also finds 'unintended narratives' which 'destabilised the relationship between colony and metropole' (p. 149).

The discursive destabilisation of the certainty of imperial superiority is the subject of Chapter 6. Here, Pearson is interested in how the writing of William Makepeace Thackeray on the Great Exhibition published in *Punch* contained opposition to the journal's patriotism. Thackeray mediated his poetic accounts of the Exhibition through 'Other' voices. Creating narrators who were not British subjects, the literary device employed by Thackeray (and other commentators) to glorify and ridicule the exhibits and visitors of 1851, made the objects of such praise or criticism less certain, 'ambivalent', to use Pearson's term.

Thus, *The Great Exhibition of 1851* examines the strategies and structures of its official and oppositional interpretations, setting out some of the mechanisms through which a temporary exhibition, open in Hyde Park for only six months, acquired such enormous historical significance. The historical detail presented in this volume will, of course, add to the status of the Great Exhibition, but it is intended to perform the work of historical demystification by demonstrating the political content and historical context of successful Great Exhibition accounts and that of its more neglected sources. The intention of this book, then, is to clarify, as well as contribute to, the struggle over meaning.

Notes

1 See for example: F. Bedarida, *A Social History of England 1851–1975*, (London and New York, Methuen, 1979); G. Best, *Mid-Victorian Britain. 1851–1875* (London: Weidenfeld and Nicolson, 1971); R. Bowlby, *Just Looking. Consumer Culture in Dreiser, Gissing and Zola* (New York and London: Methuen, 1985); R. R. Brettel, *Modern Art 1851–1929* (Oxford: Oxford University Press, 1999); A. Briggs, *Victorian People. A Reassessment of Persons and Themes 1851–67* (Middlesex: Penguin, 1967); A. Briggs, *Victorian Things* (London: Penguin, 1990); A. H. Miller, *Novels Behind Glass: Commodity Culture and Victorian Narrative*, (Cambridge: Cambridge University Press, 1995); N. Pevsner, *Pioneers of Modern Design* (Middlesex: Penguin, 1960); N. Pevsner, *The Sources of Modern Architecture and Design* (London: Thames and Hudson, 1968); B. Porter, *Britannia's Burden. The Political Evolution of Modern Britain. 1851–1990* (London: Edward Arnold, 1994); T. Richards, *The Commodity Culture of Victorian England. Advertising and Spectacle. 1851–1914* (London: Verso, 1990). A recent conference entitled 'Exhibiting Empire. Visual and Material Representation of British Imperialism from 1851', held at the National Maritime Museum, Greenwich, 15–16 October 1999, should also be mentioned here.

2 Briggs, *Victorian People*, p. 23.

3 Pevsner, *Sources*, p. 11.

4 For an early analysis of Crystal Palace architecture, see: H. Muthesius, *Style-Architecture and Building-Art: Transformations of Architecture in the Nineteenth Century and its Present Condition* (Santa Monica: Getty Center, 1994). First published 1903, p. 73.

5 M. Berman, *All That Is Solid Melts Into Air. The Experience of Modernity* (London: Verso, 1983), p. 220. Berman describes Feodor Dostoevsky's response to Crystal Palace.

6 S. Johansen, 'The Great Exhibition of 1851: a precipice in time?' *Victorian Review* 22:1 (summer 1996), p. 61.

7 *Ibid.*, p. 61.

8 M. Nesbitt, 'Ready-made originals: the Duchamp model', *October* 37 (summer 1986), p. 54.

9 Berman, *All That Is Solid*, p. 238.

10 *Ibid.*, p. 238.

11 J. Saville, *1848, The British State and the Chartist Movement* (Cambridge: Cambridge University Press, 1987), p. 202.

12 T. Bennett, *The Birth of the Museum* (London: Routledge, 1995), p. 62.

13 P. Corrigan and D. Sayer, *The Great Arch. English State Formation as Cultural Revolution* (Oxford: Blackwell, 1985), p. 119.

14 See C. Duncan, *Civilizing Rituals. Inside Public Art Museums* (London and New York: Routledge, 1995), p. 11, for a discussion of museum space as 'liminal'.

15 Bennett, *Museum*, p. 210.

16 F. D. Klingender, *Art and the Industrial Revolution* (Chatham: Evelyn, Adams and Mackay, 1968), p. 165.

17 H. Cole, 'Introduction', *Official, Descriptive and Illustrated Catalogue of the Great Exhibition of 1851* (London: William Clowes and Spicer Brothers, 1851), pp. 1–35.

18 Y. Ffrench, *The Great Exhibition: 1851* (London: Harvill Press, 1951); C. H. Gibbs-Smith, *The Great Exhibition of 1851*, (London: HMSO, 1951). C. Hobhouse, *1851 and the Crystal Palace* (London: John Murray, 1950) seems part of this group but was first published in 1937. P. Beaver, *The Crystal Palace*, (London: Hugh Evelyn, 1970) and A. Bird, *Paxton's Palace* (London: Cassell, 1976) also follow 'the making' narrative form. K. Luckhurst, *The Story of the Exhibitions* (London: Studio, 1951) is an exception here. Clearly contributing to the interest in the Great Exhibition generated by the Festival of Britain, it contextualised its formation within a wider history of international industrial displays.

19 H. Cole, 'On the International Results of the Exhibition of 1851', *Lectures on the Results of the Great Exhibition of 1851* (London: David Bogue, 1852), p. 425.

20 Cole, 'Introduction', *Official Catalogue*, p. 1.

21 Cole, 'International Results', *Results*, p. 423.

22 J. A. Auerbach, *The Great Exhibition of 1851. A Nation on Display* (New Haven and London: Yale University Press, 1999) notes 'that free trade would foster peace, formed one of the core beliefs of the Manchester School' (p. 162). Richard Cobden, Manchester liberal, orator, MP, one of the lead figures of the Anti-Corn Law League, was also a member of the Royal Commission. 'Of the ideological links between the exhibition and the Manchester School' writes Auerbach, 'there can be no doubt'. (p. 163).

23 M. Digby Wyatt, 'The construction of the building', *Official Catalogue*, p. 49.

24 Pevsner, *Pioneers*, p. 41 and p. 42.

25 *Ibid.*, p. 44, p. 45 and p. 46.

26 N. Pevsner, *High Victorian Design. A Study of the Exhibits of 1851* (London: Architectural Press, 1951), p. 45 and p. 49.

27 *Ibid.*, p. 15.

28 See A. Forty, *Objects of Desire* (London: Thames and Hudson, 1986) p. 6.

29 Klingender, *Art and the Industrial Revolution*, p. 164.

30 C. Harvie, G. Martin and A. Scharf (eds), *Industrialisation and Culture 1830–1914*, (London: Macmillan, 1970), p. 12. See also Aaron Scharf's invaluable *Art and Industry* (Bletchley: Open University Press, 1971) pp. 8–71, unit 33 of the Humanities foundation course.

31 J. Golby and S. Meikle, *The Great Exhibition and Re-reading 'Hard Times'* (Milton Keynes: Open University, 1986), p. 19.

32 Klingender, *Art and the Industrial Revolution*, p. 169.

33 Bennett, *Museum*, p. 65. Chapter 2 'The exhibitionary complex' was first published in *New Formations*, no. 4, 1988.

34 M. Foucault, *Discipline and Punish. The Birth of the Prison* (London: Penguin, 1979), pp. 195–228. Johansen's essay in *Victorian Review* (see note 6) draws upon Foucault's model of discourse to interpret the Great Exhibition's industrial agenda.

35 Bennett, *Museum*, p. 68.

36 *Ibid.*, p. 63.

37 Foucault, *Discipline*, p. 205.

38 Bennett, *Museum*, p. 61.

39 The primacy of the function of representation in commodities is described in K. Marx, *Capital. Volume 1* (London: Penguin, 1988) as 'fantastic': p. 163.

40 W. Benjamin, 'Grandville or the World Exhibitions', in *Charles Baudelaire. A Lyric Poet in the Era of High Capitalism* (London: Verso, 1989), pp. 165–6.

41 *Ibid.*, p. 166.

42 G. Debord, *Society of the Spectacle* (Detroit: Black and Red, 1983).

43 Bowlby, *Just Looking*, p. 1.

44 Richards, *Commodity Culture*, p. 3.

45 *Ibid.*, p. 18.

46 *Ibid.*, p. 4.

47 *Ibid.*, p. 35.

48 D. Slater, *Consumer Culture and Modernity* (Cambridge: Polity Press, 1997), p. 15.

49 Pevsner, *High Victorian*, p. 9.

50 T. Richards, *The Imperial Archive. Knowledge and Fantasy of Empire*, (London: Verso, 1993) p. 117.

51 P. Greenhalgh, *Ephemeral Vistas. The Expositions Universelles and World Fairs, 1851–1939* (Manchester: Manchester University Press, 1988), p. 52. Greenhalgh notes that work by Eric Hobsbawm first published in 1968 recognised the imperial aspects of industrial affairs. See E. Hobsbawm, *Industry and Empire* (London: Penguin, 1990) and E. Hobsbawm, *The Age of Capital. 1848–1875* (London: Abacus, 1977), especially p. 47.

52 C. M. Hinsley, 'The world as marketplace: commodification of the exotic at the World's Colombian Exposition, Chicago, 1893' in I. Karp and S. D. Lavine (eds), *Exhibiting Cultures. The Poetics and Politics of Museum Display* (Washington and London: Smithsonian Institute Press, 1991), p. 345. For other formulations of the Great Exhibition project as imperial see T. Barringer, 'The South Kensington Museum and the colonial project', in T. Barringer and T. Flynn (eds), *Colonialism and the Object. Empire, Material Culture and the Museum* (London: Routledge, 1998), pp. 11–27; A. Hasam,

'Portable iron structures and the uncertain colonial spaces at the Sydenham Crystal Palace', in F. Driver and D. Gilbert (eds), *Imperial Cities* (Manchester: Manchester University Press, 1999), pp. 174–93.

53 Bowlby, *Just Looking*, p. 1.

54 E. Said, *Orientalism. Western Conceptions of the Orient* (London: Penguin, 1991) p. 7 (emphasis in original). S. Hall, 'The spectacle of the 'Other', in S. Hall (ed.) *Representation: Cultural Representation and Signifying Practices* (Milton Keynes: Sage, 1997), discusses the influence of Gramsci's concept of hegemony on Said's work as well as Foucault's discursive frameworks, p. 260.

55 See, for example: L. Nochlin, *The Politics of Vision* (London: Thames and Hudson, 1991); A. McClintock, *Imperial Leather* (London: Routledge, 1995).

56 Both P. Greenhalgh, 'Education, Entertainment and Politics: Lessons from the Great Exhibitions' in P. Vergo (ed.), *New Museology* (London: Reaction Press, 1988), pp. 74–98, and A. E. Coombes, *Reinventing Africa. Museums, Material Culture and Popular Imagination* (Yale: Yale University Press, 1994) make this point.

57 See notes 1, 32, 33 for histories which relate the Great Exhibition to department stores, and L. Purbrick, 'South Kensington Museum: the building of the house of Henry Cole' in M. Pointon (ed.) *Art Apart. Art Institutions and Ideology across England and North America* (Manchester: Manchester University Press, 1994), pp. 69–86, for one which connects it to museums.

1

The accumulation
of knowledge
or, William Whewell's eye

STEVE EDWARDS

> accumulated knowledge, like accumulated capital, increases at
> compound interest.[1]

In 1851 the *Illustrated Exhibitor* described the Great Exhibition as
a 'great Open Book' in which the reader would discover an account
of 'the industry of our brethren of the north, the south, the east
and the west'.[2] But, if the exhibition can be seen as a book, it is not
an easy one to read. This is probably because it was difficult to
write. The Great Exhibition provided an important opportunity
for the intellectuals of the new industrial capitalist society to come
to terms with their world. Working out an order for things in the
middle of the nineteenth century can not have been a simple task.
As Asa Briggs has noted, Charles Babbage and William Whewell
might have looked longingly at the interchangeable parts on
display in the Machinery Court but this gaze existed alongside the
different kind of attention solicited by Pugin's Medieval Court.[3]
The spectacle of machinery played a prominent role in the
exhibition but there was still plenty of handicraft on display. It
was, as the historians are keen to point out, an uneven world. The
reading of the exhibition that I am going to offer is a partial
account: I am concerned with the exhibition as an industrial
representation, a picture of capitalist culture, or more specifically
with possible structures of middle-class spectatorship.

THE POUND AND THE SHILLING.

"Whoever Thought of Meeting You Here?"

1.1 'The Pound and the Shilling'

As a way of proceeding, I want to bring two fragments into a pattern of adjacency: William Whewell's essay 'The general bearing of the Great Exhibition on the progress of art and science'[4] and an image from *Punch* titled 'The Pound and the Shilling' (see figure 1.1).[5] This montage method stems from a rather literal-minded interpretation of T. W. Adorno's comments on Walter Benjamin's Baudelaire project. In one of the great exchanges of modernist Marxism, Adorno argued that instead of establishing the necessary mediations between social processes, categories, and texts, Benjamin proceeded by means of adjacency: he simply placed his materials next to each other.[6] Whatever strengths there are to this argument, it is easy to miss the extent to which Adorno's comments stem from a radically different estimation of the powers of montage to Benjamin. For Adorno montage simply repeated the fragmentary logic of commodity fetishism. For Benjamin, in contrast, montage was an exemplary form – probably the form – of the 'dialectical image' that, he believed, could establish the kinds of connections between ideological forms and social relations that might cut through fetishism and propel thought into the future.[7] I want to proceed by taking Adorno's comment at face value as if it really *were* Benjamin's method. I do not think that my chosen texts will have the kind of shock value that Benjamin advocated but, by establishing a new constellation for these individual shards, a dialectical image might be brought into view. I hope that by pasting these bits together two familiar representations of the exhibition can be seen again and made to illuminate patterns of class looking.

'The Pound and the Shilling'

I want to begin not with the exhibition as an image but with an image of the exhibition. The *Punch* caricature 'The Pound and the Shilling' appears frequently both in histories of the mid-nineteenth century and in commentaries on the Great Exhibition. But if this odd picture is often reproduced it appears, all too frequently, as an illustration, providing a kind of visual punctuation for dense pages of text. Clive Behagg, uniquely, has something to say about the image. Behagg's emphasis on the continuity of social division leads him to see it as a structural homology for those works of social history that view the period as one of equilibrium or equipoise. If the exhibition represented 'the visibility of progress', Behagg argues, it did so for 'many people' and not all of them. He writes:

> Punch published its famous cartoon on the theme, 'The Pound and the Shilling', celebrating the fact that the upper and lower classes could be brought together by a visit to the Exhibition. This may have been wishful thinking. In a variety of ways the Exhibition could be said to have epitomised the problems of mid-century society as well as its best aspirations. The trains that carried the visitors to London were rigidly divided into first, second and third class compartments. ... Similarly, entrance to the Exhibition cost a shilling from Monday to Thursday, two shillings and sixpence on Fridays and five shillings on Saturdays. By avoiding 'shilling days' the upper classes could be certain not to have to mix with working people.[8]

The point is well made. Behagg is surely right to emphasise the continuity of mid-Victorian class contradictions. An era of social harmony did not appear like a new dawn with the waning of Chartism. The transformation of social relations was, and is, a dynamic and contradictory process: one in which class identities and class relations are made and remade. The problem with Behagg's analysis is just that the 'wishful thinking' is swept away a little too quickly. The point, I think, is that if this image offers a fantasy of reconciliation it is one that attests to the enormous labour of psychic disavowal involved in this conception. For one thing, given Behagg's point, we need to account for why Punch thought a staging of this meeting might be worthwhile.

I want to try to account for this image as a representation of social relations in the middle of the nineteenth century. What follows is a rather clumsy analysis, since a full account of this image would require the philological attention of a historian of political caricature (something I am not). This is because at least some of the figures depict specific individuals rather than generic social types. One indication of this is the fact that 'The Pound and the Shilling' appeared as a full-page image, a usual clue to the magazine's allegorical intent. The military man on the right almost certainly represents the Duke of Wellington. Punch's characteristic way of depicting Wellington was well established by this time.[9] It is possible that the upper-class woman in the foreground represents a youthful Victoria, but it is more likely that she depicts Wellington's daughter-in-law the Marchioness of Douro in whose company he had been pictured visiting the exhibition in the *Illustrated London News*.[10] If the figures on the right represent specific persons, then it is probable that those on the left, who stand for the working community, also illustrate identifiable characters in a political allegory. Until the identity of these figures is established any account of this image will read only *one* level of allegory's twice-told tale. In the absence of this information all we can do is make a beginning.

The 'pound' and the 'shilling' are two of the metonyms through which social class was registered in debates on the exhibition.[11] It ought to be apparent, however, that despite the meeting of the different social worlds that it stages this is not an image of class conflict, or confrontation. There are two figures in this image that *do* convey a sense of social unease. The woman on extreme right peers around the shoulder of her compatriot and looks apprehensive; while on the extreme left edge we can see a raucous figure who seems like an invader from a novel by Henry Fielding. It is probably significant that these figures are pushed out to the extreme margins of the frame since the central drama is of an altogether different kind. The principal actors in this scene face each other in mutual recognition. If they appear to be fascinated by the marks of social difference and distinction they do so within a framework of reciprocal respect. On one side the navvy and the carpenter (recognisable from their distinctive dress) appear neither hostile nor cowered in this meeting with their 'betters'. Rather, they stand their ground wrapped in an aura of respectable independence and exude self-assurance. The navvy appears to half smile. The carpenter, perhaps, casts a glance toward the woman in the foreground. On the other side, the military figure looks pleased at this meeting. The central upper-class women appear confident and at ease. But for all the apparent comfort in each other's company, there is a gulf between these figures. The central shaded portion of the image marks a 'no-man's land' between two self-contained worlds. This void ensures that that there is no physical contact between the principal actors. There may be no hostility on display in this image but each figure occupies his or her place in an established pattern of relations and differences.

I take it that 'The Pound and the Shilling' is an allegory of class relations, but it is by no means certain that this is what it is. Or, at least, it is not clear that it is only this. If this is an image of social reconciliation at the middle of the century it is one where class dynamics are played out through a series of gendered exchanges. Many of the looks exchanged by the characters in this drama are indeterminate, but there is no mistaking the admiring glance cast over the navvy's broad chest by the upper-class woman in the centre (he appears to return this look). The gaze of the woman in the foreground also seems fixed (or even fixated) on this figure, and as I have already suggested the carpenter might be looking at the woman in the foreground. An interchange of this kind suggests an 'economy' of desire.

The basic grammar of this image is established around a series of couples: the military man and the woman in the foreground, the navvy and the carpenter, the two pairs of children (who may provide a significant clue for an interpretation of this drama). The construction may be based on binary differences (principally masculine/feminine) but because these couples reflect, or replay, each other's roles, complex patterns of identity are suggested. In at least one instance this hall of mirrors works to problematise the gender identity of one key figure. The two sets of adult figures appear to be mirror reflections of each other. The carpenter's right arm and the left arm of the upper-class man are virtually identical, the navvy and the principal woman both place their arm in that of their partner. The delicately linked arms of the working men are particularly striking in this respect. This contact is probably intended to suggest a community of work produced out of the union of skill and strength. It is difficult, though, not to see this as a sexualised contact. The word 'union' here takes on a particular significance since it carries connotations of marriage as well as of a labour organisation. The sexual identity of the navvy, a figure who often represented a form of manly English-ness in the period, would seem to be secure, but what are we to make of the carpenter?[12] Despite all we have come to expect about skill as a property of the male working class, there is a real sense that this image constructs the carpenter as a feminised figure.[13] The image seems to offer three reasons for thinking this. Firstly (and most trivially) the carpenter seems to be the only male figure in this tableau who doesn't sport side-whiskers. Secondly, the inverted structure of the image locates the carpenter as the corresponding figure to the foreground woman. Thirdly, and I think most convincingly, his place in the drama of the four children, who replay the roles of the adults, is taken by a small girl. However, an alternative interpretation of these gendered positions also seems plausible. It is possible that while an upper-class masculinity can be encapsulated, or contained, in the single figure of the military man – who seems to puff out his chest to match the stout build of the navvy – labouring masculinity is doubled or split. While *he* unites strength and intelligence, these features become separate attributes when applied to *them*. Perhaps this is why there are two upper-class women in this drama? There is visual evidence to substantiate both of these accounts: neither is secure; both are troubling.

The patterns of desire unleashed by this image are clearly out of the ordinary. If the gender of the carpenter admits some ambiguity, how are we to read his position in the tableau? Is he the counter-part for the woman in the foreground, or the counterpoint of the military man? Either way his relation to the military figure strikes me as rather queer. The relation of the working men and upper-class women is equally problematic. Françoise Barret-Ducrocq has suggested that the halls of the Great Exhibition provided an important place where working-class women and men first met each other and began love affairs.[14] A few middle-class adventurers, no doubt, enjoyed the sport. But while some upper-class men might have walked the exhibition in search of working girls, the 'exchange of women' suggested in this image would seem to be taboo. I suspect that what is at stake here is a rather clumsy attempt to figure a socially unified Nation.

These difficulties find at least partial resolution with the depiction of the children. As I have suggested, the four small children repeat the adult drama. There is a small navvy dressed like his father/self except for the hat. There is a small upper-class woman related in a pattern of metonymic contiguity to the adult women by her parasol (the connection here seems to be almost umbilical). The two smaller figures, behind the first two, similarly substitute for the military man and carpenter. But if the children replay the roles of the adults they do so with a significant difference. The sexual drama that remains latent among the adults is made explicit with the children. The small navvy offers the small upper-class woman a bunch of flowers; she extends her hand to accept them. And behind them, actual contact takes place as the little military man takes the hands of the little carpenter and gazes into her eyes. In this sexual labyrinth illicit and potentially threatening social relations are displaced from the world of the adults to that of the children where they can seem innocent or amusing. In the process, rigid patterns of difference – social and sexual – are loosened. Children, as yet untouched by traditional allegiances or modern fears, could be made the vehicle for a time beyond class antagonism and social conflict. 'The Pound and the Shilling' is, I think, a tale of court-ship and generation, of class relations allegorised through sexual desire. It would make for a neat argument to suggest that the working figures are wooed by the representatives of the upper classes; the skill and the strength of labour, previously excluded, welcomed into the nation. I am tempted by this account, not least because it could be concluded with a rhetorical 'seduced and abandoned'. The problem is that I can see no reason to read this courtship in a unilateral direction. 'The Pound and the Shilling' remains, then, a deeply peculiar image, one that seems to propose an ultimate reconciliation: a moment, projected in the immediate future, when class difference will be abolished through the healing powers of love. For the generations of the future, *Punch* seems to suggest, there will be no class barriers to the utopia of personal happiness: what a shame that it was all 'wishful thinking'.

We have returned, more-or-less, to the point from which we set out, with an image of the mid-century class settlement, though we should now be able to see the intense and convoluted effort necessary to stabilise this fantasy. One troubling problem, how-ever, has been left out of my account. 'The Pound and the Shilling' is framed by a question: 'Whoever thought of meeting you here?' But whose voice is this? Who is the subject and who the object of this sentence? There seems to be no visual evidence for attributing this question to any of the available characters. My hypothesis is that this voice is located outside the frame of the image, or, more precisely, that it *constitutes* that frame. The presence of this invisible narrator suggests a viewing position distinct from the actors visible in the meeting. Deictic words like 'you' are, by definition, slippery, shifting their focus from one 'you' to another. It is possible that this 'you' refers not to the depicted figures but to the reader. Alternately, and more probably, this voice secures a position for the 'imaginary spectator' outside the represented action: it is the spectator that speaks. This question, in appearing to coincide with the space of the spectator, introduces a third term into the composition and provides an imaginary point of coherence from which represented difference can be remodelled. The figure of Punch on the balcony corresponds with this third position outside of the immediate drama. It is, I believe, a middle class space and voice. That the ideal viewer of *Punch* was middle class is hardly a revelation. Through a reading of Whewell's text, however, I want to suggest that the taxonomy of the exhibition played an important role in shaping this space.

The industrial series

Before discussing my second fragment – Whewell's essay – it is worth briefly establishing the taxonomic order of the exhibition. In the present intellectual climate this is not an easy task. Since the publication of Michel Foucault's *The Order of Things*, taxonomy has become a dirty word among many cultural historians.[15] As such, I want to be clear that my engagement here involves a *specific* case of ideology critique and not a rejection of taxonomic knowledge. The prevalent attitude towards taxonomy, it seems to me, is made up of two very different elements. One component, which is eminently justified, consists of a critique of the role of classifying intellectuals in the grimy operations of social power. By mobilising taxonomic knowledge to sift persons according to spurious categories of race or class some intellectuals have played their part in the construction of normative discourses of self and other. At the far end of this process lies the horror of Nazi race theory. This use of taxonomic knowledge should never be forgotten or forgiven. The second component, however, strikes me as much less convincing. In the relativist or perspectivalist epistemologies now prevalent, all taxonomic knowledge – that dealing with the classification of plants as much as with the isolation of 'degeneracy' – is ridiculed. This argument presents us with an array of scientific intellectuals who, it is implied, failed to comprehend that the reality they were sorting and classifying was an effect of their own categories. In this anti-realist account scientific knowledge appears simply as a ruse of the will to power or the projection of desire. In reality, however, taxonomic systems are inescapable. Without them subjects would encounter every object as if for the first time. If this anti-taxonomic attitude were ever to move out from the classroom or conference venue it would make Lysenkoism seem like a party game. In criticising the taxonomy used in the Great Exhibition, then, I certainly do not mean to suggest that all classificatory knowledge is just an 'overreaching' pretence.

It is one of the abiding mythologies of the Great Exhibition that Prince Albert devised the organising structure for the displays. In fact, the taxonomy of the exhibition was designed, or at least co-ordinated, by Lyon Playfair. Playfair was one of a small group of professional administrators who came to public prominence with the Exhibition of 1851. Trained as an organic chemist he was, at various times, secretary of the Chemical Society, Professor at the Royal School of Mines, and chair of Chemistry at Edinburgh. He sat on numerous Royal Commissions, ranging from that on the herring fisheries to the one that investigated the Irish 'Potato Blight', before becoming a prominent Liberal Member of Parliament. He was a Gladstonian, and supporter of Irish home rule who would become chairman and deputy speaker of the House during the Irish disruption of Parliament. In 1885 he was, effectively, Minister for Education. But Playfair's real project was as an energetic campaigner for the professionalisation of science and for scientific and technical education.[16] Playfair, a Liberal advocate of the application of science and technical knowledge to industry, was as pure an example of the modernising capitalist intellectual as we are likely to find in mid-nineteenth-century England.

According to his biography (compiled from his own notes by Wemyss Reid) Playfair inherited a rather rough tripartite structure from Albert: the raw materials of industry, the articles manufactured from them, and the art involved in their decoration (that dismal nineteenth-century category of 'art-manufactures').[17] Reid suggests that Playfair was co-opted as 'Special Commissioner' to organise the exhibition when its forward momentum looked to be in danger of stalling. Reid's account argues that many manufacturers were at best lukewarm about the exhibition. The principal reason for this was said to be Albert's structure. Playfair felt that the categories of the proposed taxonomy blended into each other and, therefore, failed to produce stable categories for the organisation of the manufacturers' wares. While iron ore could be seen as the basis of cast iron, cast iron was itself the condition for all the other categories employing iron. Would a particular machine appear in one place or several? Would the manufacturer of ironware find his products alongside those of his competitors or next to some completely different commodity of process?[18]

Playfair addressed this issue by building the taxonomy around the categories of the manufacturers. This was stated clearly enough in the *Illustrated Catalogue*: 'Eminent men of science and of manufacture in all branches were invited to assist in drawing each one of the boundaries of his own special class of productions.'[19] According to the *Official Descriptive and Illustrated Catalogue*, sixty-five local committees decided on the wares to be submitted from their region.[20] Playfair's job was to sift these submissions into some form of order. He liaised with the committees and built his taxonomy out of the patterns of adjacency suggested by their categories. The exhibition was produced through this dialogic exchange, and it is probably more accurate to see Playfair as the editor rather than the author of the display. The effect of the dialogue was to construct the exhibition, or at least its British section, according to the manufacturers' conception of things.[21] Playfair was happy to see this picture of Britain organised around capital, manufacture and science.

Playfair's solution to the unease of the manufacturers was twofold. Firstly he added a fourth term, machinery, into the existing taxonomy. Iron might appear in *Section I. – Raw Materials* as an ore, in *Section II. – Machinery* as the apparatus that would work it, and in *Section III. – Manufactures* as a finished artefact, before appearing, transfigured by the impress of genius in *Section IV. – Fine Art*. The real advantage of Playfair's taxonomy, however, hinged on his second innovation: in addition to these four sections – raw materials, machinery, manufactures and fine

art – he introduced thirty subsections or *classes*. These sub-
divisions enabled a much finer pattern of resemblance and difference to be established than in previous exhibitions. This
structure allowed a particular commodity to be followed through
the successive stages of its production while simultaneously
allowing it to be compared to similar commodities within its
class. The respective manufacturers' iron-goods could thus be
judged against each other as well as participating in the story of
iron. As such, the manufacturers would find their wares grouped
with others of a similar kind rather than forced into pre-existing
categories that were either arbitrary or so broad as to be meaningless. The subdivision into classes also meant that as industrial
society continued to grow, and as the division of labour gained
pace, new classes could be added without disturbing the general
taxonomic structure. Since the idea of a world in which everything was as it always had been had broken so many taxonomies,
the importance of this should not be underestimated.

A moral geometry

The Rev. Dr William Whewell inhabited a different intellectual
world to Lyon Playfair. A Tory in politics, Whewell was one of
the towering intellectual figures of his era: sometime 'man of
science' and Anglican priest, he held the posts of Professor of
Mineralogy, Professor of Moral Philosophy, and Master of Trinity
College, Cambridge, and on two occasions he was Vice Chancellor
of Cambridge University. He also held a number of elected and
honorary positions including those of Fellow of the Royal Society,
Fellow and President of the Geological Society, and President of
the British Association for the Advancement of Science. Whewell
is best known as a historian and (idealist) philosopher of the
inductive sciences but, like the Victorian sages to whom he is
best compared, his interests and influence cannot be confined
within specialist parameters. In addition to writing monumental
works on the history and philosophy of science he was also a
theological partisan, an intellectual opponent of Utilitarianism
and Ricardian political economy, and a central figure in the
politics of educational reform.[22] A sketch like this merely touches
on his activities, but it should indicate the cultural authority that

he brought to his consideration of the exhibition.

Whewell was hostile to the view of utilitarian science represented by Playfair. Commenting on Sir David Brewster's review of his own *The History of the Inductive Sciences* Whewell wrote that Brewster's 'uproar about steam-boats and gas and railways shows that he has not at all comprehended the nature of the book'.[23] Whewell constantly targeted this kind of utilitarian conception of instrumental science, linking it to the dangerous theories of sensationalist philosophy and French materialism. Whewell's account of scientific thought is wide ranging and complex.[24] His project involved a search for secure epistemological grounds for the inductive sciences. Whewell worked from within a perspective of natural theology in which the first principles or 'fundamental ideas' of science would testify to the existence of God. As such, a foundation for inductive reason would also secure moral foundations for human actions. I don't intend to expound on this philosophy here, but the distance from Playfair's industrial taxonomy should be apparent.

Whewell's text is more than usually figurally dense. Franco Moretti has recently suggested that the frequency of tropes in the nineteenth-century novel tends to increase as narratives encounter national borders.[25] I want to stretch this point and suggest that the figural pulse of a text rises when a thinker attempts to grapple with a difficult ideological problem, when they try to make their conceptions fit awkward, or novel, phenomena. Heavily tropic language can be seen as an index, or symptom, of ideological upheavals (and in some cases of a realist impulse). Whewell attempted to make sense of the new industrial society, to see how its parts fitted together. The over-abundance of tropes attests to the strain involved in this project. What follows is merely an initial attempt to read some sections of Whewell's essay.

Whewell suggested that 'despite of the maxims of antiquity' the exhibition had demonstrated that, after all, there was 'a Royal Road to knowledge'.[26] His lecture was delivered in the presence of Albert and the comment suggests a form of social creeping – it would fit with his politics. But he also meant it since he saw the exhibition as a snapshot of all the worlds' knowledge. He wrote:

if we could suppose some one of the skilful photographers whose
subtle apparatus we have exhibited there, could bring within his
whole field of view the surface of the globe, with all its workshops
and markets, and produce instantaneously a permanent picture, in
which the whole were seen side by side.[27]

This is an interesting image that conveys an important theme of
the essay – the instantaneity of the display brought under a
detached gaze. The metaphor that appears more frequently, however, is that of the exhibition as a text (a play, a poem, a work of
criticism). It will turn out to be a book of capital, and it seems a
good point from which to begin my account of Whewell's essay.

From the time of wonderment to the time of criticism
Thomas Richards has been led by the frequency of the word
'spectacle' in Whewell's text (it occurs eight times) to read this
essay as evidence for treating the Great Exhibition as a key
moment in the development of the society of the spectacle.[28]
Richards, however, responds to the word spectacle in Whewell
without sufficient textual attention. Richard Yeo, in contrast,
notes that of the many metaphors used by Whewell, the image of
theatre holds centre stage.[29] The spectacle in Whewell is not *the*
spectacle but a tableau or a drama. The Great Exhibition, he suggests, is a 'first act' which, now completed, provides the basis for
'the series of scientific morals' to be presented in these lectures.

For Whewell the development of knowledge followed a
pattern from affect to understanding. As Aristotle comes after
Sophocles or Longinus after Homer, he suggests, so language is
poetic before it is critical: 'language is picturesque and affecting
first; it is philosophical and critical afterwards: – it is first concrete,
then abstract: – it acts first, it analyses afterwards'.[30] First we
experience language; we feel its effects directly on our emotions
before we grasp its significance or meaning. Whewell presents
this passage from the emotive to the reflective, from poetry to
criticism or philosophy, as a general pattern of knowledge, one
that is applicable beyond the particular confines of language.
More specifically he reads the objects and processes on display in
the Great Exhibition metaphorically, attributing to them the
characteristics of a poetic text. The exhibited items were, he
wrote: '… utterances, articulate utterances of the human mind,

no less than if they had been audible words and melodious sentences'.[31] On the same page he suggests that the exhibition 'contained a multitude of compositions – not of words, but of things ...'.[32] It is an unsurprising metaphor since there is a close link between the central object of his essay – taxonomy – and grammar. What needs accounting for, however, is the movement that he repeatedly describes from poetic text to critical reading. To take another example of this, Whewell wrote of his task of lecturing on the exhibition after its closure: 'those days of wonderment at the creations of such a poetry being gone by; the office of reading and enjoying being over; the time for criticism seems to have arrived'.[33]

Whewell's decision to treat the exhibition as a text might be unremarkable, but the passage from affect to understanding, when applied to the exhibition, has some surprising ramifications. The movement Whewell establishes presents the things in the exhibition – the commodities at the centre of Playfair's worldview – as the precondition for a more important work of critical reflection. In one sense this is an ordinary point: what is the role of an exhibition if not to be looked at or thought about? The logic of Whewell's argument, however, drives him to a disturbing conclusion: he emphasises the role of intellectuals over that of the manufacturers. In this account, thought would appear to take precedence over the glorification of things. Whewell's text suggests that the exhibition be experienced immediately, through a kind of bodily and imaginative insertion into the labyrinth of things. In this sense, his evocation of the kind of experience that a viewer might have when traversing the exhibition runs remarkably parallel to modern accounts of its fetishistic mechanisms.[34] The 'wonderment' he describes seems to be an effect of phantasmagoric things. But this 'wonderment' is only one register of the text – he was also concerned with how these things could be fitted together, what could be made of them, what kind of society they depicted, and what kind of role there was for men like himself.

Whewell suggests that, while the exhibition left impressions on the viewer, understanding the stories it told entailed a secondary labour of critical and synthetic reflection. This understanding required a perspective outside, or above, the exhibition itself.

Rather than an immersion in the exhibition, a serious viewer needed a distance from it. You could experience the things immediately, but understanding their connections took time. The distinctions he mobilises here imply an opposition between symbolic and allegorical modes of representation.[35] The exhibition, like poetry, constitutes a symbolic form whose meanings are instantaneous. What I am calling the secondary labour on the exhibition, in contrast, depends on an allegorical form of reading – it requires time and distance. One key aspect of Whewell's text was to inscribe a viewer, a perspective from which the myriad things and experiences might cohere. Whewell was, of course, one of the few serious philosophical idealists writing in Britain at this time, and it should be no surprise that for him things held together in thought and not experience.

As I have argued, Whewell was not a simple prophet of technological progress. His interest was not really in the things on display but in discovering 'what the laws of operative power are, after having had so great a manifestation of what they do'.[36] Again, we see the same movement from mundane things to their mysterious laws. He drew the general point from this distinction and suggested that the relation of criticism to poetry and that of science to the Great Exhibition were 'two cases of succession connected by a very close and profound analogy'.[37] In the past, art (by which he means the mechanical arts) had preceded science; people worked metals or fermented wine, before the chemical principles on which these processes are based were understood. Because of this, he argued: 'Art was the mother of Science: the vigorous and comely mother of a daughter of a far loftier and serener beauty.'[38] Scientific knowledge, in this account, assumes priority over the feminine display of things.

Whewell believed that the 'great spectacle of the works of material art' ought to teach a 'scientific moral'.[39] This moral (and it was one he thought would be as secure as the 'axioms of geometry') involved a conception of natural theology.[40] The order of steam-hammers probably suggested to him the hand of God. But the labour of secondary reading plays a different, if related, role in producing a space for Whewell himself as an 'unconnected spectator'.[41] The metaphor of the eye occurs frequently in this essay: the exhibits that eluded the mind were displayed, he tells us, before the 'bodily eye' of the viewer.[42] The exhibition was a symbol of all that was 'present to the eye'.[43] Whewell, in another context, described himself as a 'looker-on' in science.[44] His allegorical reading works to establish a spectatorial position outside, or above, the chain of contiguity. John Barrell has noted that the 'philosophic eye' central to Adam Smith and political economy was 'borrowed from the discourses of natural science', which, because it was disembodied, could sustain the pretence that it represented no particular interest.[45] Barrell suggests that the problem Smith confronted – how to make a market society, where each subject pursues his or her own interest at the risk of the complete social fragmentation, seem rational – required a position outside it for its solution. In order to sustain the claim of objectivity (freedom from specific social interests) political economy needed its 'hidden hand' or its 'philosophic eye'. These fetishistic abstractions hold the system together and enable the theorist to comment on society from a position seemingly outside it. Whewell worked with a remarkably similar set of concerns to Smith and the political economists. It was one of his main objectives to prevent science from splintering into a variety of mutually incomprehensible specialisms. He did so by constructing what Yeo calls, a little too politely to my mind, a 'metascientific' perspective.[46] Science could be held together by a labour of secondary reflection that drew out the common inductive principles shared by the different areas of investigation. This in turn required a new kind of labour conducted by the metascientific theorist. The paradox here is that it requires the work of a specialist to prevent science from fragmenting into so many specialisms. Middle-class 'experts' from Smith to Whewell and beyond have sought to secure for themselves this space seemingly beyond interests. From this fantastic place intellectuals establish their legislature: decreeing existing society to be just, or fair, or the best pragmatic solution. This account of Whewell's text suggests that the exhibition provided an important site on which some middle-class intellectuals could negotiate a role for themselves.[47]

This disembodied spectator was central to Whewell's conception of the exhibition, which he believed was arrayed for a gaze, allowing specialists to survey simultaneously every part of the world.[48] I am going to pass over the section of Whewell's text concerned with establishing the superiority of industrial society to 'ruder and more primitive' societies. It is a fascinating and deeply troubled component of his argument that requires a different (if related) critical argument to the one I am pursuing here.[49] It is worth noting, however, that in this section of the essay he pursues a series of significant oppositions between the hand and the eye, and between the manual and the mental. In each of these oppositions the objects of the display occupied a lowly mechanical position to be surveyed from the superior perspective of the abstract observer.

The problem of Babel

The central section of Whewell's text addresses the vexed problem of industrial taxonomy. If the determination of 'resemblances' and 'differences' were not 'skilfully and happily devised', he argued, the result would be 'intolerable incongruities and even impossibilities'.[50] As evidence of this problem he described the taxonomic conundrums encountered in staging a series of French exhibitions of 'art and industry' between 1806 and 1844. This was not simply because of the four central classes, but, as we noted earlier, because his 'gradations of classification' allowed for a complexity of organisation.

By assuming fixed and uniform principles of classification, he argued, 'we can never obtain any but an artificial system, which will be found, in practice, to separate things naturally related, and to bring together objects quite unconnected with each other.'[51] As an example he recalled the exhibition in which:

> the cotton-tree, the loom, and the muslin, stood side by side, as belonging to *vestiary* art; or when woven and dyed goods were far removed, as being examples, the former of *mechanical*, the latter of *chemical* processes. Suitable gradation is the *felicity* of the classifying art, and so it was found to be in this instance.[52]

This was exactly the problem that Playfair had set out from in his attempt to prevent the arbitrary distribution of the manufacturers' goods. Whatever the wider ideological differences between them, Whewell was particularly impressed that each of Playfair's thirty subdivisions could be further broken down by the use of alphabetical and numerical sub-categories. The interested observer of agricultural grain would, for instance, find millet displayed in Section I. – Raw Materials, Class 3 – Substances for Food, Division A. Cereals, as subsection 3.

Whewell fervently hoped that Playfair's system might permanently fix the order for things. The advantage of a 'permanent and generally accepted classification of all the materials, instruments, and productions of industry', he argued, would be to facilitate collective labour, since, he believed, a 'diversity and ambiguity in the language used' prevented the co-operation that was necessary for work.[53] In order to illustrate this problem he drew on Milton's account of the construction of the tower of Babel. Milton, we are informed, thought work ceased on the tower because the workmen couldn't understand each other's languages: 'when one of them asked for a spade, his companion brought him a bucket; or when he called for mortar, handed him a plumb-line; and that, by the constant recurrence of these incongruous proceedings, the work necessarily came to a stand'.[54]

The possession of a common language was, Whewell believed, a necessary condition for modern forms of work. He wrote:

> It is not only necessary that they should call a brick a brick, and a wire a wire, and a nail a nail, and a tube a tube, and a wheel a wheel; but it is desirable, also, that wires and nails, and tubes, and wheels, should be classified and named, so that all bricks should be of one size, so that a wire number 3, or a tube section 1, or a six-inch wheel, should be constructed so as to correspond to such significations; and even, except for special purposes, no other than such.[55]

This is a fascinating passage in which Whewell's distance allows him to see the necessity of systematising industrial production. The transformation of diverse and everyday practices into this kind of systematic 'high knowledge' is never a disinterested affair.[56] Accustomed, as we now are, to standardised patterns of large-scale and international production it is difficult to conceive of the barrier that irregular components presented to industrialisation. If picking up a cog and not knowing in advance that it would mesh with another led to difficulties in the workshops, it became a substantial fetter on the development of a trade in machine parts. The standardisation of components, no doubt, played a significant role in the development of the productive forces, but, predictably, Whewell has framed this problem in class terms. The 'settled and common language', he insisted, was necessary so 'that the manufacturer, the man of science, the artisan, the merchant' would be able to converse.[57] It should be apparent that the example of Babel is misleading. The problem Whewell was addressing was not one of diverse national languages but one of different class knowledges. Presumably, the language of the workshop was, if not settled, at least held in common between its members. This standardisation of terminology and the classification of industrial components became necessary only at the point where an external spectator who desired to take control of the labour process confronted the knowledges of the working community. Standardisation was a weapon deployed against worker skill and artisanal knowledge since regular components of production did away with reliance on an individual's judgement when it came to cutting two gear wheels or gauging a screw thread.[58]

The role the international exhibitions played in the transformation of the labour process and the development of a national economy has gone unnoticed. The display provided an impetus to further standardisation by establishing points of intersection in the manufacture of commodities. In laying out the artefacts of industry the exhibition allowed specialists of production to determine points of resemblance and difference, to see what had been achieved and what remained to be done. As Reid suggested, the Great Exhibition provided 'an enormous impetus' to the 'reform of our industrial methods' and revolutionised technical education.[59] Standardisation, which here appears as the product of an external eye, also contributed to making a space for this detached point of view. Simon Schaffer has noted that the kinds of abstract laws of production that interested a man like Babbage required a position outside the customary culture of the workshop from which they became visible.[60] Whewell made his contribution to the redefinition of workshop practice by offering a vantage point from which to survey production and find the lack of fit between its parts irrational. The rationalisation of industrial production could then be seen to depend on a position outside the 'restrictive' view of the workshop.

We have noted the taxonomy of the exhibition was ordered around the categories of the manufactures. 'It was determined

that within each of the four sections the divisions which had
been determined by commercial experience to be most convenient should be adopted.'[61] Playfair's fine category distinctions,
which allowed for the location of objects as diverse as walking
sticks and millet, were built around the knowledge of these men.
It can easily be forgotten how utterly banal and intensely partisan the arrangement of the exhibition was. As Whewell noted,
Playfair was aided in his creation of the sub-divisions by the
'practical experience' contained in the 'Trades' Directories of
Birmingham and Manchester, and other great manufacturing
towns.'[62] It would, of course, take more than an exhibition to
transform the labour process. What the exhibition did do, however, was produce a representation of production from which the
worker was conspicuously absent. This occlusion allowed the
spectator to imagine, or to fantasise, a system of making that
provided no resistance to the manufacturers' desires. If artisans
were to participate in the 'settled and common language' alongside manufacturers and men of science, their role here is that of
student and not teacher. The dialogue takes place between
manufacturers and technical experts; it becomes a moralising
monologue at the point it encounters the worker. The exhibition
did more than occlude labour in a display of spectacular things; it
ordered those things according to a logic that was hostile to the
particular knowledge of the working community. William
Whewell's eye, like Adam Smith's eye, or Andrew Ure's eye, was
one guarantor of the supposed objectivity and social neutrality of
this structure of representation.

A short point of conjuncture

I ended my analysis of the 'The Pound and the Shilling' by
suggesting that its point of (imaginary) coherence was located in
a middle-class spectator. Whewell and Playfair represented very
different conceptions of both science and politics and yet they
agreed not only that the Great Exhibition was a representation of
an industrial middle-class world, but also that this was a good
thing. It is significant that the imaginary meeting depicted by
Punch occurs within this middle-class space. I have referred to
the figures on the right-hand side of the image throughout this

essay with the deliberately vague term 'upper class'. By 1851 the integration of the middle class and the aristocracy was well advanced, but Wellington and his daughter-in-law can not, straightforwardly, be made to represent the manufacturers. Rather, it seems to me, 'The Pound and the Shilling' is able to suggest a new era of class harmony, and a new coherence to the nation, because the actors are brought together by a middle-class structure of representation. It is noticeable that no representative of the industrial bourgeoisie appears in the picture. Or rather they are not a visible part of it. The taxonomy through its metonymic relation to the industrial middle class provides the frame for this image.

This space depended on the fetishistic labour of the new type of intellectual. Whewell and Playfair, like Henry Cole and Robert Hunt, are absent from the categories of the exhibition. Their wares do not fit into any of the taxonomic categories, and yet these men are visible everywhere in it. Reid described the Commissioners for the Exhibition as 'good fairies' who secured for English industry and art the position they held.[63] Magic – that perpetual marker for commodity fetishism in the modern world – covers a more prosaic reality. If the taxonomy of the Great Exhibition constitutes a representation of industrial capitalism it is one only partly made by the industrial class. This work also depended on men like Playfair and Whewell. In making themselves these men defined a place for middle-class commerce seemingly beyond interests where exchange took place between equal agents. It is in this space that the voice of the narrator and the eye of the viewer coincide. On the one side of the image stand aristocratic representatives of the state, on the other the personnel of labour, but it is the middle class, the image suggests, that can encompass and unite these diverse interests. Society holds together as a community of peace and plenty under the hegemony of those outside the image. The absent middle class provided the glue that held pictures and exhibitions together.

Reading this image with Whewell's text makes for a last surprising connection. Whewell was the son of master carpenter from Lancaster who entered Cambridge on a £50 scholarship. Through his participation in the network of science he was able to make a spectacular social rise, becoming Vice-chancellor of

Cambridge University and marrying into the aristocracy.[64] It is an image of him as he is of it. From his point of view – at once middle class and beyond interest – so many things held together.

Notes

Adrian Rifkin first made the problem of taxonomy in the international exhibitions a vivid issue for me. I would like to thank him, though the reader may not. Caroline Arscott has been the recipient of numerous inquiries during the writing of this essay; she also constrained some of my wilder speculations. I can't thank Caroline enough. I am indebted to Gail Day who read the text and discussed an obscure image. Louise Purbrick deserves special thanks as a sympathetic and patient editor throughout the troubled history of my text.

1   C. Babbage, *The Exposition of 1851: Views of the Industry, the Science, and the Government of England* (London: John Murray, 1851), p. 211.

2   Quoted in A. Briggs, *Victorian Things* (Harmondsworth: Penguin, 2nd edn, 1990), p. 61.

3   A. Briggs, *Victorian People. A Reassessment of Persons and Themes 1851–67* (Harmondsworth: Penguin, 1965), p. 47.

4   W. Whewell, 'The general bearing of the Great Exhibition on the progress of art and science', *Lectures on the Results of the Great Exhibition of 1851, Delivered Before the Society of Arts, Manufactures and Commerce* (London: David Bogue, 1852), pp. 3–34.

5   *Punch*, 20 (1851), p. 193.

6   See T. W. Adorno, 'Letters to Walter Benjamin', in E. Bloch *et al.*, *Aesthetics and Politics* (London: Verso, 2nd edn, 1980), p. 128.

7   Walter Benjamin's work on Baudelaire is published in English as *Charles Baudelaire: A Lyric Poet of High Capitalism* (London: Verso, 1983). Adorno and Benjamin's differing evaluations of montage are most evident in their respective essays on Surrealism: see W. Benjamin, 'Surrealism: The Last Snapshot of the European Intelligentsia', in W. Benjamin, *One Way Street and Other Writings* (London: Verso, 2nd edn, 1985), pp. 225–39; T. W. Adorno, 'Looking back on Surrealism', *Notes to Literature: Volume One* (New York: Columbia University Press, 2nd edn, 1991), pp. 86–90; for a good discussion of Benjamin's theory of the 'dialectical image' see S. Buck-Morss, *The Dialectics of Seeing: Walter Benjamin and the Arcades Project* (Cambridge, Mass: MIT, 1989).

8   C. Behagg, *Labour and Reform: Working Class Movements 1815–1914* (London: Hodder and Stoughton, 1991), pp. 76–8.

9   See for example 'The Chartist Petition according to the signatories of the Petition', *Punch*, 14 (1848), p. 175. In this image Punch imagined a demonstration comprised of its notoriously dubious signatories. Wellington appeared 17 times, with the lead Wellington – in a gesture redolent of 'The Pound and the Shilling' – linked arm in arm with Queen Victoria.

10 The *Illustrated London News* of 26 April 1851 includes an illustration of Wellington and the Marchioness touring the exhibition. The illustration appears on page 327 and the accompanying text on the next page.

11 An extensive article in the *Illustrated London News* took two more metonyms – the district of St Giles and that of St James – to figure class difference. 'Five Shilling Days and One Shilling Days', *Illustrated London News* (19 July 1851), pp. 100–2.

12 For the navvy as a figure for the heroic and manly Englishman see C. Arscott, *Social Classification and Pictorial Deconstruction in Ford Madox Brown's Work* (unpublished MA Dissertation, Leeds: The University of Leeds, Department of Fine Art, September 1979), p. 29; see also T. Coleman, *The Railway Navvies: A History of the Men Who Made the Railways* (Harmondsworth: Penguin, 1968).

13 For debates on class, gender and skill see C. Hall, 'The tale of Samuel and Jemima: gender and working-class culture in early-nineteenth-century London', in C. Hall (ed.), *White, Male And Middle Class: Explorations in Feminism and History* (Cambridge: Polity Press, 1992), pp. 124–50; K. McClelland, 'Time to work, time to live: some aspects of work and the reformation of class, 1850–1880', in P. Joyce (ed.), *The Historical Meanings of Work* (Cambridge: Cambridge University Press, 1987) pp. 180–209; and the same writer's 'Some thoughts on masculinity and the "representative artisan" in Britain, 1850–1880', *Gender and History*, 1:2 (summer 1989), pp. 164–77. These arguments, which I find convincing, drive home just how odd the gendering of the carpenter is here.

14 F. Barret-Ducrocq, *Love in the Time of Victoria: Sexuality and Desire Among Working-Class Men and Women in Nineteenth-Century London* (Harmondsworth: Penguin, 1992), p. 77.

15 M. Foucault, *The Order of Things: An Archaeology of the Human Sciences* (London: Tavistock, 1990).

16 W. Reid, *Memoirs and Correspondence of Lyon Playfair. First Lord Playfair of St Andrews, PC, GLB, FRS, &c* (London: Cassell, 1899). I use the names of Playfair and Reid interchangeably when referring to this text since, without a detailed comparison of Playfair's notes and the final text, there is no way of identifying a definitive author.

17 *Ibid.*, pp. 115–16. The *Official Descriptive and Illustrated Catalogue* attributes all four of the final categories to Albert and credits Playfair with the introduction of sub-categories. See H. Cole, 'Introduction', *Great Exhibition of the Works of Industry of All Nations, 1851: Official Descriptive & Illustrated Catalogue in Three Volumes* (London: Spicer Brothers, 1851), p. 22.

18 See Reid, *Memoirs*, pp. 115–16.

19 *Official Descriptive and Illustrated Catalogue*, 'Introduction', p. 22.

20 *Ibid.*, p. 18.

21 In the final event only the British section of the exhibition followed Playfair's logic: the numerous foreign sections were organised according to their own criteria. This effectively introduced a second taxonomy of

national classification into the exhibition. It has often been suggested that
the national taxonomies meant that Playfair's system had a purely notional
existence. There is some truth to this claim but it should be noted that the
original intention was to distribute the different national submissions
according to his categories. The national sections were introduced as an
expedient only when the lack of time and poor system of international
communications meant that information could not be submitted in time for
all items to be ordered according to this logic. On this question see: the
Official Descriptive & Illustrated Catalogue, pp. 23–5.

22 For a comprehensive account of Whewell's intellectual concerns see R. Yeo,
    *Defining Science: William Whewell, Natural Knowledge and Public Debate in
    Early Victorian Britain* (Cambridge: Cambridge University Press, 1993).

23 Letter to R. Jones, October 1837, cited in Yeo, *Defining Science*, p. 225.

24 There is an enormous literature on Whewell in the history and philosophy
    of science. I have found Yeo's work particularly helpful for an under-
    standing of the wider parameters of Whewell's project.

25 F. Moretti, *Atlas of the European Novel 1800–1900* (London: Verso, 1998),
    p. 47.

26 Whewell, *Lectures*, p. 4.

27 *Ibid.*, pp. 13–14.

28 T. Richards, *The Commodity Culture of Victorian England* (London: Verso,
    1990).

29 Yeo, *Defining Science*, p. 156.

30 Whewell, *Lectures*, p. 5.

31 *Ibid.*, p. 6.

32 *Ibid.*

33 *Ibid.*

34 The ur-form of the reading of the international exhibitions as a site of
    pilgrimages to commodity fetishism is W. Benjamin's, *Charles Baudelaire:
    A Lyric Poet in the Era of High Capitalism* (London: Verso, 1983). See also
    C. Asendorf, *Batteries of Life: Things and their Perception in Modernity*
    (Berkeley and Los Angeles: University of California Press, 1993); and
    T. Richards, *Commodity Culture*.

35 Whewell, as a reader of Coleridge, Wordsworth and the German
    Romantics, would have been acquainted with arguments on the symbol/
    allegory distinction. For Whewell's engagement with romanticism see Yeo,
    Defining Science, pp. 65–71.

36 Whewell, *Lectures*, p. 7.

37 *Ibid.*

38 *Ibid.*, p. 8. In another metaphor on this page he presents science as the
    developed blossom from the bud of art.

39 *Ibid.*, p. 9.

40 Yeo, *Defining Science*, and the same writer's 'William Whewell, Natural Theology and the Philosophy of Science in Mid Nineteenth Century London', *Annals of Science*, 36 (1979), pp. 493–516.

41 These arguments are connected because an intellectual capable of grasping the coherence of things constitutes an important proof for the existence of God in this scheme of things. On this point see Yeo, *Defining Science*, p. 119.

42 Whewell, *Lectures*, p. 12.

43 *Ibid.*, p. 11.

44 William Whewell, Letter to Johm Herschel, 1 November 1818, quoted in Yeo, *Defining Science*, p. 52.

45 J. Barrell, 'Visualising the Division of Labour: William Pyne's Microcosm', *The Birth of Pandora and the Division of Knowledge* (Basingstoke: Macmillan, 1992), p. 91.

46 See for example Yeo, *Defining Science*, pp. 110–11.

47 Many of the most influential texts on industrial society from Smith to Ure, Babbage to Whewell, have as a primary drive the inscription of a professional middle-class identity. For wider considerations of the way that middle-class experts made themselves, see the important recent studies by R. Gray, *The Factory Question and Industrial England 1830–1860* (Cambridge: Cambridge University Press, 1996); and M. Poovey, *Making a Social Body: British Cultural Formation, 1830–1864* (Chicago: Chicago University Press, 1995).

48 Whewell, *Lectures*, p. 10.

49 For an account of Whewell's views on India see the essay by Lara Kriegel, Chapter 6 in this volume.

50 Whewell, *Lectures*, p. 20.

51 *Ibid.*, p. 22.

52 *Ibid.* (emphasis in original).

53 *Ibid.*, p. 26. The word 'permanent' is a complex and multivalent term in Whewell's philosophy of science. For a discussion of his idea of the permanent sciences see Yeo, *Defining Science*, pp. 215–17.

54 *Ibid.*, p. 26.

55 *Ibid.*

56 For an account of 'learned' or 'high knowledge' in these terms see C. Ginzburg, 'Clues: roots of an evidential paradigm', *Myths, Emblems, Clues* (London: Hutchinson Radius, 1990), pp. 96–125. Whewell was an advocate of high knowledge in science, contrasting this with the works of mere observers. For this see Yeo, *Defining Science*.

57 Yeo, *Defining Science*, p. 25.

58 The literature on the transformation of the labour process is now too vast to list. Louise Purbrick's article on geometry, drawing and standard-isation, however, seems of particular relevance here. Geometry was for

Whewell one of those key subjects that were grounded in 'fundamental ideas'. This he thought made it suitable for the education of gentlemen. As Purbrick demonstrates, geometry played an important role in the presentation of machinery at the exhibition. It seems likely that geometry as a form of ideal and abstract knowledge also played a significant part in mediating the ethereal space of the intellectuals to the task of standardising production and validating capitalist control of work. Louise Purbrick, 'Ideologically technical: illustration, automation and spinning cotton around the middle of the nineteenth century', *Journal of Design History* 11:4 (1998), pp. 275–93.

59 Reid, *Memoirs*, p. 110.

60 S. Schaffer, 'Babbage's intelligence: calculating engines and the factory system', *Critical Inquiry*, 21 (autumn 1994), p. 210.

61 Whewell, *Results*, p. 23.

62 *Ibid.*, p. 24.

63 Reid, *Memoirs*, p. 110.

64 Yeo, *Defining Science*, pp. 15–21. Also, on p. 102, Yeo notes that Whewell's own financial interests were bound up with Trinity as a powerful landlord. His Toryism might be seen in this light.

2

An industrial vision: the promotion of technical drawing in mid-Victorian Britain

RAFAEL CARDOSO DENIS

In his oft-quoted lecture on the results of the Great Exhibition, the Reverend William Whewell confidently announced that the great task of the Victorian age was to arrive at 'a permanent and generally accepted classification' of the myriad things displayed in the Crystal Palace, which could serve as a 'common language [in which] the manufacturer, the man of science, the artisan, the merchant' could communicate their varying needs and requirements.[1] Throughout the ensuing decade, authors of drawing manuals and other educational authorities were to take up this challenge with a remarkable literal-mindedness, characterising drawing as the exact language for this purpose.[2] A veritable national campaign for the promotion of drawing instruction came into being in the wake of 1851, primarily but not exclusively under the auspices of the Department of Science and Art, at South Kensington, an entirely new branch of government which derived its very institutional existence directly from the Great Exhibition and which can, with much justice, be regarded as the most enduring result of that famous event.[3] The essential nature of this campaign can be gleaned from an 1853 circular by the Committee of Council on Education underlining the shift in views regarding drawing instruction and stating firmly that it

'ought no longer to be regarded as an accomplishment only ...
but as an essential part of education'. By the mid-1860s, this
philosophy had become so entrenched that drawing was being
taught to over 90 per cent of British schoolchildren as well as to a
large proportion of working-class adults.[4] There can be little
doubt that drawing was elevated to a new centrality within the
arena of educational provision at this time; what remains to be
explained is exactly why this transformation took place when it
did and as quickly and powerfully as it did.

The present essay argues that drawing came to fulfil a
strategic purpose in the nineteenth century's view of itself as an
industrial age, especially after 1851 when an awareness of that
status became common currency. Drawing was widely seen to
provide a material language of industry which, being universally
understood, could mediate the unprecedented flow of information
and knowledge required by the extraordinary transformations
taking place in communications, transport and the means of
production and consumption.[5] This essay further suggests that
drawing instruction was used not only to disseminate an industrial language but also to inculcate an industrial vision, and one
erected on the foundation of an underlying division of mental
and physical labour, as manifested in endless discussions regarding
the training of eye and hand. Jonathan Crary has drawn attention
to the importance of investigating and regimenting the capacities
of the eye as one aspect of the drive towards a rational organisation of time and movement in production, surveying the links
between nineteenth-century psychological research into attention
and the problem of attentiveness within the context of industrial
work.[6] Educating vision for the purposes of minute observation
and the perception of a whole new set of formal qualities and
relations indeed constitutes a fundamental preoccupation in
nineteenth-century drawing manuals, particularly those of a technical bent.[7]

The aim of this essay is to provide a concrete historical
analysis of the relationship between vision and learning around
the time of the Great Exhibition, underlining the importance of
drawing instruction to broader currents in nineteenth-century
culture and society. The old functionalist argument that education was promoted in the nineteenth century because of the need

for a literate working population has fallen into a deserved state of disrepute. Less impetuous research has demonstrated convincingly that the correlation between literacy and industrial employment is much more vague than that suggested by the likes of Halévy or Durkheim.[8] Care must be taken, however, not to throw out the baby with the functionalist bathwater. Although the role of literacy as an element of industrial training may have been exaggerated over the years, the very real importance of *visual literacy* has been neglected to perhaps an even more dangerous extent, distorting historical readings of what was at stake in the promotion of art and design education. The process of inculcating an industrial vision through drawing instruction possesses profound ramifications in terms of the separation between intellectual and manual labour, particularly between the industrial designer and the worker who executes the design. In this sense, it is a topic vital not only to the comparatively limited concerns of educational theory but to the very nature of work in an industrialised society.

Even more disturbing in the present cultural context are the powerful parallels between the late nineteenth century's promotion of drawing as an industrial language and the late twentieth century's insistence on the merits of electronic media and their 'languages'. Computer literacy is constantly invoked in our day as a panacea for building up a workforce attuned to the changing demands of the information revolution, and the same creepily circular arguments about hand–eye co-ordination are often invoked to justify exposing children to a flashier yet still mind-numbing routine.[9] There is a suspicious continuity between past and present in the discourse of programming people and machines for work; and, although its importance can be exaggerated in hindsight, this connection is bolstered by the fact that a comparatively short historical interval witnessed the introduction and adoption not only of card-driven mechanical devices such as the Jacquard loom and the stereoscope, but also the massive dissemination of visual aids for learning such as drawing copies and cards. The evolution of cards, and later disks, as physical bearers of information and concrete stimuli of a sequence of pre-determined actions or reactions, mostly virtual or abstract, is a chapter which remains to be written in the material history of our programming culture.

Working drawings

As the nineteenth century progressed, drawing instruction came to be seen increasingly as an adjunct of work rather than of leisure. By the 1840s, writers on mechanical and engineering drawing were quite explicitly asserting the monetary value of drawing as a raw material of industry, highlighting its particular importance as a part of the process of designing new machines. By working out technical arrangements on paper, the inventor's expenses were reduced to the marginal cost of drawings as opposed to the greater cost of building models. No less an authority than Charles Babbage upheld this view, citing mechanical drawing as one of the 'requisite' powers in developing machinery.[10] Similar views continued to prevail three decades later, one writer going so far as to assert that Britain wasted much time and money on 'defective castings' due to a lack of knowledge of machine drawings. The impact of such economic considerations on drawing instruction was unambiguous: writing in the late 1850s, William S. Binns – then teacher of mechanical drawing at South Kensington – noted an increase in the demand for knowledge of geometrical drawing, precisely because of its applicability to industrial work.[11]

From the 1830s on, writers on drawing persistently advanced a discourse identifying technical drawing as a useful means of intercommunication between those involved in industrial work, especially insofar as it was credited with a perceived ability to express 'things' and not just 'ideas'.[12] Through the insistent repetition of such notions, drawing came to be perceived as a medium by which ordinary working men could communicate in the universal language of machinery. The idea that certain types of knowledge were better transmitted visually than verbally was certainly not new. John Locke had famously invoked the representation of machines among those objects which could be registered through the descriptive power of drawing but 'which being committed to words are in danger to be lost'.[13] Nineteenth-century writers latched on to this passage, focusing on the importance of purely visual information as a means of registering mechanical facts. Studying 'the devices of ingenious machines', Andrew Ure suggested in 1835, should 'form an essential part in the education of all classes of society; of the noble and rich, as well as the humble artisan' since these devices were, after all, the implements of modern manufacture and, therefore, the basis of modern wealth.[14]

Although Ure's invocation to the noble and rich was soon forgotten, by mid-century a conviction had taken shape that drawing should be taught to all workers – even agricultural ones – as a means of acquiring a better understanding of machinery and construction:

> Drawing is useful; and if *every* labourer cannot learn it, many a labourer may, and may thus get a clearness of ideas most beneficial to himself and his fellows. For there is no practice which so disentangles the ideas, and makes them distinct and plain as drawing. It materially assists the understanding of machinery, not only by illustrations, but by teaching the mind to separate the parts of a whole and to note their relation; and if farmers want hands to use machines, they will acquire what they want if the hands be guided by eyes that would reduce the machine to a diagram.[15]

Locke's heirs clearly believed that drawing possessed a unique power to disentangle ideas, particularly certain rather dangerous ones. Reduced to the abstraction of a diagram, the explosive threat of the machine as an agent of unemployment was defused. Drawing, as argued by the quotation above, could teach the worker the relations of each part to the whole, thereby ensuring the docility of hands/labourers to the eyes which oversaw them. The study of machinery was not only an end in itself, wrote Robert Scott Burn in *Mechanics and Mechanism*, but a means of teaching 'the value of system, and the advantages of doing the right thing in its right place'.[16] Seeing, drawing and understanding machines could have a moral effect, providing a concrete example of system and subordination. More importantly, familiarity with machinery, it was hoped, would encourage a love of it. Thus, drawing manuals not only provided depictions of the machines themselves but sometimes even geared their exercises in practical geometry to echo the forms of machinery (see figures 2.1–2.2).

The Society of Arts declared in 1853 that industrial instruction was not a charity but, rather, 'a duty that cannot be safely resisted'. As the ignorant poor were displaced by industrial progress, they tended to 'resort to machine-breaking, rick-burning, and land-steward shooting as practical remedies'.[17] The solution was to educate them; and mechanical drawing must certainly be a part of that education. Addressing colleagues and students in the Department of Science and Art in 1857, Richard Burchett likewise pointed out that drawing could serve as an important means of easing the transition from agricultural to industrial labour: 'drawing will be found a potent auxiliary', he stated, in supplying the greater knowledge of mechanical powers which was needed now that 'the labour of men's hands' was constantly being 'superseded by machinery'. The diffusion of this kind of education, he went on to note, 'may tend in no small degree to avert evils that have heretofore been heavily felt in this country, when mechanical and animal power have been strongly put in opposition'.[18] Although machine-breaking was little more than a distant memory by this time, its spectre apparently still loomed large in the minds of those concerned with educating the working classes. As an activity at once physical and mechanical, drawing was ideally suited to reconcile these two antagonistic poles in the worker's mind.

There was, furthermore, a strong perception among writers on drawing instruction that the supply of skilled labour was insufficient to meet the demands of manufactures and that workers would, therefore, have to be trained, or re-trained, for industrial production. Although this notion seems little grounded in the facts of an economy which was undergoing a long-term process of de-skilling in many trades as well as fairly regular cycles of redundancy and labour glut, a perceived need to equip workers with new skills is explicitly stated in various texts on art and design education. Horace Grant's *Directions for Introducing the First Steps of Elementary Drawing in Schools, and Among Workmen* (1852) casts the 'powers of observation' of rural labourers in a wretched light, highlighting 'their astounding ignorance of the commonest forms, and utter incapacity of imitating them'. According to Grant, 'a large portion of the agricultural population' were in a state of ignorance so complete that their mechanical powers extended no further than the 'rude use of a few rude agricultural tools'. In his natural state, 'the poor peasant-boy' was described as 'a quadruped, scarcely able to stand on his hind legs, or use his paws or faculties except to clutch a stick or stone for petty annoyance or destruction.' All this could be turned around, Grant suggested, through practical lessons in drawing. The erstwhile 'quadruped' would be 'improved for life as an appreciator and concocter of forms' and

2.1 'Steam engine' from Armengaud, Armengaud and Amouroux

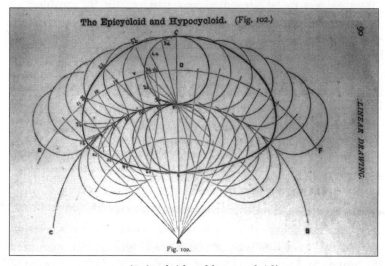

2.2 'Epicycloid and hypocycloid'

would probably become, if nothing else, 'a better blacksmith than his father'.[19] There appeared to be little doubt that workers had much to gain by improving their powers of observation.

An elemental concern with adapting vision to the demands of factory production can be noticed in conjunction with the rise of technically orientated drawing manuals. The 'progression of the British system of industry', as Andrew Ure phrased the problem in his classic *The Philosophy of Manufactures*, relied upon a course of action under which 'every process peculiarly nice, and therefore liable to injury from the ignorance and way-wardness of workmen, is withdrawn from handicraft control, and placed under the guidance of self-acting machinery'.[20] Ure was a technological optimist, and it soon became evident that machines capable of handling every process peculiarly nice were still a long way off. As this realisation sank in, educational writers turned their attention to the other factor in Ure's equation, evincing greater concern for transforming the 'wayward' and 'ignorant' worker into a new paragon of industrial efficiency. Charles Toplis, vice-president of the London Mechanics' Institution, was an early advocate of the 'careful cultivation of the eye' as an essential element in many branches of manufacture. He was followed in that opinion by numerous others, including James Nasmyth, David Ramsay Hay and George Wallis. Mechanical drawing was to be presented as a panacea for the problem of transforming agricultural and other pre-industrial labourers into a disciplined workforce equipped with the skills required for factory work. Whether or not such workers actually constituted the main source of labour for manufacturing industry is only partially relevant; from the educational standpoint, the eyes and hands of Britain needed to be trained anew.

During the 1850s and 1860s, writers of drawing manuals consistently complained that workers were incapable of under-standing technical plans, patterns and diagrams, evincing the increasing importance of such representations as command texts in the context of work. Hannah Bolton complained in 1850 of the 'ignorance of the English operative, in connexion with diagrams and pictorial illustrations' which, she wrote, 'will be acknowledged by every one who, through their agency, has attempted to convey an idea of the form of an object'. The 1860s edition of

Horace Grant's *Drawing for Young Children* lamented that operatives were 'not only unable to sketch the form they are about to
make, but really cannot understand a representation of it',
occasioning a loss of 'time, labour, and money'.[21] Almost all
agreed, furthermore, that such knowledge was essential to the
business of manufactures. A steep growth in the supply of
manuals and books containing technical drawings after the 1850s
bears witness to the fact that artisans and mechanics were
increasingly required to read and understand them as a routine
part of their work.[22] By the 1860s, a new visual literacy was
already widely disseminated among a certain segment of the
working-class public, which took for granted that readers
possessed a basic familiarity with plans, sections, elevations and
other such schematic representations. A book like Robert Scott
Burn's *Handbook of the Mechanical Arts* – originally prepared for
the exclusive use of colonists and emigrants – presupposes a
knowledge of geometrical drawing, orthographic projection and
architectural drawing well beyond what might be expected of
the average 'quadruped' farmer. As William S. Binns pointed out
in his *Elementary Treatise on Orthographic Projection*, orthographic
projection had become more than just one among several systems
of representation. It was by that time the accepted conventional
form of communicating knowledge about machines, without
reference to models or to the machines themselves.[23]

It has been suggested that mechanical drawing came to
function as a dividing line between different spheres within the
technical community, creating a social distance 'between the
engineer in his drafting room and the mechanic on the shop floor'
based on the distinction between being able to decipher this
'graphic mode of expression'.[24] This thesis deserves to be given
serious consideration outside the limited context of the French
machine-building industry to which it refers. Although manuals
of mechanical drawing and orthographic projection were accessible
to many working artisans and mechanics in mid-Victorian
Britain, most never acquired the enhanced professional status of
the new breed of professional engineers. If at least some workers
were 'fluent' in the new graphic idiom, what bearing does this
have on the eventual differentiation by social class of 'engineer'
from 'mechanic' and of 'designer' from 'artisan' which took place

in Britain as well as in France? A distinction between different levels of visual literacy seems to be necessary if knowledge of mechanical drawing is to be understood as a dividing line between the activities of thinking and those of doing or making.

Analysing the ways in which machine drawings became codified during the nineteenth century, Louise Purbrick has drawn attention to a crucial epistemological difference between orthographic projection and perspective representation: the former aims to *conceptualise* an object by calculating the mathematical relationships between its parts in abstract space, while the latter seeks to *visualise* an object by representing it mimetically as it would be seen from a given viewpoint.[25] This dichotomy between 'conceptual' and 'visual' is absolutely crucial because it takes into account the fundamental characteristic that distinguishes representations of machines in plan, section and elevation from those in perspective – i.e., an *intellectual abstraction* of spatial relationships based on mathematical calculation, or what one contemporary writer described as 'the geometrical faculty'.[26] Reading geometrical projections involves a process of seeing that which cannot be observed, of grasping an impossible view which is not a likeness but a translation of the object, breaking it down into parts which can only be joined together again in the mind of the observer. Mechanical drawings based on orthographic projection differ, therefore, from their perspective predecessors because they possess an inherent level of mathematical abstraction. Thomas Bradley, professor of geometrical drawing at King's College and at Woolwich, made this difference explicit by distinguishing 'pictorial' from 'graphical' representations. While the former depicted apparent forms, he stated, the latter could 'only suggest the thing represented to a mind trained to interpret rightly the mode of representation'.[27] Unlike perspective representations, which, theoretically at least, can be understood even by the uninitiated, projections can only be 'read' by those who have learned the code. The knowledge of mathematics required to understand them is, however, much inferior to the knowledge required to produce them which, in turn, is vastly inferior to that required to calculate physical relationships in the abstract. In a rather fuzzier sense, then, knowledge of mechanical drawing should be taken not as a dividing line between the engineer/designer and the mechanic/ artisan but as a common space, comprising a complex range of gradations, which both allowed supervisors and workers to communicate and effectively codified the social distance between them according to a mutually accepted standard.

Although geometric and mechanical drawing were made available to a working-class public through technically orientated manuals, information was presented on varying levels of complexity, usually staggered according to price, the cheapest manuals tending to restrict themselves to the most elementary knowledge. Between the 1830s and 1850s, relatively few drawing manuals with a technical bent were published; and, by the 1870s and 1880s, the professional space defined by the highest level of technical drawing had become more neatly codified, mainly through the growth of formal technical education as well as unions and other professional bodies. Although the intervening decades witnessed a remarkable proliferation of technically orientated manuals at a time when the class attribution of terms such as 'designer' and 'engineer' was still largely ambiguous, there is no evidence of an unusual amount of social permeability based on professional status during this period. The increased diffusion of technical drawing at the time would seem to indicate, rather, a crucial point of transition in the process by which 'designer' and 'engineer' acceded from the status of trades to that of professions. Mechanical drawing was made available in different ways to different groups, and this sense of variegated purposes must inform any understanding of its functions in mid-Victorian Britain. As Thomas Bradley made clear, though, a theoretical knowledge of mathematics constituted the true dividing line between thinking and making: without such knowledge, he warned, a student would remain 'a mere copier of buildings, machinery, or constructions which he certainly does not rightly understand'.[28]

Young artisans and mechanics were more likely to engage in mechanical drawing as a part of courses in general or elementary drawing which concluded with basic notions of how machines looked than they were to undertake a complete study of orthographic projection accompanied by adequate instruction in mathematics, mechanics and physics. As late as the 1860s, for instance, there were virtually no cheap books available providing instruction in this form. At the upper end of the scale, advanced and exhaustive books such as Woolley's *Elements of Descriptive Geometry* (1850), Bradley's *Elements of Geometrical Drawing* (1861–62) or Rankine's *Manual of Civil Engineering* (1865) were reserved for an elite of professional practitioners, many of whom frequented the new institutions of higher technical education. Woolley's book, directed to naval engineers, cost 20 shillings; Bradley's, 32 s. At a lower but still exclusive level of the pricing scale, a book like Binns's *Course of Geometrical Drawing* (1863) – costing 9s.6d. – provided a general and useful introduction to orthographic and isometric projection. Although Binns encouraged the inclusion of geometrical drawing as a branch of national education, pointing out its utility to 'those who shall hereafter be engaged in the arts of industry', he lamented that it was actually made available in very few schools.[29] At the more accessible price of 1s.6d., the second series of Chambers' *Drawing and Perspective in a Series of Progressive Lessons* (1851–55), authored by Robert Scott Burn, offered basic notions of mechanical and isometric drawing, but with a greatly reduced amount of explanatory text, if compared to Binns. At the bottom end of the scale, *Vere Foster's Drawing Copy Books* [1868] – various of which covered mechanical drawing – provided little more than plates to be copied, but at the bargain price of 3d. each. By price and by format of books and manuals, working-class practitioners were generally obliged to approach mechanical drawing more from the vantage point of art than of science: that is to say, they tended to spend more time copying flat depictions of machines than studying the principles by which they operate. It was not until the 1870s that a modicum of the 'intellectual' aspects of mechanical drawing began to filter down to the working artisan, often through the efforts of individuals who had already helped themselves up the ladder of knowledge.

Educating the eye

Parallel to such developments in drawing instruction, interest in vision and the physiology of the eye reached a new level of intensity, with a corresponding increase in both theoretical and practical knowledge of the subject.[30] Writers on art and design education were certainly not oblivious to the transformations going on in the sciences relating to vision. In his landmark *Essay on the Education of the Eye*, John Burnet remarked that the eye, like other parts of the body, acquires 'strength and perfection from frequent use of the muscles'. Sportsmen and sailors, therefore, were particularly suited to seeing at a distance, 'while those whose professions lead them to close examination, see better at small distances'.[31] A later writer on ophthalmology concurred, suggesting that nearsightedness was extremely rare among labourers, excepting 'those artisans and mechanics whose peculiar work demands a constant, and therefore injurious, strain … upon the eyes'. He added, however, that nearsightedeness did possess the advantage of rendering close-up vision 'particularly keen', making it useful in drawing and penwork.[32] In light of such quasi-Lamarckian notions of the correspondence between physiological development and physical activity, the education of the eye was a subject not to be taken lightly.

Attentiveness and accuracy of sight were widely deemed to number among the most important acquirements of drawing instruction. Drawing's purported ability to endow learners with a meticulously focused vision became a highly prized aspect of elementary education, evoking even more concern at times than reading and writing. According to many educational texts of the period, drawing provides excellent opportunities for inculcating habits of accuracy and neatness in children as well as for remedying deficiencies of observation in adults, because of its ability to educate the eye, cultivate the mind and train the hand. In fact, the discourse of the 'educated eye' and the 'trained hand' became so pervasive and so prominent, that it can be readily singled out as the most conspicuous ideal advanced by nineteenth-century drawing instruction. To say that drawing enhances powers of observation and manipulation is, of course, no historical anomaly. Drawing has been valued for these advantages for as long as it has been practised and remains serviceable in this capacity today. What can perhaps be seen as anomalous is the exaggerated way in which these aspects were highlighted, as well as the emphasis on their particular suitability to the working classes and to the purposes of industrial work.

Drawing's perceived ability to instil habits of accuracy and precision was routinely overstated to an extent which seems almost ludicrous today. One translator of Louis Benjamin Francœur's classic textbook on linear drawing suggested that its practice was capable of imbuing the eye and hand with an extraordinary degree of precision, 'almost equal to that of ordinary instruments'. George Wallis, headmaster of the Birmingham School of Art, took this comparison one step further, arguing that the eye was, 'mechanically speaking', nothing more than a camera obscura and the hand, 'an exquisitely constructed pair of compasses'.[33] Equipped with such precision instruments, there was no limit to what the properly educated mind could do. Mechanical exactitude was perceived to be not only useful but an increasingly necessary possession in the context of factory work. As has been seen in the previous section, Andrew Ure set a standard for panic – which educationists were keen to capitalise upon – by asserting that the principle of the factory system was 'to substitute mechanical science for hand skill'. All processes requiring 'peculiar dexterity and steadiness of hand' would be withdrawn from the '*cunning* workman, who is prone to irregularities of many kinds', predicted Ure, and placed in the charge of a machine 'so self-regulating that a child may superintend it'. Skilled labour would be progressively superseded and replaced by 'mere overlookers of machines' (see figure 2.3). The grand object of the modern manufacturer, he concluded, was 'to reduce the task of his work-people to the exercise of *vigilance and dexterity*, – faculties, when concentrated to one process, speedily brought to perfection in the young'.[34]

Whether to save workers from this sad fate or better to equip them for the exercise of vigilance and dexterity, art educationists after Ure focused even more resolutely on the applicability of drawing to purposes of work. As one writer of the 1840s put it:

> From the anvil of the smith to the workbench of the joiner, to the manufacturer of the most costly productions of ornamental art, [drawing] is ever at hand with its powerful aid, in strengthening invention and execution, and qualifying the mind and hand to design and produce whatever the wants or the tastes of society may require.[35]

2.3 'Workmen operating lathes'

In 1852, the Council of the Society of Arts likewise affirmed 'that there is hardly any handicraft in which a workman can be engaged, ... which would not be greatly improved by an ability to perceive the form of objects correctly, and represent it with precision'.[36] Not surprisingly, since he was a leading member of that council, the future superintendent of the Department of Science and Art, Henry Cole, agreed. In a more or less contemporaneous speech, he asserted that a bricklayer's skill was determined by 'his power of seeing correctly, his power of measuring distances, and his ability of making his hands work correctly according to his knowledge'. Drawing, Cole pondered, would make him a better bricklayer and a better member of society, as well as earning him higher wages.[37] Still not satisfied that they had given due attention to the subject, the council of the Society of Arts appointed a committee to inquire into industrial instruction. The report of that committee belaboured even further the point that the continued progress of industrial production in Britain depended on cultivating habits of observation among workmen. As James Nasmyth put it in a letter to the committee, '[n]ine tenths of all the bad work and botches that occur in our business of engineers and machine makers, results from the want of that mere power of comparison and "*correct* eye," which is so rare amongst such class of workmen'. In light of the *'commercial* value' of such knowledge and the huge losses entailed by 'crooked work', something needed to be done urgently. Nasmyth expressed his distress at 'how totally neglected is the education of the eye in our schools' and recommended drawing as the route to 'the perfection of the manufactures of the country'.[38]

Drawing was particularly advised as a preparation for factory work, which required a heightened attention to minute detail and the ability to perceive minimal variations in pattern and surface. Ralph N. Wornum, of the Department of Practical Art, made a clear-cut case for the art education of factory workers in the *Art-Journal* in 1852, arguing that good manufactures relied more upon 'correctness of eye and proper appreciation of forms' than upon 'any mechanical quality whatsoever'. The case of the silk-weaver provided him with the chance to expound this idea more fully:

> He cannot give uniformity to his pattern except by paying the strictest attention to his work; some may be too close, and some loose, even with a uniform weft, but suppose he should accident-ally have given to him, or carelessly take, a wrong weft too coarse or too fine, if he understands his pattern, he will instantly detect an alteration in its shape, he will find it contracting or elongating, and will stop; but suppose he cannot appreciate the figure he is working, he will go on unconscious of the change, and spoil a whole valuable piece of silk, or, at least, considerably reduce its price; and those who are above such mistakes are the exception.[39]

The following year, *The Home Companion* told its mainly working-class readership that art education could provide the artisan with the power of seeing 'rightly and truly' and the ability 'to perceive many qualities and relations which would otherwise be overlooked or not properly understood'. Signifi-cantly, these statements emphasise the value of drawing to vision alone, relegating touch to a position of inferiority. 'Correctness of eye', it was widely believed, would effect definite improvements in the taste and design of manufactured objects, by keeping sloppy hands in check.[40]

The question was not simply one of training workers to pay attention to their work, though this was already a major source of concern at the time and has remained as such to this day. The early to mid-nineteenth century witnessed a broader restructuring of the regime of vision, moving from what was bold, expansive and globalising to what was meticulous, confined and detailed. In terms of optical inventions such as stereoscopy, photography and even improvements in lenses and spectacles, 'looking in', 'looking through' and 'looking at' were acquiring new directional meanings too focused and particularised for an activity as generic as just 'looking'.[41] The phrenologist George Combe revealed something of the contemporary sense of uneasiness with the world beyond ordinary appearances when he wrote of the 'disgust' which too great an intensity of vision might provoke: under a powerful microscope, he remarked, 'the cheek of beauty becomes coarse, and the water of the crystal stream is filled with impurities and life'.[42] Alongside such developments, scientific interest in minute differences of appearance was on the rise in astronomy, geology, botany, zoology and even anthropology, as systems of identification and classification were refined to degrees previously unimaginable. Scientists were widely credited with the ability to observe 'distinctions so minute as to escape the vulgar eye', as one drawing manual put it. A biographical essay on William Hyde Wollaston – who patented the camera lucida in 1807, among other achievements – similarly dwelt on the scientific precision of seeing which allowed him to make out details 'so minute as to be scarcely perceptible by ordinary eyes'.[43] As the noted scientific writer Robert Hunt pointed out in his essay on *The Importance of Cultivating Habits of Observation*, there were no accidents in science; learning to observe 'closely and accurately' was the key to great discoveries.[44] Observation was subtly being transmuted into something of a moral quality, implying a superiority of character which distinguished great men from the unseeing masses.

Panacea that it was, drawing was invoked by writers of manuals as the ideal means of cultivating these desired habits of scientific observation. John Clark's *Elements of Drawing and Perspective* lumped together drawing, mechanics and natural science as different means of seeing what was hidden to ordinary view:

As he who has acquired a knowledge of Botany feels a new
pleasure in examining the parts of a plant; as he who has acquired a
knowledge of Geology feels a new pleasure in passing along a road,
the side of which, perhaps, displays a deep section of rock, or from
which he may view granitic elevations; as he who has acquainted
himself with the principles of Machinery experiences an enjoy-
ment in contemplating the intricacies of some great engine, which
another knows nothing of; so does he who has studied the art of
Drawing discover a source of new and most innocent gratification
in the innumerable forms and tints of external nature.[45]

Throughout the middle part of the century, manuals continued
to emphasise the importance of drawing in inculcating 'habits of
observation and of contemplation' and to link this to the
painstaking examination of detail in the natural sciences and in
technological subjects.[46] Drawing was fulfilling its brief as a
universal language of visual description not only for industry
and commerce but for science as well.

This association of the various branches of industry,
commerce and science was set out in Cassell's *The Technical
Educator: An Encyclopaedia of Technical Education* (1870) and
placed within reach of a wide audience. Alongside essays on technical drawing by Ellis A. Davidson, on design by Christopher
Dresser and on colour by A. H. Church, the *Technical Educator*
contained articles on applied mechanics; civil engineering; commercial products animal, mineral and vegetable; and a vast range
of mechanical and scientific subjects. In this instance and others,
drawing instruction was unambiguously presented within a global
context of learning to view detailed images of all sorts closely and
to read plans and diagrams correctly.

Although the new visual literacy promoted through technical
drawing instruction was being applied to objects and purposes
wider than the representation of machines, manufacturing processes remained very much at the heart of the endeavour. The
vast majority of the illustrations contained in encyclopaedic
volumes like Burn's or Cassell's referred either to the raw materials
of industry or to the machines and processes by which they were
transformed into commodities. What is truly remarkable about
these images, though, is the homogeneity of treatment involved
in their depiction (see figures 2.4–2.5). Regardless of nature and

2.4 'Lathe'

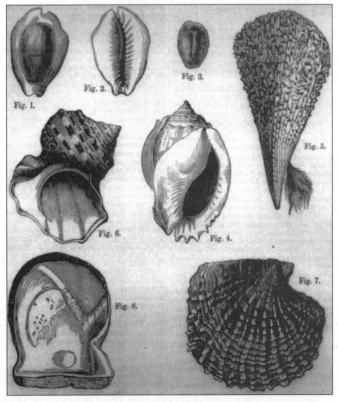

2.5 'Shells'

purpose, these 'objects' – including shells, animals, machines, weapons of war, the odd diagram of a toilet – were all presented as specimens of a vague and generic 'technical knowledge', detached from any background or function, as if on display in an imaginary museum or exhibition of the mind. The nature of the representations themselves reflects a curious duality of concern with three-dimensional structure as well as an exaggerated focus on pictorial or surface detail. To possess at a single glance so much knowledge of the internal and external arrangements of a shell, to see a whole lathe in perspective and yet see it so closely that it is possible to count the teeth on a gear wheel – these are impossible views, uniting near and far, inside and outside, surface and structure, in ways that the eye could not do (at least not without the assistance of fingers to touch and a mind to remember), yet all these levels of knowledge are subsumed within single images of an encyclopaedic nature.

A concern with the tension between surfaces and structures seems to underpin much of the debate on drawing instruction throughout the mid-Victorian period. Seeing the true nature of objects was a power 'laboriously attained', wrote the architect Thomas Morris in his manual of perspective: 'we cannot comprehend the character and principles of things, their special anatomy, structure, and peculiarities, at a glance'.[47] Morris's statement bears comparison to John Ruskin's concern with drawing the 'vital facts of form': those underlying structures beyond superficial appearances. Ruskin contrasted the bad draughtsman who sees only the irregularity of tiles in an old roof with the good one who sees 'all the bends of the under timbers'.[48] There is a fundamental difference between representing, illusionistically, that which can be seen and representing, abstractedly, that which cannot be seen at all: a difference perhaps first addressed within the field of architectural drawing through the complementary use of perspective views and plans. As Nesbitt has noted, perspective drawing deals only with appearances as they can be seen by the naked eye, while mechanical drawing deals with the 'truth' behind surfaces.[49] Neither Ruskin nor Thomas Morris was concerned with teaching mechanical drawing, yet both expressed a desire to use drawing as a means of moving from surface to structure. The solution they offered, in slightly varying degrees, was an eminently 'artistic' one, involving the strategic magnification and suppression of pictorial detail. The common ground shared by Ruskin and Thomas Morris, by Cassell's *Technical Educator* and Burn's 'object teaching' and by mechanical drawing, as it encompasses both orthographic projection and linear perspective, is a desire to accede to that which cannot be seen or touched, to the factors beyond appearances which can only be grasped abstractedly by the intellect, to the minute, particularised, microscopic elements that are the building blocks of the visible universe, but, simultaneously and impossibly, without ever losing sight of the more global view.

Conclusion

To conclude simply that technical drawing instruction served to separate hand and head would be not only historicist but also somewhat misleading. The head/hand distinction certainly dates back much further than the popularisation of technical drawing in the mid-nineteenth century. If that were the case, furthermore, how would it be possible to explain that middle-class practitioners of technical drawing such as architects, engineers and eventually designers rose to a position of social parity with painters, sculptors and other professionals? Clearly, technical drawing was not in itself stigmatised, only certain practitioners of it. Since mechanical drawing was made available to at least some working artisans and mechanics, how was the 'dividing line' between their knowledge and the knowledge of their 'betters' defined? As has been seen in the previous section, the differentiation of levels of knowledge took place not so much around a single, definitive, dividing line – an unbridgeable gap between knowing and not knowing – as along a gradated hierarchy in which the two extremes were clearly defined while the various intervening spaces remained contested sites. The main purpose of popular drawing instruction – as it was made available both institutionally and through manuals – was to flesh out those intermediary stopping points between no knowledge at all and the expert knowledge of a fine artist or a scientific engineer.

As the main sensorial point of translation between subject and object, vision came to represent a sort of middle ground in

the relationship between manual and intellectual. The relationship of eye to hand was often taken as the metonymic representative of drawing instruction itself, as an idealised site for
mediating the conflict between operative and ruling classes.
Writers on drawing spoke of the eye as the 'sure and intelligent
monitor' of the hand, while the hand was 'in a manner paralyzed'
without the guidance of the eye.[50] Just as the eye guided the
hand, both were in turn equally governed by the head; the task
of drawing was, therefore, 'to acquire, by strict manual exercise,
a habit of prompt obedience to the will', a combination that could
only be achieved through the 'universal accuracy of the eye'.[51]
On a rather unsophisticated, but none the less cogent, level of
metaphor, this hierarchy of bodily parts reflects an evolving
vision of society in which the tensions between rulers and ruled
were mediated by typically middle-class concerns with education,
reform and philanthropy. On a more profound level, the conspi-
cuousness of the union of 'educated eye' and 'trained hand'
bespeaks a process of subsumption of the latter by the former,
through which hands acting alone were perceived to be rendered
obsolete. As has been seen, workers themselves seemed for a time
– notably, between the 1830s and 1850s – to be losing their
relevance within the process of labour. With the advance of
mechanisation, the value of their labour would cease to depend
on manual dexterity or mechanical strength and become reduced
to their powers of vision – as mere overlookers of machines.
Similarly to the encyclopaedic depictions of objects provided in
the manuals they read, the immense variety of craft knowledge
workers had once been expected to possess was now broadly
subsumed within the single skill of observing accurately and
precisely. As eyes became ever more sovereign, hands became
inevitably more idle.

     This new culture of vision came eventually to engender a new
vision of culture, fostering art schools, museums and public
libraries under the auspices of the very institutional agents which
had first been charged with the task of teaching workers to draw
– namely, the Department of Science and Art and its offshoots.[52]
Though the authorities at South Kensington very soon began to
falter in their attempts at providing technical education, they
quickly slipped into a new and much more profitable role as a

vehicle for the distribution of government subsidies and favours. Alongside the established civic institutions of exclusion and repression, the latter half of the nineteenth century witnessed the rise of standardised institutions of inclusion and leisure.[53] From today's vantage point, this precedent of transforming technologies of enhanced productivity into spaces of leisure and entertainment possesses a particular resonance. As the ideal of virtuality lures us ever deeper into a parallel universe of abstracted visual experience, it is difficult not to wonder what will become of the very real pleasure of hands-on interactivity with people, places and things.

Notes

1 W. Whewell, 'The general bearing of the Great Exhibition on the progress of art and science', *Lectures on the Results of the Great Exhibition of 1851 Delivered Before the Society of Arts, Manufactures and Commerce* (London: David Bogue, 1852), pp. 2–12.

2 See, for example, Mrs [Mary P.] Merrifield, *Handbook of Light and Shade, with Especial Reference to Model Drawing* (London: George Rowney & Co., 1855), p. 40; E. A. Davidson, *Drawing for Elementary Schools* (London: Chapman and Hall, 1857), p. vi.

3 After playing an essential part in organising the Great Exhibition, Henry Cole was given the post of superintendent of the newly formed Department of Practical Art in 1852, the name of which was changed to Department of Science and Art in 1854. A part of the surplus funds from the Exhibition were used to purchase objects for the Schools of Design, absorbed into the new Department, as well as to acquire the Kensington Gore Estate, which later became the site of the South Kensington Museum and headquarters of the Department after 1856. For a summary history, see C. Frayling and C. Catterall (eds), *Design of the Times: One Hundred Years of the Royal College of Art* (Shepton Beauchamps, Somerset: Richard Dennis Publications/Royal College of Art, 1996), esp. pp. 14–23.

4 *Art-Journal*, 1853, p. 98; and F. E. Hulme, *Art Instruction in England* (London: Longmans, Green & Co., 1882), p. 71.

5 Molly Nesbitt has posited the existence of a 'language of industry' geared towards purposes of work and commerce in late nineteenth-century France, tracing this phenomenon to the Ferry reforms of the educational curriculum which imposed Eugène Guillaume's method of drawing instruction on French schools. Nesbitt's analysis is only enriched by the realisation that the same process was at work in Britain as early as the 1850s, especially bearing in mind that Guillaume's pedagogical methods were heavily influenced by South Kensington. See M. Nesbitt, 'Ready-

made originals: the Duchamp model', *October* 37 (1986), pp. 53–9. The same subject is taken up in greater detail in M. Nesbitt, 'The language of industry', in T. de Duve (ed.), *The Definitively Unfinished Marcel Duchamp* (Cambridge: MIT Press, 1991), pp. 353–6.

6 J. Crary, 'Unbinding vision', *October* 68 (1994), pp. 22–4.

7 On the history and importance of such sources, see my 'A preliminary survey of drawing manuals in Britain, c.1825–1875', *Journal of Art and Design Education* 15 (1996), pp. 263–75.

8 For a summary and dismissal of the functionalist argument, see A. Green, *Education and State Formation: the Rise of Educational Systems in England, France and the USA* (London: Macmillan, 1990), pp. 36–40.

9 On the widespread abuses of computers in education, see T. Roszak, *The Cult of Information* (Berkeley: University of California Press, 1993).

10 C. Babbage, *On the Economy of Machinery and Manufactures* (London: Charles Knight, 1832), pp. 136–7, 207.

11 C. Ryan, *Systematic Drawing and Shading* (London: Cassell, Petter and Galpin, 1868), p. 12; W. S. Binns, *An Elementary Treatise on Orthographic Projection* (London: E. & F. N. Spon, 1857), pp. iii–iv.

12 See, for example, J. Clark, *Elements of Drawing and Perspective* (Edinburgh: William and Robert Chambers, 1837), pp. i–ii; J. G. Chapman, *The Elements of Art* (London: David Bogue, 1848), p. 4; *The Engineer and Machinist's Drawing Book* (Glasgow: Blackie & Son, 1855), p. iii; Ryan, *Systematic Drawing*, p. 11.

13 J. Locke, *Some Thoughts on Education* (London: J. Hatchard and Son, 1836), pp. 242–3.

14 A. Ure, *The Cotton Manufacture of Great Britain Investigated and Illustrated* (1861) [1835], p. lxxiv.

15 '"An unlearned people" made learned in "common things"', *Spectator* 29 (1856), p. 1080.

16 R. Scott Burn, *Mechanics and Mechanism* (London: Ingram, Cooke, and Co., 1853), pp. vi–viii.

17 Society of Arts, *The Report of the Committee Appointed to Inquire into the Subject of Industrial Instruction* (London: Longman, Brown, Green and Longmans, 1853), pp. 25–6.

18 R. Burchett, *On the Central Training School for Art* (London: Chapman and Hall, 1858), pp. 8–9.

19 H. Grant, *Directions for Introducing the First Steps of Elementary Drawing in Schools, and among Workmen* (London: Chapman and Hall, 1852), pp. 4–5.

20 A. Ure, *The Philosophy of Manufactures* (London: Charles Knight, 1835), pp. x–xi.

21 H. Bolton, *Drawing from Objects* (London: Groombridge and Sons, 1850), p. 2; H. Grant, *Drawing for Young Children* [1862], p. xiv.

22 For an explicit statement of the importance of working drawings, see C. B. Allen, 'A proposal for an art result society', *Journal of the Society of Arts* 12 (1863–64), pp. 435, 565.

23 Binns, *Elemetary Treatise*, p. viii.

24 J. M. Edmondson, *From Mécanicien to Ingénieur: Technical Education and the Machine Building Industry in Nineteenth-century France* (New York: Garland, 1987), p. 511.

25 L. Purbrick, *Machines and the mechanism of representation: the display of design in mid-nineteenth-century Britain* (unpublished D.Phil. dissertation, University of Sussex, 1994), pp. 102–4. See also L. Purbrick, 'Ideologically technical: illustration, automation and spinning cotton around the middle of the nineteenth century', *Journal of Design History* 11 (1998), pp. 275–293.

26 R. Willis, 'On machines and tools for working in metal, wood, and other materials', in Society of Arts, *Lectures on the Results*, p. 297.

27 T. Bradley, *On Practical Plane and Descriptive Geometry* (London: Eyre & Spottiswoode, 1860), p. 3.

28 *Ibid.*, pp. 13–15.

29 W. S. Binns, *A Course of Geometrical Drawing* (London: John Weale, 1863), pp. iii–iv.

30 For more on this, see A. Briggs, *Victorian Things* (Harmondsworth: Penguin, 1990), esp. ch.3.

31 J. Burnet, *An Essay on the Education of the Eye* (London: James Carpenter, 1837), p. 68n.

32 R. Hengist Horne, 'Eyes and eye-glasses. A friendly treatise', *Fraser's Magazine* 14 (1876), pp. 698–9.

33 W. B. Fowle, 'Introduction', in L. B. Francœur, *An Introduction to Linear Drawing* (Boston: Hilliard, Gray, Little, and Wilkins, 1830), p. iv; and G. Wallis, *Drawing Book for the Use of Artizans* (London: Chapman and Hall, 1859), pp. 7–8.

34 Ure, *Philosophy*, pp. 8, 19–22 (emphasis added).

35 Chapman, *Elements of Art*, p. 4.

36 Cited in D. R. Hay, *A Letter to the Council of the Society of Arts, on Elementary Education in the Arts of Design* (London: William Blackwood and Sons, 1852), pp. 3–4.

37 [Handwritten text of a speech, c.1851] in H. Cole, *Miscellanies*, v.11 (1851–66), pp. 34–42 [housed in the National Art Library/V&A].

38 Nasmyth cited in Society of Arts, *Report into the Subject of Industrial Instruction* (1853), p. 172; see also pp. 25–6, 89.

39 R. N. Wornum, 'The Government Schools of Design', *Art-Journal*, 1852, pp. 38–9.

40 *Home Companion* 2 (1853), p. 311; H. Krüsi and W. J. Whitaker, *A*

Progressive Course of Inventive Drawing on the Principles of Pestalozzi (London: W. F. Ramsay, 1850), p. 1.

41 On the new vision, see J. Crary, *Techniques of the Observer: On Vision and Modernity in the Nineteenth Century* (Cambridge: MIT Press, 1990).

42 G. Combe, *Phrenology applied to Painting and Sculpture* (London: Simpkin, Marshall, and Co., 1855), pp. 2–3.

43 B. Waterhouse Hawkins, *The Science of Drawing Simplified* (London: Smith, Elder and Co., 1843), p. 5; and W. Walker, *Methods of the Distinguished Men of Science of Great Britain Living in the Years 1807–8* (London: W. Walker & Son, 1862), p. 219.

44 R. Hunt, *The Importance of Cultivating Habits of Observation* (London: Eyre & Spottiswoode, 1851), p. 19.

45 Clark, *Elements of Drawing*, pp. ii–iii.

46 C. E. Butler Williams, *A Manual for Teaching Model-drawing from Solid Forms* (London: John W. Parker, 1843), pp. 18–19.

47 T. Morris, *A Popular Outline of Perspective or Graphic Projection* (London: Simpkin, Marshall, and Co., 1869), p. 11.

48 J. Ruskin, *The Elements of Drawing* (1857), in E. T. Cook and A. Wedderburn (eds), *The Works of John Ruskin* (Sunnyside: George Allen, 1903–12), v. 15, pp. 91–6.

49 Nesbitt, 'Ready-made' (1986), p. 59.

50 C. F. Blunt, *Polytechnic Drawing-book* ([London]: n.p., [1841]), p. ii; Burnet, *Essay*, p. 2.

51 R. Peale, *Graphics; a Manual of Drawing and Writing* (London: W. Molineux, 1835), p. 7.

52 See my 'Teaching by example: education and the formation of South Kensington's museums', in B. Richardson and M. Baker (eds), *A Grand Design: The Art of the Victoria and Albert Museum* (New York: Abrams, 1997), pp. 107–16.

53 For a fuller analysis, see my *The educated eye and the industrial hand: art and design instruction for the working classes in mid-Victorian Britain* (unpublished Ph.D. dissertation, Courtauld Institute of Art/University of London, 1995), pp. 218–26.

3

Entrepreneurship and the artisans: John Cassell, the Great Exhibition and the periodical idea

BRIAN MAIDMENT

Introduction

This chapter is centrally concerned with three half-yearly volumes of the weekly periodical *The Illustrated Exhibitor* which was published by John Cassell in the eighteen months between July 1851 and December 1852. The first thirty issues of the magazine (volume 1) were published throughout the second half of 1851, and were intended to accumulate into both a catalogue and an interpretation of the significance of the Great Exhibition which was, of course, open to the public during the same period. The second series (volumes 2 and 3) comprised 52 weekly issues and occupied 1852. Although the second and third volumes of *The Illustrated Exhibitor* were published under the same title, the function of the periodical was bound to change as a result of the closure of the Exhibition. The changes made to the periodical – to ensure its survival not as an Exhibition catalogue and a topical commentary on the Exhibition but rather as an embodiment of the values and ideas it suggested – form the central interest of this chapter.

Putting this intention in a wider context, this chapter describes the way in which what might be called 'The Exhibition Idea', as both constructed and scrutinised by the 1851 *Exhibitor*, was sustained, analysed, and ultimately transformed by Cassell's periodicals during the period of, and the months immediately following, the Exhibition. In this context 'The Exhibition Idea' is meant to stand for a complex alliance between ideological vision, new illustrated periodical genres based on the exploitation of high technology modes of production in combination with a range of both established and innovative content, and the recognition of a clearly defined artisan readership. Making use of the organisation of knowledge and the understanding of the socio-cultural implications of industrialism which the Exhibition embodied, *The Illustrated Exhibitor* can be best understood as an attempt to validate and sustain a culture in which a progressive artisan elite would live out the visions of internationalism, rational progress and industrial imperialism represented by the Crystal Palace and its contents. It also needs to be understood as an original and in many ways a radical formulation of the periodical idea by a progressive and increasingly successful pioneer of cheap illustrated journalism.

But if the main thrust of this chapter is to offer a descriptive account of *The Illustrated Exhibitor,* there is a wider argument at stake. It is possible to describe *The Illustrated Exhibitor* as a periodical that to some extent resisted the commodity fetishism and rampant imperialism which Tony Bennett, for example, sees as deriving from, and as structured by, the Great Exhibition.[1] The *Exhibitor*'s vision of the artisan presence in the processes of production – and of the democratising, rather than imperialistic, power of mass production and its trans-national technological processes – were, in Bennett's terms, a throwback to what were rapidly becoming outmoded values. Bennett suggests that many previous exhibitions, especially those mounted by such working-class organisations as Mechanics Institutes, 'placed considerable stress on the centrality of labour's contributions to the processes of production which, at times, allowed a radical appropriation of their message. "The machinery of wealth, here displayed," the *Leeds Times* noted in reporting an 1839 exhibition, "has been created by the men of hammers and papercaps; more honourable than all the sceptres and coronets in the world".'[2] Accordingly, taken in the wider context of Cassell's expanding list of periodicals aimed at both drawing on and defining artisan culture, the

Exhibitor's celebration of artisan achievement and way of life can
be read as more generous, more visionary, perhaps even more
progressive than the 'stupefying' power of commodity culture
might have been expected to permit. Although primarily a
commercially astute entrepreneur, and thus himself a representative of a vigorously expanding commodity culture, Cassell none
the less offered his artisan readers an account of their own world
which was largely constructed out of an optimistic, creative and
essentially *participative* sense of the potential of the new technocratic working classes. Much of the argument of this chapter
must be structured by this sense of duality – Cassell's grasp of
the artisan market-place and commercial potential of magazines
is in complex dialogue with his determination to create a version
of artisan culture which is not simply a result of the hegemonic
drive of what Bennett identifies as the dominant ideological project of exhibitions at this time – the transformation of 'displays of
machinery and industrial processes into material signifiers of
progress – but of progress as a collective national achievement
with capital as the great co-ordinator'.[3] The power of such exhibitions, he claims, 'subjugated [its spectators] by flattery' and
'inveigled [them] into complicity'.[4]

  I find it difficult to identify Cassell with such a hegemonic
project on the evidence of *The Illustrated Exhibitor* at least. Like a
number of other entrepreneurs of mass publishing for artisans in
this period - the Chambers brothers and William and Mary
Howitt provide obvious examples – Cassell saw artisans both as
consumers and as a significantly progressive element within
industrial society. Such duality is complicated by the relatively
lowly social origins of all these people. This chapter seeks to use
such ambivalence as a structuring device to explore not just the
account of the Great Exhibition which emerges from Cassell's
magazines, but the wider place of *The Illustrated Exhibitor* in the
history of artisan culture in mid-Victorian Britain.

John Cassell and periodicals for the artisans

The evolutionary process that transformed *The Illustrated Exhibitor*
from an annotated catalogue into a magazine which represented a
broader tradition of artisan self-educational endeavour needs to

be placed briefly in a number of contexts if its full significance is to be understood. The first of these is the entrepreneurial career of its publisher, John Cassell.

John Cassell's name is, and was, extremely well known from the title pages of many Victorian books and periodicals, especially those which found their way into the homes of ambitious, respectable artisans keen to make their mark in a newly technocratic culture.[5] He was, like other entrepreneurs such as William Howitt or the Chambers brothers who developed print culture outside of propagandist institutions and organisations for an emergent artisan readership,[6] himself of a relatively poor background, and stood in a somewhat awkward relationship to the working men on whom he relied for his large profits. *Cassell's Illustrated Family Paper* in particular is often seen as exemplifying a widely held middle-class vision of what the respectable working classes might read and, through the assimilation of their reading, think.[7] Other of his hugely successful publications from the 1850s, such as *The Working Man's Friend and Family Instructor*, *The Popular Educator* and *The Historical Educator*, laid out self-educative and self-improving programmes for artisan readers drawing on the widely held belief in the value of 'useful knowledge'.

Cassell's early career was both practically and emblematically bound up with the Great Exhibition of 1851, held when Cassell was a struggling young businessman of thirty-four.[8] Simon Nowell-Smith notes that 'Cassell exploited the exhibition to the full'[9] not just as a publisher but also as an entrepreneur alert to the emergent spending power of artisans. Recognising at an early stage that the Exhibition would be of huge appeal to artisans, Cassell's immediate response to the business opportunities represented by the Exhibition was to launch a scheme for accommodating large numbers of artisans in cheap lodgings.[10] Quite aside from the entrepreneurial opportunism of Cassell's venture, his lodgings scheme attests to his clear-sighted recognition that artisans were beginning to become an identifiable social group in a number of significant ways. As well as a sense of their own centrality to the maintenance and development of an increasingly technological society, artisans were beginning to show some awareness of their opportunities for social mobility. Such a new sense of social identity was recognised partly in their increasing power as consumers, especially as buyers of 'cultural' and educational products which would, they hoped, themselves prove valuable in furthering the economic and social rise of their purchasers.

By 1851 Cassell had already launched the first of his 'artisan' periodicals, the unillustrated, small format, dour, and cramped 1d. weekly, *The Working Man's Friend and Family Instructor*.[11] A miscellany in the tradition of *Chambers's Edinburgh Journal*, the first series of *The Working Man's Friend* nevertheless explored radical new potential in encouraging its artisan readers to submit their own work which the magazine 'from time to time ... shall select articles which will alike reflect credit upon that important Order, and render essential service to the great Body of which they are such worthy representatives'.[12] Even at this early stage of his mass circulation publishing career, Cassell was both identifying and exploring the nature and potential of the artisan 'Order' as a distinct cultural formation in contemporary society.

The first seven volumes of *The Working Man's Friend*, with their radical stress on giving artisans access to print, gave way to a new series in October 1851. By this time, the prior launch of *The Illustrated Exhibitor* had given Cassell the formal blueprint he needed to develop his artisan publications – a double-columned quarto page using large wood-engraved illustrations, and a contents list which extended a range of factually based and extended explicatory articles beyond the human and physical sciences into the fields of manufacture, natural history, biography and, to a limited extent, fiction. But however attractive and successful the new format of *The Working Man's Friend* may have been, the second series of this periodical ostensibly dissociated itself from the earnest sense of cultural and political endeavour which had characterised the first series. Quite aside from the loss of the supplements dedicated to contributions sent in by working men,[13] the second series replaced sections starkly called 'Law and Politics', 'Biography', 'Tales' and 'Science' with the more temptingly titled 'London Scenes and Characters', 'Historical and Biographical Notices' and 'Glimpses of the People of All Nations'. As well as replacing baldly presented information with sections more obviously dependent on narrative and on 'snippets', the reformulated *Friend* announced its more overtly entertaining and

diversionary project with the introduction of both advertisements and copious illustration, set out on a larger quarto page
with increased opportunity for display.

Even with these significant changes which moved the magazine more into a mainstream format, *The Working Man's Friend*
itself became incorporated in 1853 into the most immediately
successful of Cassell's early periodicals, *The Popular Educator*
(launched in 1852), which concentrated largely on information
rendered entertaining by both diversity and illustration.[14] The
success of *The Popular Educator* in turn led to the founding of the
The Technical Educator and *The Historical Educator* (1854), which
both used the same layout and tone to address slightly more
specialised interests within the same potential readership. The
more entertaining and 'life-style' elements of *The Working Man's
Friend*, however, were transferred by Cassell into his most
famous periodical, *Cassell's Illustrated Family Paper*, which
began publication in 1853.[15]

This complex of periodicals is important to this article for a
number of reasons. First, it shows Cassell quickly grasping the
importance of a combination of cheapness, profuse, attractive
illustration in modes beyond the simply explicatory or diagrammatic, and the kind of habitual, frequent publication suggested
by a weekly issue. Second, it shows him slowly separating out
'information' and 'self-education' from more 'life-style' elements.
Third, Cassell was beginning to segregate his audience into very
precisely identified 'market sectors'. Finally, the publisher seemed
to pull back from his more radical ideas – access to print for
artisan authors, dialogue and discourse as part of a magazine's
editorial process – in order to implement a safer definition of
what might supply the reading needs of ambitious artisans.

What then of the *Exhibitor* itself? Its specialism had been the
delineation and celebration of technological process within a socio-
cultural context. But on the abandonment of the title at the end
of 1852 the more technical aspects of this project were incorporated into *The Popular Educator* and *The Technical Educator*,
while the more socio-cultural elements went to *The Illustrated
Family Paper*. These changes left the *Exhibitor* centrally interested
in illustration itself, and in 1853 Cassell re-launched the title as
The Illustrated Magazine of Art, a 2d. weekly. This project was an

attempt to capitalise on the efforts of entrepreneurs such as the Howitts and John Saunders to champion the cheap and accessible reproduction of 'fine art' as a form of mass entertainment and education. Nowell-Smith suggests that *The Illustrated Magazine of Art* was 'born before its time'[16] but significantly pre-figured developments in art journalism in the 1880s and 1890s.

To some extent, then, *The Illustrated Exhibitor* can be seen not just as a piece of commercial opportunism, but actually as a crucial experiment for Cassell in trying to extend the idea of the artisan journal, using the kinds of technological changes exemplified by the Great Exhibition, and the enthusiasm generated by them, as its unifying principle in defining what an artisan might read. Any such extension of interests required to sustain *The Illustrated Exhibitor* on beyond the Great Exhibition inevitably had to be into the socio-cultural context in which commodities were produced, robbed of precise political significance, but nevertheless giving the human presence a crucial role in the heroic commodification of British culture.

The excitement generated by the technological triumphalism of the Exhibition combined with the opportunities for cheap serial publication offered by the long-running show pressed Cassell in a number of innovative directions in formulating his periodicals. These innovations are especially clear in terms of the use of illustration, where Cassell exploited the full range of mass production image making which had been pioneered in the 1830s and 1840s by such successful and emblematic periodicals as *The Penny Magazine*, *The Saturday Magazine*, *The Illustrated London News* and *Punch*.[17] *The Illustrated Exhibitor* thus combined a number of key ideas into what was to prove an immensely successful formula: a recognition that artisans represented a new, potentially high-spending group with especial interests in self-educative reading; a brilliantly opportunistic awareness of the potential of *seriality* as a mode of publication for self-educative texts; an innovative use of the latest technology to produce profusely and interestingly illustrated texts at low cost. It is within these contexts of change and innovation in artisan reading that *The Illustrated Exhibitor* needs to be considered.

The Illustrated Exhibitor – Volume 1 July–December 1851

The first volume of *The Illustrated Exhibitor* was published in weekly parts between 7 June 1851 (five weeks after the Exhibition had opened) and 27 December in the same year, when the thirtieth number, a double issue, completed the 556-page volume. It cost 2d. a week,[18] and for your twopence you got twenty (sometimes sixteen) close printed double-column pages liberally illustrated with wood-engraved vignettes of varied size and shape. While the periodical's large circulation – Cassell claimed the first issue had sold 100,000 copies[19] – and use of new technology for the illustrations ensured that it remained cheap, Nowell-Smith reminds us that the capital investment required was a considerable one for Cassell. The illustrations for each number cost £50, and the advertising campaign Cassell ran on first publication was, at a cost of £100, extravagant enough to generate friction between Cassell and his staff.[20] On ten occasions a fold-out plate was distributed free with the periodical.[21] On completion at the end of 1851, the series was re-issued in volume form with a considerable amount (44 pages) of prefatory material – extracts from the closing speeches at the Exhibition, the official list of awards (which reinforced the organising pattern of the exhibits), and a list of the principal contents which names two authors: Charles Fowler, who wrote a series of nine pieces on the construction and building of the Crystal Palace,[22] and a French writer, Blanqui, who contributed a short series of 'Letters on the Great Exhibition'.[23] A concluding section of 'Binders' Instructions' emphasises the serial nature of the entire project, and suggests ways in which the shape and scope of the publication had grown in its making.

There is an immediate tension, then, between *The Illustrated Exhibitor* as a serial publication which was to some extent improvised and re-invented during its publication, and *The Illustrated Exhibitor* as a deliberately conceived and permanent monument to the Exhibition. Any assumption that serial publications are more ephemeral, more vulnerable to incompleteness and impermanence, than volumes was here challenged by the deliberate monumentality and self-consciousness of *The Illustrated Exhibitor*, which clearly saw itself as something more complete, more significant, and more enduring than a memento.

The concluding remarks to the introductory, celebratory, paragraphs of the first issue of the *Exhibitor* make the following claims:

> One word of ourselves. In this our book we shall from week to week endeavour to instruct the reader by effort of pen and pencil; till, in the end, we shall have produced a complete historical, pictorial, and literary description of the Great Exhibition – interesting alike to those who visit it and those who stay at home. Our plan will be more fully developed as we proceed. Like the ideas we illustrate, our tendencies are cosmopolitan.[24]

The serial then was meant to be both catalogue and commentary. It also sought to construct an experience of the Exhibition which could be either a memorialising of a visit, a rendering permanent of the actual experience of the Exhibition, or else a substitute experience, a virtual Exhibition, which might legitimately replace a visit to London with a different but no less worthwhile domestic Exhibition experience. In fact, as the tripled features of the 'historical', the 'pictorial', and the 'literary' suggest, the *Exhibitor* sought to render the Exhibition experience as something closer to a *hypertext* than a virtual reality. Each of these three elements in the magazine attempted to unify a considerable range of diverse purposes – to describe the artefacts in the exhibition accurately; to re-create the experience of the Exhibition from the point of view of the visitor and spectator; to contextualise commodities and machinery into their broader socio-historical (and national) contexts; and to offer commentary on the ideological, propagandist, and cultural polemics associated with the Exhibition. To achieve these purposes, the *Exhibitor* clearly had to step beyond Hyde Park in its range of interests and concerns.

The 'historical' concerns of the magazine were both local and wide reaching. Immediately, in its second number, the *Exhibitor* offered a brief history of the Exhibition idea[25] which, while seeming to be a generous acknowledgement of previous endeavours, served largely, both in text and illustration, to emphasise the huge differences in vision, scale, and ambition between the Crystal Palace and all its predecessors. Other articles rendered the building history of the Crystal Palace in precise detail.[26] But the magazine takes a much wider view of history as well, and one

of its central concerns was to illustrate the socio-political contexts
of commodities and their manufacture. In particular, as we shall
see in more detail later, the *Exhibitor* is interested in the
commercial and social history of Ireland.

The 'pictorial' elements of the *Exhibitor* are even more diverse
in their interests. The illustrations themselves comprise a number
of types which are all dependent on the technology of the wood
engraving, which, by the 1850s, had become established as easily
the best, perhaps the only, method for the mass production of
images, even where the precise rendering of technical detail was
required. In its total reliance on wood engraving, the *Exhibitor*
stands in contrast to many of the other catalogues and industrial
commentaries produced as a response to the Great Exhibition.
Charles Knight's two volume *Pictorial Gallery of Arts*, for example, presumably aimed at a somewhat similar readership to the
Exhibitor, prefaces the text with some self-consciously artistic
steel engravings, and masses its extraordinarily profuse small
woodcut illustrations on to separate double-page spreads, as if to
maintain the tradition of separate page illustration enforced by
metal engraving or etching even when illustrations could be
dropped into the text to sit alongside the appropriate paragraph
of text.[27] Similarly, the *Cyclopaedia of Arts,* edited by Charles
Tomlinson and published by George Vertue in 1854, which
acknowledged its debt to the Great Exhibition both by a long
prefatory account of it and by the organisation of its contents
through the structures used by the Exhibition, also combines
delicately drawn steel plates with rather more robust wood-
engraved vignettes.

Despite the use of the more sophisticated detail and tonal
potentiality of steel engraving in similar publications, however,
the wood engravings in the *Exhibitior* use the form triumphantly
rather than apologetically. Many of the vignette illustrations are
very large. Although they are dropped into the typeset page
alongside the appropriate text, they often seem to impose further
and further on to the page, sometimes relegating the text to a few
apologetic lines, and occasionally filling the whole page up to its
containing double-ruled border (see figure 3.1). The kinds of
small, rather orderly vignettes that Knight organises on to his
mammoth pages in *The Pictorial Gallery of Art* are used by Cassell

For beauty of design and delicacy of execution this exquisite statue is inferior to nothing in the Great Exhibition. It represents an historical fact in all but the chains, for it *was* the custom to expose female slaves in the bazaar of Constantinople. Observe the shame and scorn, the sad melancholy rebuke upon the face of the beautiful girl exposed to such ignominy: see with what modesty the pure high-minded Greek stands before her voluptuous purchasers;—verily, the purpose of the sculptor was aimed high when he conceived this noble idea. He has failed not in his task of reading a lesson of shame and scorn to the traffickers in the dreadful trade. Appealing to the sensibilities of our better nature, rather than to those feelings which yield delight, he has successfully overcome the difficulties of his subject, and won our admiration by the touching beauty and unexaggerated ideality of his subject. It was no easy task to place a young, beautiful, and high-minded female in such a position without a chance of offending; but the great charm of Mr. Powers' statue is, that it repels all thoughts but those of sympathy and compassion for the victim,

and execration of those who could make merchandise of the beauty and innocence of the fairest of God's creatures:

" As if their value could be justly
    told
By pearls and gems, and heaps
    of shining gold."

The Greek Slave was first exhibited in 1845, in the rooms of Messrs. Graves, of Pall-mall, and excited universal approbation by the excellence of its execution and the beauty of its conception.

While admitting the truth that genius exclusively belongs not to age nor race, and that its elements are as likely to dwell in the minds of the untutored savage as in the more favoured inhabitant of a civilised state, the first sight of this statue—coming from the hand of a sculptor whose country has hitherto made comparatively little progress in this, the highest department of Art—afforded us no little surprise, but it also gave us infinite pleasure. We had not often heard of the name of Hiram Powers, and were consequently astonished to find so fine a work from one whose fame had not already reached the shores of England. But we subsequently learned that he had been studying for a considerable time in Florence. In his studio here, Captain Grant

THE GREEK SLAVE.

saw a small model of the Greek Slave in plaster, and was so struck with the beauty of the subject, that he immediately gave a commission to the sculptor to execute it in marble. The result was triumphant.

3.1 'The Greek slave'

Profane writers also make mention of early specimens of sculpture. Herodotus visited Babylon while it was in a state of tolerable preservation, and in describing the temple of Jupiter Belus, he says, " In a chapel which stands below, within the temple, is a large image of gold, representing Jupiter sitting upon a throne of gold, by a table of the same metal ; " he alludes also to another statue of solid gold, twelve cubits high, which, he says, was not seen by him, but described to him by the Chaldeans. According to Diodorus Siculus, the weight of the statues and decorations in and about the temple amounted to five thousand talents in gold ; and their value has been estimated at about one hundred millions of dollars. The vessels and ornaments are supposed to have been those which Nebuchadnezzar had brought to Babylon from Jerusalem ; for he is said to have dedicated in this temple the spoils of that expedition.

Semiramis, the wife of Ninus, finished the stupendous walls of Babylon, which were reckoned among the seven wonders of the world, and her palace is celebrated by historians for the emblematical sculptures, with which the walls were covered, and for the colossal statues of bronze and gold of Jupiter Belus, of Nimrod, and of herself, with her principal warriors and officers of state.

We shall continue this interesting subject. Meanwhile, we may well direct attention to the beautiful design shown on the first page. It will be found in the south-east corner of the British Sculpture Room, and is entitled " The Pastoral Age." Its execution shows the sculptor, Mr. W. B. Kirk, of Dublin, to be possessed of both taste and imagination ; for who can gaze on the face of the shepherdess, singing to her lover's music, without acknowledging the poetry and grace of Nature's children ?

Somewhat removed from the realms of sculpture, but still allied to it, is the carved figure of " The Gladiator," by Mr. Fletcher. In this object the *utile et dulce* are well united. It will be found in the main avenue, just outside the British Furniture Court.

MR. MURPHY'S GREAT BELL.

Mr. Murphy, of Dublin, exhibits two capital specimens of bell-founding, the larger of which is here shown. It is worthy of mention, to the honour of this gentleman, that he was the first who attempted bell-founding in Ireland, and though he commenced the business only some six or seven years ago, so successful has he been, and to such perfection has he brought the art, that he already exports very largely, particularly to the colonies. The larger of the two bells here exhibited, which measures some three feet in height and diameter, is placed in the centre of the eastern nave, and may be heard daily striking the hours—being acted on by the hammer of Mr. Dent's turret clock—for the benefit of Her Majesty's faithful lieges. Round the bell is this quaint inscription—

" At length hear joy resound from Erin's voice-
Albert commands, and Irish bells rejoice."

Mr. Murphy also contributes a pair of church bells, and the octave in a peal of eight, both maiden bells—that is, cast in tune from the furnace, without the aid of artificial means, by cutting or chipping after leaving the mould.

3.2 'Mr. Murphy's great bell'

in a much more assertive manner in the *Exhibitor*. They seem to invade the page aggressively, creating large, often irregular, white spaces which emphasise the scale and autonomy of the objects displayed at the Exhibition even without any obvious graphic indication of size. There seems to be little self-doubt as to whether these images can adequately render the complexities of mass-produced objects or the intricacies of high-tech machinery. These confident vignettes are reinforced by the ten folding plates,[28] which illustrate, with considerable attention to detail and tonal complexity, crowds of visitors at various Halls in the Exhibition. These large illustrations, while specifically located in the accumulated text by the binders' instructions, must, nonetheless, in many cases have been taken out of the periodical and pinned to walls or framed as more permanent visual emblems of the Exhibition.

The *Exhibitor*, then, is a periodical which has entirely grasped the visual and commercial potential of the most advanced contemporary wood-engraving techniques for illustrative purposes. Using many separate blocks to build up extremely large images, and stretching the traditionally small vignette into something more assertive and substantial, the illustrations in the *Exhibitor* show a highly developed awareness of the centrality of mass-produced image-making to the development of an artisan readership, especially in a publication in which a 'participative' reader was required.

Some of the diversity of what is represented in these illustrations has already been suggested. The large fold-out plates concentrate on trying to represent the experience of viewing the Exhibition, and a good number of the vignettes also include spectators. The Exhibition experience is essentially rendered as an orderly procedure (even the representation of a crowded day on p. 357 suggests a rather static process rather than a vast flow of people). Class differences are scarcely acknowledged (there is little attempt to differentiate between the crowds at the 'shilling' days and more genteel spectators). But if issues of class are backgrounded in the more general rendering of the human press, the crowds are carefully differentiated both in terms of nationality and of social groupings. There is considerable stress on family groups of various kinds (mother/children, father/mother/children, and so on). The central concern of these images, however, is to suggest the harmonious *internationalism* of the Exhibition's spectators. Thus it is no surprise to find Mr Murphy's Irish 'great bell' being viewed by a genteel family group of a man and two women from one angle and by what appears to be a Cossack soldier from another[29] (see figure 3.2). Equally, in some of the more panoramic fold-out views, national costume or other forms of distinctive dress picks out certain individuals among the slowly circulating groups. The plate of *The Great Eastern Avenue* for example,[30] despite the loftiness of the viewpoint, permits the viewer to identify various military uniforms, both British and foreign and a turbaned, apparently Indian, spectator engaged in conversation with a European visitor among the familiar throng of family groups. The large presence of women is widely acknowledged. One function of the illustrations, then, is to reinforce a notion of Exhibition spectatorship as a decent, orderly activity which was as appropriate to men, women, and children alike, and in which class, cultural, and racial differences were subordinated to a general sense of intelligent interest, international harmony, and discreet wonder.

The majority of the vignette illustrations serve different purposes. Many are largely diagrammatic in function, seeking to render accurately the shapes, construction, and implicit function of isolated objects or machines. This documentary function has to be achieved within the relatively poor tonal reach of wood engraving. Illustrations of this kind largely isolate objects both from their place within the spectatorly space of the Exhibition itself and from the social contexts in which they are used. Sometimes the size of the object is very hard to gauge, as the image contains nothing to suggest scale. A considerable number of the vignettes introduce some small element of spectatorship, although the viewers in these images are carefully drawn so as not to direct the reader's gaze away from the proffered object at the centre of the image. The linearity of wood engraving sometimes makes it hard to render the texture or material of the displayed object with any clarity. But there is a general confidence in these kinds of image that the nature of the objects depicted has been adequately represented.

The most interesting images in the *Exhibitor*, and those which

3.3 'The punching machine and shears'

press the periodical on beyond a catalogue towards it being a kind of Victorian proto-hypertext, are those illustrations that depict manufacturing processes which occur outside the Exhibition within the wider cultural contexts of industrial societies. These kinds of images, of course, by 1851 lie within a lengthy tradition of rendering industrial processes as graphic narratives, narratives which are polemical and propagandist as well as documentary and informative, and which, by their nature, are forced to posit some kind of significant relationship between machine and the working human presence.[31]

Interestingly enough, such a series of illustrations, which show the manufacturing process as a managed sequence of human interactions with machines, seem to derive in the *Exhibitor* (as it had in *The Penny Magazine*) from a self-referential impulse. Charles Fowler's eight articles on 'The Great Exhibition Building', which form a central part of the opening issues of the *Exhibitor*, began as simple descriptions of technological inventiveness, but were quickly forced to stress process rather than machine (see figure 3.3). Here, for example, is a description of a drilling machine:

The workman, having arranged the iron in the right position under the drill, presses his foot upon the tread, thereby raising the counter-pointed end of the upper lever and lowering the point of the drill, which is of a spear-head form, down upon the iron. The operation necessarily causes a great heat from the friction between the drill and the iron, and to prevent the point from thus losing its hardness, it requires to be frequently moistened during the operation; to protect the point of the drill when it has passed the bar, a piece of tough wood is placed underneath the iron to be drilled. It requires the same number of men to work this machine as for the punching machine. Both these pieces of machinery were worked on the spot.[32]

Both the text and the illustration suggest a clear hierarchy of purpose: the machine constructs the human activity needed to make it effective, and its function demands its location on site. The vignette organises and reiterates this hierarchy both in its composition and its tone. The machine is rendered entirely at the centre of the image in the deepest tones, while the two operatives, rendered in increasingly less detail and tonal weight, slide backwards and sideways out of the scene. They are, nevertheless, depicted with a certain heroic presence – the rolled sleeves

3.4 'Roving machine'

and muscular posture of the machine operative suggest the necessity of human labour to manage and maintain even the most ingenious machines. Fowler's articles describe and illustrate mechanical and manufacturing processes *separately* within the complex overall project of building the Crystal Palace. The stress, inevitably, is on prefabrication, technical ingenuity, and the contribution of inventive local technology within the massive visionary framework of the Exhibition.

But the representation of industrial process within its socio-economic context becomes an increasingly apparent, and indeed ultimately central, feature of the *Exhibitor*. Within these representations, there is an increasingly evident evolution away from wondering, detached spectatorship towards a recognition of the human presence within the process, so that the representation speaks not just of manufacture and commodities but also of lived experience. These developments can be seen in the *Exhibitor* within a few pages. Pages 260–2 feature 'Nottingham Lace Machinery at the Crystal Palace'. This article is in many ways a classic assembly of Exhibition images – the fetishised machines, represented in the tonally simple linearities of the wood-engraved vignette which separates them from any context or background, stand entirely detached from all sense of their function or presence (see figure 3.4). The exception is a single image in which an imposing machine (the warp lace machine) is being contemplated by a respectful and genteel couple who are rendered entirely static presumably by a combination of awe and incom-

3.5 'Warp lace machine'

prehension (see figure 3.5). But most of the representational narratives of machinery in the *Exhibitor* recontextualise the machines within their industrial setting. Between pages 206 and 209, for example, there is a detailed description of steel making in the pre-industrial context of India which uses six vignette illustrations to explicate the various stages of the process. The reader is asked here to acknowledge the dominance of the workforce

3.6 'Tilt hammers' and 'Making crucibles for melting'

over the machinery – only in the first image and to some extent the last, are the machines given any visual dominance (see figure 3.6). Thus the *pre-* or *proto*-industrial qualities of the manufacturing process are fully acknowledged. But a few pages later a description of cotton manufacture using eleven detailed vignettes establishes a different set of relationships. Here the images are dominated by large and complex machines with the human presence acknowledged but represented largely as ancillary or even, in one vignette, as ghostly (see figure 3.7). The machinery is placed clearly if sketchily within its factory locale through a perfunctory, thinly drawn background of beams, doorways, or walls. But despite the use of such a large repertoire of representational possibilities, the 1851 *Exhibitor* has as one of its central purposes the re-contextualising of machinery out of its spectatorly, fetishised presence at the Crystal Palace back into the factories, and indeed the lives, of its readers.

Similar variety can be seen in the 'literary' content of the 1851 *Exhibitor*. While a considerable amount of the text is spent on retailing celebratory and to some extent self-referential anecdotes about the Exhibition, the greater part of the text is descriptive either of individual objects, machines, or commodities or, more

3.7 'Lapping finisher'

widely, of industrial processes. The text, then, uses the same repertoire of possibilities as the vignette illustration. This repertoire allows for spectatorly contemplation, in which the machine or commodity is detached from social processes, for awestruck recognition of the technical achievement of industrial culture, and, increasingly and to some extent unusually, for the projection of human experience back into the reified, commodified, and fetishised nature of the 'Exhibitionary idea'. But the *Exhibitor* also gives some sense of the ways in which industrialisation works as a 'civilising' force. As well as essentially celebratory accounts of the role of labour in even primitive industrial societies, as in the account of Indian steel making already cited, the *Exhibitor* also pursued an exhortatory nationalism. A prominently placed lead article on 'Ireland's Contribution to the World's Fair', for example, combined a somewhat bathetic description of the Irish contribution alongside some visionary rhetoric:

> THERE IS HOPE FOR IRELAND
> In no political or party spirit do we use these words – for politics and party have no place in *The Illustrated Exhibitor*. But we repeat There is Hope for Ireland – strong, vigorous, lively hope; hope, in the warm, generous, kindly hearts of their people; Hope in the industry of hard hands, and the energy of thoughtful minds ... Hope in the evidences of enterprise and skill exhibited in every object which she has placed in the Glass Palace of Hyde-park.[33]

If hardly progressive, these comments do at least associate industrialism with the development of human qualities, and offer a generous internationalism which was not characteristic of many accounts of the Exhibition.

What, then, in summary, were the dominant characteristics of the opening volume of *The Illustrated Exhibitor*? Firstly, it saw itself as an exploit which, if not quite the Exhibition itself, none the less could bear comparison with Hyde Park. The act of reading *The Illustrated Exhibitor* was, the periodical argued in the Preface and elsewhere, an experience comparable to a heroic visit to the Exhibition itself. This experience was the collaborative achievement of the editorial team and the reader. There is a strong sense of 'we' in the making of the magazine – the editorial team as working on behalf of an active, participatory audience and readership.

Second, there was an improvised quality about the production and development of the magazine. There was no clear initial sense of quite what the project would be, or what it might require. Hence the magazine depended on the eventual construction of itself more as a 'hypertext' ramifying out from the Exhibition itself rather than slavishly attempting to re-create the Exhibition in literary and graphic equivalents.

Third, the magazine did try to enact one of its original declared aims: 'Our tendencies are cosmopolitan' as the Preface put it. The magazine does maintain its attempt to reject a narrow nationalism in favour of a vision of the internationalism of labour.

Finally, *The Illustrated Exhibitor* comes to reject a triumphalist narrative of production of machinery and commodities and instead insists that industrial processes must be represented within a socio-historical context. The narratives of manufacture must encompass the human. It was this broader, potentially progressive view of the objects and values represented in the Great Exhibition which allowed *The Illustrated Exhibitor* to sustain its project on into a post-Exhibition society eager to continue to read hopeful narratives of the relationship between manufacture and the artisans.

The Illustrated Exhibitor – second series

It has already been established that the second series of *The Illustrated Exhibitor*, which comprises the two six-monthly volumes of weekly issues for 1852,[34] represents a substantially changed project from the original volume which, in complex ways, annotated and re-presented the Great Exhibition to its artisan readers. Such changes are immediately identifiable from the title page of the first issue of the new volume. The title has changed significantly so that the periodical has added a new, somewhat ambiguous and generalised dimension to its previous purpose – it has now become *The Illustrated Exhibitor and Magazine of Art*. 'Art' in this context was left undefined, largely because Cassell wanted the word to combine notions of 'fine art' with ideas of domestic and industrial production as something given the status of 'art' by its recent history. Simply, he wanted to give the 'art' in 'artisan' a higher social and cultural status, and used the discussions engendered by the Great Exhibition to legitimate this purpose. In terms of practical outcomes in the make-up of the journal, the 'art' of the new title was immediately translated into a wide range of illustrations which encompassed the reproduction of fine art images into wood-engraved versions, the representation of the industrial arts through annotated pictorial narratives, and a new emphasis on 'domestic arts' – lace-making patterns, embroidery designs, and fashion illustrations, for example.

Immediately below the suggestive, if vaguely defined, new title of the second volume of the *Illustrator* was a full-page wood engraving of 'The landing of the Saxons in Britain' framed within a clear linear border (see figure 3.8). In opening the volume in this way, Cassell offered the reader a number of new challenges. First, the image – in its rounded-off frame and dramatic placing on the page, as well as its size – announced itself as an 'art' image rather than a diagram or a documentary representation of an event. Second, the image ostentatiously had nothing at all to do with industry, manufacture or the Great Exhibition. The *Exhibitor* has begun to deny its origins in the precise context of the 'exhibition' in pursuit of a broader expository function. 'Show' in this context has lost its precise exhibitionary connection but gained a wider social role as a form of explanation – artisans are to be shown the world through expository illustrations. Third, the image is a didactic as well as an 'artistic' one. The accompanying leading article is offered under the headline 'Historical Events', and it is immediately apparent that the periodical has become centrally interested in the categorisation and delineation of information. Such an opening sequence of illustration and lead article was, in effect, a prototype for *The Historical Educator*, and Cassell quickly recognised that such a project could form a successful independent publication.

Given these evident, indeed self-publicising, changes to the *Exhibitor*, it is perhaps most accurate to regard the second series of the periodical, published throughout 1852, as a transitional periodical within Cassell's wider project. The first volume of *The Illustrated Exhibitor* gathered together as its implied readership the technically literate, socially ambitious, and self-educating elements within the artisan classes. The successful construction

THE
ILLUSTRATED EXHIBITOR
AND
Magazine of Art.

JANUARY 3, 1852.

THE LANDING OF THE SAXONS IN BRITAIN.

DRAWN BY J. GILBERT.   T. BEAVISDE, SC.

Hither came from eastern shores
The Angles and Saxons over the broad sea—
Fierce battle-smiths—and Britain sought;
O'ercame the Welsh, most valiant earls,
And gained the land.

                              OLD SAXON POEM.

3.8 'The landing of the Saxons in Britain'

3.9 'Manufacture of glass'

3.10 'Manufacture of glass'

GRAND CUT-GLASS CHANDELIER, AND GROUP OF OBJECTS, MANUFACTURED AT MESSRS. PELLATT AND CO.'S GLASS-WORKS.

3.11 'Manufacture of glass'

of such a readership outside the overtly ideological and sectarian 'information' offered elsewhere in mass circulation periodicals must have assured Cassell of his market. Accordingly, the revised *Exhibitor* of 1852 allowed him to begin to develop the pattern of specialised, carefully targeted, didactic and educational periodicals which emerged, with staggering speed and effectiveness, under the Cassell imprint in the 1850s. Thus the two volumes which form the 1852 *Exhibitor* comprise a compendium of possibilities, alluding back to the Great Exhibition, but essentially concerned with defining and satisfying the cultural ambitions of the audience predicated by the Exhibition rather than maintaining a precise focus on the Crystal Palace and its significance.

In a chapter of this length it is not possible to offer a full analysis of the contents and significance of two full volumes of the second series of *The Illustrated Exhibitor*, but it may be possible, within the context of the account of the magazine's evolution contained in the previous paragraphs, to point to some key features. The first of these is the clear compartmentalising and categorising of knowledge which forms a central defining strategy of the revised *Illustrator,* and which provided Cassell with the map of his wider educational project. The categories comprised fields of knowledge as defined by traditional educational principles (History, Science, Natural History, Architecture); by new developments in industry and commerce as embodied in the Great Exhibition (Machinery and Inventions, Manufacturing Processes, Needlework); by branches of the fine and applied arts (Architecture, Portraits, Historical and Landscape Painting); and by the kind of general information typical of eighteenth-century periodicals (Topography, Travel). Fiction and anecdote are conspicuously absent, though more obvious still is the lack of anything approaching the 'political' not just in terms of current affairs but also as a form of historical understanding. But in these categories, as already suggested, lay the blueprint for the subsequent extraordinarily successful development of Cassell's particular concept of 'useful knowledge', with several categories forming the basis of separate publications – *The Historical Educator, The Technical Educator* – as well as staple elements in the more generalised *Popular Educator* and *Illustrated Family Paper*. The impetus to, and re-categorising of, human knowledge and understanding implicit in the conception and organisation of the Great Exhibition, is mirrored in Cassell's vision of popular education, social utility, and the market potential of the inform- ative periodical. Cassell's definition of what an artisan might want to know, and how such knowledge might relate to wider understanding of the world, was a powerfully polemical one, partly because it was given legitimacy through the ideals and practices of the Great Exhibition.

Other elements of the revised *Exhibitor* spoke of new pur- poses and new audiences. The introduction of lace and needle- work patterns formed part of a concerted attempt to identify women as potential readers and to offer them participative roles within Cassell's technocratic vision of post-Exhibition Britain. While practical home-based crafts had long been a staple element of magazines specifically addressed to women, the fact that Cassell linked them with wider industrial and social change is important. While well-established magazines such as *The Ladies' Treasury* contained practical advice on knitting, needlework, and other domestic crafts,[35] the second series of the *Exhibitor*, through the development of its 'Ladies' Department', attempted to link the role of women as productive and energetic homemakers with wider industrial and commercial change. The underlying purpose of the 'Ladies' Department' was to heroicise small-scale domestic productivity through its association with the kinds of industrial heroism described elsewhere in the *Exhibitor*. The role it offered women, however circumscribed, nevertheless sought to project them beyond diversionary or hobby productivity into a more collective vision of useful making.

Other new elements in the new *Exhibitor* were primarily adaptations of successful features from other periodicals. By the time of its second series the magazine had begun to formulate its descriptive accounts of manufacturing processes, which had been a central element in the *Exhibitor* from its inception, in terms of familiarising 'visits' to factories. This kind of article, a staple of many periodicals throughout the nineteenth century, derived immediately from *The Penny Magazine*, but had its origins further back in the explanatory encyclopaedias of the eighteenth-century Enlightenment, with their delicate copper plates and rationalist optimism. But using the 'visit' format had the immediate effect of humanising industry and rendering it accessible. The danger was, however, that the curious visitor would be subjugated into awestruck and passive spectatorship by the scale, complexity and mechanisation of the productive process. The *Exhibitor* sought to avoid these dangers by elaborating social narratives out of the manufacturing process which stressed the relationship, indeed the necessary interdependence, of people and 'things' rather than merely celebrating commodities as industrial accomplishments. Such narratives were largely constructed visually through multi-image full- or double-page spreads which stressed, through the organisation of the images, the interdependence, co-operation and human activity required to produce a single 'thing'. The 'Visit to Apsley Pellatt's Flint Glass-works'[36] provides a typical example of how the *Exhibitor* managed this kind of article (see figures 3.9–11). The illustrations form complexly massed double pages which are sandwiched between two lengthy texts. The text deals with glass in a kind of humanised encyclopaedia fashion – beginning with a historical account of the discovery of glass amongst ancient civilisations, the article offers a technical description of glass before actually proceeding to describe a 'visit' to a glass works and the various processes involved in its manufacture. The description is formulated in characteristically *Exhibitor* terms. The account of the visit begins by describing the complex of emotions and physical responses to be found in the uninitiated visitor – awe, alarm, heat, chaos, wonder – which stresses the vicarious thrill of the industrial 'other' to curious readers. Much of the classic imagery of literary description of industry is to be found here – images of Hell in particular. But the visitor, in the persona of the journalist, quickly recovers his equilibrium and proceeds to a very orderly, detailed, and technical account of the manufacturing processes. In characteristic encyclopaedia mode, this account completely omits human labour, except for a careful account of the work of the high-status engraver which concludes the two articles. But the illustrations pursue a quite different narrative: one which restores, indeed emphasises, the role of the workforce.

The first double page of illustrations is rendered as two multi-image blocks contained within an arched frame. But within these two blocks the images are organised complexly. There is no simple chronological representation of the various stages of the manufacturing process, but rather a mixture of images in which no clear hierarchy of machine over men or men over machine is clear. Some images represent machines or kilns alone. Others show people tending machines. Still others show men performing industrial processes against a backdrop of machinery or furnaces. Two line-engraved vignettes, situated in clear contradistinction against the darker tonality of most of the images, centrally depict human figures. So the subordination of men to machine is not a clear intention here, nor is there any attempt to construct anything approaching the clear and logical, process-by-process account of glass making that the text builds up. Even more ambiguously, the central image of the right-hand page is framed by a pair of furled curtains which perhaps suggest theatrical spectacular as much as naturalistic reportage. These images of industry, then, are not simple celebrations of industrialisation or the wonders of a commodity economy. Nor are they unambiguously heroic accounts of manual labour, or figurative rehearsals of traditional Victorian images of labour. The framing, placement and deployment of these images, to say nothing of their tonal and formal variation, build more complex narratives of the relationship between people and things than are commonly found elsewhere at this time

Other important innovations in the second series of the *Exhibitor* deserve more sustained attention than can be given here – the role of the periodical in sustaining interest in the reproduction of art works for a mass audience pioneered by *Howitt's Journal* in the 1840s, for example, or the early use of photo-reprographic techniques, which changed the entire tonality of the illustrated page. But enough should have been said to suggest the key changes which Cassell had made to his magazine to ensure that the audience he had established for the 'Exhibition idea' remained faithful to the new, more generalist *Exhibitor* he introduced in 1852. It was from the basis of this, very considerable, audience that his expanding list of artisan journals in the 1850s was built.

The *Exhibitor* and after – a few conclusions

It has been noted that Cassell abandoned the title *The Illustrated Exhibitor* after 1852. There were good reasons for this. The Great Exhibition was receding in people's memories and Cassell had already begun to develop his broad portfolio of niche-marketed artisan magazines each of which had drawn upon particular aspects of the *Exhibitor*, thus collectively rendering it redundant. The *Exhibitor* did have a direct successor in *The Illustrated Magazine of Art*, but perhaps, as Nowell-Smith suggests, the time for a specialist art magazine for a mass readership was somewhat in the future.[37] Yet, despite its short life of three half year volumes, *The Illustrated Exhibitor* seems to me an extremely interesting periodical. To my mind, it is no less interesting or influential than Cassell's much more celebrated journals such as *The Popular Educator* and *Cassell's Illustrated Family Paper*. As I have tried to show, the nature of the periodical's importance was, and is, complex. Cassell used the magazine to begin to define the variety of artisan interests which his complex of periodicals subsequently exploited with huge success. Further, the *Exhibitor* was extremely innovative in the development of its illustrated page, and drew on the most progressive thinking available in developing its physical presence. It constructed, additionally, one of the most interesting versions of the Great Exhibition, which, I believe, offered a challenge to the notion that the Great Exhibition was primarily interpreted to artisans as an awesome, subjugating spectacle of the power of commodities. It is in such complex and sustained response to the Great Exhibition as *The Illustrated Exhibitor* rather than in the immediate and direct reactions of visitors and commentators, that the literary legacy of 1851 can be found.

Notes

1 T. Bennett, 'The Exhibitionary Complex' in *New Formations* 4 (Spring 1988), p. 94.

2 T. Kusamitsu, 'Great Exhibitions before 1851', *History Workshop* 9 (1980), quoted in Bennett, 'Exhibitionary Complex', pp. 93–4.

3 *Ibid.*, p. 80.

4 *Ibid.*

5 For recent accounts of Cassell and his periodicals see: S. Nowell-Smith, *The House of Cassell 1848–1958* (London: Cassell, 1958): R. D. Altick, *The English Common Reader* (Chicago: University of Chicago Press, 1956); V. Neuburg, *Popular Literature* (London: Woburn Press, 1977) pp. 205–10; P. Anderson, *The Printed Image and the Transformation of Popular Culture 1790-1860* (Oxford: Oxford University Press, 1991); R. K. Webb, *The British Working Class Reader 1790–1848* (London: George Allen and Unwin, 1955). These authors all stress the immense impact that Cassell's publications had on mid-Victorian society, especially in enabling the development of self-educative practices among the working classes. Accordingly, they lay great stress on *The Popular Educator* and *Cassell's Illustrated Family Paper*. None of them makes any substantial reference to *The Illustrated Exhibitor* or makes any acknowledgement of its central role in the development of Cassell's business. Anderson does, however, allude to the importance of *The Illustrated Magazine of Art* in the development of illustration, especially the reporduction of art works (Anderson, *Printed Image*, p. 113 and p. 188).

6 For William and Mary Howitt see: M. Howitt, *Autobiography* (2 vols, London: W. Isbister, 1889); C. R. Woodring, *Victorian Samplers – William and Mary Howitt* (Lawrence, Kansas: Oxford University Press, 1952); A. Lee, *Laurels and Rosemary: The Life of William and Mary Howitt* (Oxford: Oxford University Press, 1955). For the Chambers brothers see W. Chambers, *Memoir of Robert Chambers* (Edinburgh: W. and R. Chambers, 1872); W. Forbes Gray, 'A Hundred Years Old – 'Chambers's Journal' 1832–1932' Supplement to *Chambers's Journal* February, 1932. See also Altick, *Common Reader*, Webb, *Working Class Reader* and Neuburg, *Popular Literature*. For a brief account of the ideological and cultural significance of these kinds of journals see B. E. Maidment, 'Magazines of popular progress and the artisans', *Victorian Periodicals Review* (Autumn 1984), pp. 82–94.

7 Anderson, *Printed Image*, pp. 88–9; Nowell-Smith, *Cassell*, pp. 40–3.

8 Nowell-Smith, *Cassell*, offers the best account of Cassell's early business ventures (pp. 9–16). Altick, *Common Reader*, argues, however, that 'Cassell's story had never been satisfactorily told … and must be pieced together from a number of fragmentary and not always reliable sources' (p. 302).

9 Nowell-Smith, *Cassell*, p. 32.

10 Nowell-Smith, *Cassell*, gives an account (pp. 29–30) of Cassell's lodgings scheme which sought to give visitors to the Exhibition a place to stay in houses which had been inspected for their suitability and which charged on a reasonable uniform tariff. The over-optimism of Cassell's view of the potential offered by such a co-ordinated and co-operative approach to what was after all an astonishing commercial opportunity is pointed out by Nowell-Smith. Not for the last time, Cassell found himself caught between a genuine wish to support artisan interests and a recognition of the commercial potential of this newly self-conscious and economically significant group.

11 The first series of *The Working Man's Friend* ran for seven three-monthly volumes between 1850 and 1851.

12 Epigraph 'To Our Readers' in the volume reprint of volume 2 of *The Working Man's Friend* (London: Cassell, 1850).

13 These supplements offered artisans one of the few easy outlets for publishing their writing in mass circulation metroplitan magazines. Some scholars, notably David Vincent in *Bread, Knowledge and Freedom* (London: Europa, 1981), have argued that access to print for artisan writers had improved markedly by 1850, and, in this context, Cassell's project of offering a clearly differentiated space for the work of working men and women in *The Working Man's Friend* was an interesting and progressive one, even if Cassell soon abandoned it when he came to re-formulate the periodical in a second series begun in October 1851. For a discussion of these issues concerning access to print, see B. E. Maidment *The Poorhouse Fugitives* (Manchester: Carcanet Press, 1987), pp. 323–53.

14 *The Popular Educator* has been regarded by both contemporaries and subsequent scholarship as a key periodical for the development of cultural and educational self-consciousness among artisans, largely because it shows both the strengths and weaknesses of such developments. While the definition of 'useful knowledge' propounded by educational reformists remained factual and narrowly a-political, nevertheless the pursuit of even this kind of information was seen by artisans themselves as valuable and enabling. One balanced, and not unrepresentative, response was that of W. E. Adams writing in one of the most accomplished artisan autobiographies from the period, *Memoirs of a Social Atom*: 'John Cassell, a vendor of coffee and a lecturer on temperance, had tried several small ventures in periodical literature before he commenced his famous *Educator*. One of these was the *Family Friend* ... But *The Popular Educator* was the great enterprise. It came out in weekly parts. It was badly printed, and was full of blunders and blemishes; but it contained lessons to suit all aspiring tastes, and satisfied the requirements of the young folks in a manner they had never been satisfied before. Most of the self-educated people of my age and of later generations owe a deep debt of gratitude to John Cassell. It was with such aids as have been indicated, and scribblings at odd moments of the day or night, that the desire for knowledge was in some manner gratified.' W. E. Adams, *Memoirs of a Social Atom* (London: Hutchinson, 2 vols, 1903) 1, p. 113. More recent commentators who have stressed the centrality of the *Educator* include Altick, *Common Reader* (p. 303), who lists the novelist Thomas Hardy, the labour politician Thomas Burt and the philologist Joseph Wright as among those who had given testimony to the usefulness and importance of *The Popular Educator*.

15 Neuburg, *Popular Literature*, pp. 206–7; Anderson, *Printed Image*, pp. 88–9; Nowell-Smith, *Cassell*, pp. 42–4.

16 Nowell-Smith, *Cassell*, pp. 40–2.

17 One useful introduction to the development of illustrated periodicals is provided by Simon Houfe, *The Dictionary of British Book Illustrators and*

Caricaturists 1800–1914 (Woodbridge Antique Collectors' Club revised edn, 1981) pp. 13–75. Houfe discusses Cassell on pp. 73–4. It is regrettable that a recent reprint of Houfe's book has a much less extensive and informative Introduction.

18 Nowell-Smith, *Cassell*, implies that the work was always conceived as a multi-volume publication 'designed to fill four handsome volumes' but which could 'meanwhile be brought out in weekly numbers at 2d. and in monthly parts at 8d.' (p. 31). While I accept that the intention had always been to use a multiplicity of formats and that volume publication had always been intended, none the less I think that the initial priority was with establishing the serial rather than the volume format.

19 Nowell-Smith, *Cassell*, p. 31.

20 *Ibid.*

21 Cassell had used a fold-out plate before in the single illustration he had included in the first series of *The Working Man's Friend*. Significantly, that illustration had been of the projected site for the Crystal Palace.

22 *The Illustrated Exhibitor* 1 (1851), pp. 44, 63, 79, 95, 112, 130, 187, 215, 243. This title will hereafter be abbreviated to *TIE*.

23 *TIE* 1 (1851), pp. 187, 231, 251, 263, 301, 329, 341, 365, 400, 428.

24 *Ibid.*, p. 3.

25 *Ibid.*, pp. 23–9. The series was called 'The Origins of Expositions'.

26 See note 22.

27 There has not been room in this chapter to compare *The Illustrated Exhibitor* with the range of less literary, more technical specialist works aimed at describing industrial processes, which were also derived from the Great Exhibition in various ways. P. Barlow's *The Encyclopaedia of Arts, Manufactures, and Machinery* (London: J. J. Griffin, 2 vols, 1851), which contained a long introductory chapter by Charles Babbage provides one important example. Tomlinson's *Cyclopaedia of Useful Arts and Manufactures* provides another. Knight's *Pictorial Gallery* needs to be situated here, too: C. Knight, *The Pictorial Gallery of Arts* (2 vols, London: The London Printing and Publishing Company, n.d.). The relationship between metal engraving on steel and copper, the traditional method of rendering complex machinery and mechanical processes, and an emerging use of wood engraving even for difficult subjects, can be seen to change in these part-issue works.

28 The ten plates were drawn by W. Harvey and engraved by T. Gilks.

29 *TIE* 1 (1851), p. 163.

30 *Ibid.*, p. 387.

31 The most relevant precursor for this tradition is *The Penny Magazine*'s serialisation of its own production processes, which were re-issued in pamphlet form for even wider circulation in the mid-1830s.

32 *TIE* 1 (1851), p. 130.

33 *Ibid.*, p. 142.

34 *The Illustrated Exhibitor and Magazine of Art* comprises two volumes. Vol. 1 ran from January to June 1852 (26 weekly parts comprising 412 pages) and vol. 2 from July to December in identical format.

35 See M. Beetham, *A Magazine of Their Own* (London: Routledge, 1996).

36 *The Illustrated Exhibitor and Magazine of Art* 1 (1852), pp. 54–9, pp. 70–4.

37 Nowell-Smith, *Cassell*, p. 42.

4

An appropriated space: the Great Exhibition, the Crystal Palace and the working class

PETER GURNEY

Introduction: debating the Great Exhibition

In July 1851 the journalist and women's rights advocate Eliza Cook published an article on 'The Cheap Tripper' in the popular periodical she had established two years earlier to aid 'the gigantic struggle for intellectual elevation now going on'.[1] Cook sympathised with the pleasures and difficulties experienced by 'the people' in mid-Victorian England and enthusiastically described the increased leisure opportunities made possible by the railways. More and more working people, she observed, now packed into excursion trains to visit ancient cathedral cities, seaside resorts and the capital itself. Cook narrated a fictional outing taken by a young courting couple, Bessie and Tummus, who had journeyed to London for the first time from a town in the industrial north, drawn most especially by the Great Exhibition. The main attraction, Cook assured her readers, did not disappoint.

> And then, in the Great Exhibition, lo! is not the Cheap Tripper there in all his glory? He is quite lost in admiration at Kiss's Amazon, and at the specimens of Yankee india-rubber fabrics; but the 'ransepp' or transept, with the sparkling fountains there, charms him above everything else. There he uncovers his basket,

and displays his country ham and cheese, which tastes sweet after the long ramble he has had through the Austrian, Russian, French, and American departments, not to speak of the honest pride which has led him to give a less than ordinarily minute inspection to the manufactures from 'our own town' … and though the Yankee may assert that he 'beats creation', the Cheap Tripper 'caps it' by saying that 'Britain beats Yankeedom.' And then, after saying thus much, the Cheap Tripper takes a full swig from his black bottle.[2]

This not untypical representation is highly condescending as one would expect; Bessie, Tummus and cheap trippers generally are ignorant but harmless, their language restricted though rather quaint, morally lax and self-indulgent occasionally but also instinctively patriotic.

The relationship between the working class and the Great Exhibition was widely discussed at this time; as a number of social historians have pointed out, many liberal intellectuals hoped that the Great Exhibition, as an ambitious model of 'rational recreation', would fulfil a wider educative function and exert a civilising influence on the majority.[3] In his novel, *1851: or, the Adventures of Mr. and Mrs. Sandboys and Family*, Henry Mayhew argued that the Great Exhibition clearly demonstrated that labour had now achieved a recognised and respected place in society. Only a few years ago, he maintained, working men were regarded as 'mere labourers', inferior in most respects to machines: a view which was no longer tenable. Not only was the Great Exhibition 'the first public national expression ever made in this country, as to the dignity and artistic quality of labour', but the marvellous display of the 'trophies and triumphs of labour' could not fail to fill working men with pride and 'inspire them with a sense of their position in the State, and to increase their self-respect in the same ratio as it must tend to increase the respect of all others for their vocation'. Mayhew also underlined the fact that working-class visitors were enthralled by the magical structure that housed the exhibits; the Crystal Palace was 'a visual feast, and a rare delight of air, colour and space'. The designer, Joseph Paxton, embodied the idea that improvement and class mobility were now possible.[4]

The significance of the Great Exhibition as a turning point in class relations is a major component part of the dominant historical representation of the event. From the outset the Great Exhibition was made to symbolise the triumph of *laissez-faire* capitalism and British industrial hegemony certainly, but the good behaviour of the working-class crowd on shilling days was also frequently remarked upon in the bourgeois press. Those commentators most sympathetic to the working class, such as Mayhew and Cook, provided their own nuanced perspectives, though they too were relieved that the violent class conflicts which had marked British society in the 1830s and 1840s now seemed to belong only to the past; labour had been successfully pacified, temporarily at least, and was now ready and eager for improvement. Although some modern scholars have questioned the onset of an 'age of equipoise' in the early 1850s, the notion that a profound caesura in class relations occurred in the summer of 1851 still attracts considerable support.[5]

For many middle-class commentators, then, the Great Exhibition signified the possibility of class harmony as well as technological progress. It was widely believed that the former was guaranteed, in the medium to long term if not immediately, by the prospect of mass consumption.[6] This plausible argument has its merits; the department store magnate, William Whiteley, who visited the Exhibition as a young man, 'was so inspired by the glass building that he began to dream of large retail stores, "universal providers' shops", with plate glass fronts'.[7] In *Social Aspects* (1851) John Store Smith drew attention to the expanding world of goods and concluded that 'the middle-class family now possesses carpets and hangings, which would have excited great wonderment even at so recent a period as the American War'.[8] The cheapness of British goods and the expansion of a mass consumer market was often remarked upon by contemporary observers. George Cruikshank conveyed some of the hope as well as the fear generated by this transformation in a typically surreal engraving which appeared in Mayhew's fictional account. In 'The dispersion of the works of all nations from the Great Exhibition of 1851', a phantasmagoric host of commodities take on a life of their own as they explode outwards from the Crystal Palace (see figure 4.1). The problem with this argument of course is that the majority of working-class people had very little disposable income to spend on the expanding range of consumer

4.1 'The dispersion of the works of all nations from the Great Exhibition
of 1851'

goods in the 1850s and beyond. Most trod a precarious path
between scarcity and survival and we should be wary of any
over-arching interpretation that claims to discover a mythical
origin for forms of behaviour and sociality which occur in a much
later period.

Instead of reading 1851 unproblematically as a turning point
in class relations or as one of the founding moments in the making
of modern consumer society, this chapter proposes an alternative,
and less teleological, account of the relationship between the
Great Exhibition, the Crystal Palace and the working classes in
Victorian England. Firstly, some radical working-class reactions
to the Great Exhibition will be explored in order to demonstrate
that the dominant representation and meaning of the Great
Exhibition was vigorously contested at the time. Rather than
tracing the influence of the Exhibition on the development of
public museums, the bulk of the chapter then considers the fate of
the Crystal Palace itself after it was moved to Sydenham Hill in
South London in 1852 and the ways in which this magical,

authentically popular structure and space was appropriated by working people in the decades that followed. The initial struggle over Sunday opening will be considered as the heated debates over this issue help illuminate the complex attitudes toward the commercialisation of leisure and the prospect of unregulated mass consumption at mid-century. Finally, working-class uses of the Crystal Palace are discussed, particularly the great fêtes and festivals organised by various voluntary associations in the second half of the nineteenth century. The Crystal Palace captured the imaginations of working people from its inception and I shall argue that this highly significant recreational space was appropriated by and for labour, albeit in a limited and circumscribed manner, in ways that would have surprised and startled many of the bourgeois celebrants of 1851.

'The monster Exhibition humbug': some radical responses to the Great Exhibition

Working-class enthusiasm for exhibitions of industrial goods can be traced back to the exhibitions organised by the Mechanics Institutes in the 1830s, which had been designed to inculcate 'better taste' in the 'lower orders.'[9] Radical publications aimed at a popular, working-class market such as *Reynold's Newspaper*, as well as the Chartist *Northern Star*, devoted a good deal of coverage to preparations for the Great Exhibition. Large engravings of the Crystal Palace were advertised for sale in the *Northern Star* for 6d. from early January, for example, and the paper considered the building to be, 'the realisation of a fairy tale'.[10] Yet there were also critical voices; the project was vehemently denounced by *Reynold's Newspaper* from its inception. In early March the editor's brother, Edward Reynolds (writing under the pseudonym 'Gracchus'), berated the Exhibition as a 'gigantic folly' designed to distract people from the real political issues of the day. The whole show was nothing more than the expedient ruse of a foreign prince, 'brought up with all the shallow and despotic notions so characteristic of shallow German potentates', and was therefore unlikely to harmonise with the views of 'the great masses of our enlightened population'.[11] The following week G. W. M. Reynolds himself prophesied that the exhibition would have a number of 'fatal effects' on British industry and the 'work-ing class', and reminded readers that the paper had described the affair as 'the monster Exhibition humbug' from the start.[12]

The decision by the Royal Commissioners to exclude the public from the opening ceremony provoked a torrent of criticism. An editorial in the *Northern Star* in April declared 'If ever there was a building or an object that ought to have been kept free from favouritism and exclusivism, the Hyde-park Exhibition should have been undefiled by both.' Exclusion was insulting, not only to 'the people', but also to 'the SOVEREIGN herself'.[13] A similar line was taken by G. W. M. Reynolds, though he had far less sympathy for Queen Victoria: 'It appears, however, that she is to slink in to the monster building, as if afraid to face publicly the people over whom she rules.'[14] Anti-monarchist sentiment continued to mark Reynolds' interventions: immediately after the Exhibition was opened on the first of May he foretold that within a year, 'the bowings and scrapings of royalty will not blind the people to the evil results of Prince Albert's scheme'.[15] Despite such criticism the opening ceremony was covered in extensive detail, particularly in the *Northern Star*. This paper also featured a regular series of articles on 'The Crystal Palace and its Contents', from May until the Exhibition closed in October. The leaders of the Chartist movement probably found the international aspect of the event most attractive, believing that the Great Exhibition held out at least the possibility of a 'fraternity of nations'.[16]

The working class were effectively shut out from the Exhibition for over three weeks by the cost of admission and were only finally admitted on special shilling days from Monday 26 May. The attendance figures disappointed the hopes of many, as the *Northern Star* duly reported. Only just over 20,000 visited on the first shilling day and they seemed 'to belong to the middle class of society, and few fustian jackets were observed among them'. Takings saw 'an immense decline' from the previous Saturday.[17] In his novel Mayhew noted that 100,000 visitors had been anticipated and extra police drafted to keep order on this day, though the organisers failed to realise that the 'masses are busy working for their bread'.[18] The issue of attendance was disputed when the Exhibition closed in October, 'Censor' arguing, in a letter which appeared on the front page of the *Northern Star*, that the 'labouring classes' had been poorly represented. Although official sources put the total number of visitors at over 6 million, 'Censor' calculated that if season-ticket holders, repeat visits and visits by foreigners were taken into consideration about 2.25 million of the adult British population were likely to have seen the Exhibition. Despite the 'patronage and puff' of some railway directors and steam boat proprietors this was not a very impressive figure. The correspondent concluded that probably only about 1 million of these were from the 'artizan and dangerous orders' and that this relatively modest number proved 'as much the inability as the unwillingness of the many to visit it, notwithstanding the charge was but a shilling, and that people were carried four hundred miles for 5s. ... the facts are a lasting evidence of the widespread misery pervading the country'.[19]

Two linked themes recurred time and again in the radical press: the Great Exhibition was attacked as a stimulus to increased competition and would exert necessarily adverse effects on the working classes. 'Gracchus' condemned bourgeois organs such as the *Times* and the *Morning Chronicle* at the end of May for their naive, uncritical support for an event which would heighten foreign competition and therefore increase unemployment.[20] The following week he noted that *Reynold's* had initially been almost the only critical voice, though now others were coming round – the *Weekly Despatch* had recently deprecated generalised 'puffing' for instance. According to 'Gracchus' only the aristocracy stood to benefit from the affair: employing the old republican critique he emphasised once again that the Exhibition had been thought up by Prince Albert and the nobility to detract from the contemporary political crisis and the necessity for political and social reform.[21]

Similar arguments were developed at this time in a fascinating editorial in the *Northern Star* entitled 'Labour and the Crystal Palace'. The editor – most probably the Owenite George Fleming[22] – noted that 'the masses' from the manufacturing districts had not flocked to the Crystal Palace during the Whitsun holidays: middle-class and wealthy visitors were as numerous as ever but 'Lancashire and Yorkshire withheld their anticipated myriads'. He went on to argue that this was partly due to the tone adopted by the capitalist press which had trumpeted the Great Exhibition as a stimulus to competition. According to the editor this had alienated many workers who were sick and tired of competition and its effects and who looked forward instead to an alternative exhibition which proclaimed the benefits of co-operation:

> We can imagine a similar World's Show gathered together for very different purposes, but composed of precisely the same materials, to which Labour would flock gladly, as to a high Carnival, and the inauguration of a better era. If instead of avowing that this marvellous collection of skill and industry was made for the purpose of stimulating competition, it had been to ascertain what were the actual means at the command of the world, for producing wealth of all kinds, and for promoting a regulated system of distribution, which would ensure to all nations the full and fair participation in the aggregate wealth so produced, the case would have been very different.[23]

According to the *Northern Star*, then, the Great Exhibition celebrated the competitive system and 'a selfish and degraded individualism', so it was little wonder that working people preferred, in the main, to ignore it. The national Chartist leader, Feargus O'Connor, claimed that the Exhibition was irrelevant to the 'impoverished working classes' soon after.[24]

Edward Reynolds became more and more incensed at the way labour was marginalised at the Great Exhibition as the months passed. In an article entitled, 'The Imposter Representatives of England's Labour', he argued that the Great Exhibition would not have been possible without the working class but that the event had in effect been largely appropriated by the aristocracy and the capitalist class:

> The events of this year must have demonstrated to the working classes that neither the upper or the middle orders are inclined to elevate their inferiors in social position. The thousands and tens of thousands of hard-working, industrious mechanics and labourers, who perform their duties faithfully and honestly towards society, are in return only recognised as human machines in the hands of hereditary tyrants, for the production of necessaries and luxuries; or by capitalists to add to their accumulated wealth. Hence society is so much out of joint.[25]

As a number of social historians have pointed out this influential publication commonly employed a populist discourse that pitched a despotic monarchy and aristocracy against 'the people', as in the celebrated *cause célèbre* over the Tichborne Claimant.[26] Nevertheless, Edward Reynolds also used the language of class to make sense of and critique the Great Exhibition: he reminded readers that working men had made the objects housed in the Crystal Palace and sought to appropriate the event for labour, at least theoretically. An editorial following the closure of the Exhibition reiterated this point, as workers had received no mention at all in any of the speeches: 'Neither Prince, Bishop or Lord, cared to acknowledge the real source from whence the gorgeous display in Hyde Park came ... And thus ended the monster bubble of 1851.'[27]

'A great popular advertisement': rational recreation, commercial culture and the Crystal Palace

When the Great Exhibition closed, the building itself belonged to Fox and Henderson the building contractors. Paxton campaigned to leave the Crystal Palace in Hyde Park from the summer of 1851 but his scheme met with strong opposition from Colonel Sibthorpe and others. Undaunted, Paxton raised £500,000 in £5 shares, formed the Crystal Palace Company, and purchased both the building itself – for the relatively small sum of £70,000 – and two hundred acres of wooded parkland on the summit of Sydenham Hill in South London, which was to be the new site. Rebuilding began in early August 1852. The new structure was to be much larger than the one in Hyde Park; the latter had been built for little more than £150,000 but now Paxton had half a million to spend. Two more end transepts were erected and the Palace transformed from three to five stories. Digby Wyatt and Owen Jones were sent abroad to ransack art collections and make plaster casts of classical statuary for the series of elaborate courts including, among others, the Grecian, Roman, Byzantine, Romanesque, Pompeian, Chinese, Renaissance and Egyptian Courts. These were intended to provide an insight into the art of great civilisations as well as their progress and eventual decline. Exotic trees and plants, fountains, lakes and extensive flower gardens also featured on the Sydenham Hill site. Not surprisingly, more money had to be raised and the final cost came to £1,300,000. The new structure was eventually opened by Queen Victoria – who praised the project of rational recreation in her opening speech – on 10 June 1854, in the presence of some 40,000 people. An average of 2,000,000 visitors a year enjoyed the delights of the Crystal Palace in the first thirty years, conveyed to Sydenham by purpose-built railway lines.[28]

Tensions marked this ambitious enterprise from the start; the imperatives of rational recreation and commerce often pulled in opposing directions. A commitment to the former was written into the deed of settlement when the company was established; one of the explicit objects of the venture was, 'the cultivation of a refined taste amongst all classes of the community'. A ban on alcohol and Sunday opening was a condition of the Charter of Incorporation granted in January 1853. Provision was also made for the company to police and ensure the 'orderly conduct' of visitors.[29] On the other hand, the commercial potential of the Crystal Palace was exploited from the start: it became, in part, a department store. The Crystal Palace featured a host of new additions, 'The Court of Inventions', 'The Department of Building Materials and Architecture', and 'The Court of Industrial and Domestic Economy', where furniture, food and culinary utensils were displayed by manufacturers for sale. No goods were ticketed at the Great Exhibition but significantly this had now changed.[30]

The commercial potential of exhibitions was exported overseas and fully understood by some contemporary commentators.[31] The New York Exhibition of 1853 for example, which was modelled on the Hyde Park event, prompted some prescient reflections from the Reverend H. W. Bellows, congregational pastor in that city. Bellows argued that the 'moral significance' of these exhibitions was that they proved that real material advances had been made and that, 'the productive industry of the whole race will soon be required to meet the demands of the consumers; for when all the world are great consumers, all the world must be great producers.' Anticipating the arguments of some contemporary cultural historians, Bellows insisted that the Exhibition was not a 'museum for idle curiosity' but was instead 'a great popular advertisement … a scheme for creating wants by exhibiting ingenious means of supplying them, and thus developing new forms of labour and new markets for them'.[32] The contradiction between the Crystal Palace as a site for rational recreation and 'a great popular advertisement' for consumer society, between improvement and commerce, provoked heated controversy from the outset and threatened to bring financial ruin to the company many times over the following decades.

The ban on Sunday opening led to a fierce confrontation from the early months of 1853 between sabbatarians, who insisted that Sundays should be completely reserved for piety and prayer, and those who believed that secularised forms of recreation could exert a civilising influence on the majority. Public meetings were held in the metropolis and scores of pamphlets helped fuel debate. Liberal intellectuals such as Mayhew and Cruikshank and metropolitan working men were allied in favour of Sunday opening: Mayhew had denounced 'slimy bigots' such as Archdeacon Hale, who supported the ban, at a working-class meeting at St Martin's Hall in early February.[33] The opponents of sabbath-breaking were led by the Lord's Day Observance Society, an organisation that had drawn searching criticism from working-class radicals since its formation in 1831.[34] The champions and the opponents of Sunday opening were deeply divided on questions of how and where working people should spend their leisure time and what they should spend their disposable income on; thus the debate exposed some of the expectations and fears generated by the prospect of a developing consumer society and is worth therefore attending to in some detail.

A committed temperance reformer, George Cruikshank argued strongly in favour of Sunday opening in an influential pamphlet published in 1853. As vice-president of the London Temperance League, Cruikshank had written to the Crystal Palace Company for assurances – which were readily given – that alcohol would be banned from the Sydenham site as it had been from the Great Exhibition. Cruikshank regarded the Crystal Palace as an alternative to the public house and maintained that wider access should therefore be encouraged by all those interested in the elevation of 'the people'.[35] This view was supported by other advocates of rational recreation who insisted that the new venture would help build links between classes in a modern, urban environment: John Butlin, for example, suggested to sabbatarians that less money would be needed for model prisons if more was done to alleviate, 'the constant toil of the honest and industrious'.[36] Other suggestive voices were heard in the debate. John Baldwin Brown was a London minister who had made the case for Sunday opening within the Congregational Union. In his pamphlet *The Sabbath, the Crystal Palace and the People*, Brown linked the English victory over Napoleon to the Great Exhibition, which had displayed to the world the productions of forty years of peace-time industry. The new company had 'another and profounder character', was more democratic and seemed likely to exert the 'uplifting influence' which had become more pressing than ever as organised religion lost its hold over large sections of the working classes. It was no longer merely an exhibition, Brown continued, 'except in the sense in which the whole world is an exhibition'. The venture itself bore eloquent testimony to the growing belief that 'the united strengths of the intellect and wealth of the country should build a Palace, far transcending all private palaces, for the great people whose industry has made our England the queen of the kingdoms of the Earth. It is emphatically a People's Palace'.[37]

The attempt to claim the Crystal Palace as a 'People's Palace' was made contemporaneously by perhaps one of the only working-class voices to have survived. J. D. Devlin, a shoemaker provoked into print by Dr Cumming's sabbatarian pamphlet, adopted a significantly disrespectful tone and attacked the latter directly on the grounds of class: 'had I served my apprenticeship at a college, I, too, might have become a preacher – a six-day-a-week do-nothing, and a Sunday worker!' Devlin insisted that the Crystal Palace was, 'a building which may, in all justness, be proudly denominated the PEOPLE'S PALACE', and that the people, by definition, ought not be excluded.[38]

The opponents of Sunday opening drew on a well-established set of arguments. The view that working people would gain much more from Christian worship and contemplation than they would from any other activity on Sundays, especially drinking alcohol, had been articulated by sabbatarians for decades. Despite the company's assurances, many worried that the Crystal Palace would quickly become a giant public house. Moreover, the potential immorality of the crowd drawn to Sydenham Hill by the superficial and transient pleasures of consumption was also a cause for concern. The Crystal Palace, it was thought, furnished ample opportunities for 'the lovers of dress and display, the foolish, the flirting, the frivolous, the match-making mothers, and heart-breaking profligates'.[39] More interesting and significant, perhaps, were the views of those who questioned the philanthropic motives of the champions of Sunday opening. The Rev. John Hall, for example, delivered a 'Lecture to the Working Classes' at the Union Chapel, Brixton Hill, soon after Mayhew's vituperative denunciation of the sabbatarians. Hall criticised those masters who overworked their labourers so severely during the week that they had little choice but to recuperate on Sundays. For Hall the real motivation behind the campaign to open the Palace on the Sabbath was profit: 'It is tolerably well-known in our own day that when our capitalists want a good return for an outlay, they not infrequently find it to their interest to fall into a fit of philanthropy', he wrote.[40] The middle-class Leeds radical, Edward Baines Jr, shared these suspicions and opined: 'If the religious bulwark of the Lord's-day were thrown down, nothing could prevent Mammon, with all his rabble, from rushing in at the breach.'[41] Although the sabbatarians could frequently appear somewhat disingenuous themselves, many of those who opposed Sunday opening were sincerely concerned about the growing commercialisation of civil society. The Rev. Barton Bouchier, for example, asked shareholders in the Crystal Palace Company why they had failed to back demands for the Saturday half-holiday, or even introduce Saturday shilling days at the Palace, to encourage wider access at other times. Bouchier also emphasised the underlying profit-motive and wryly observed: 'I think we may see something more than the fox's tail peeping out of this hole ... I see a very suspicious slobbering of his chops, as he casts a side-glance at the poultry-yard.'[42]

In the short term the sabbatarians won the debate and the Palace remained closed on Sundays. However, the company had more success over the sale of alcohol. The Crystal Palace Company appealed to the Queen in Council to permit the sale of fermented liquor at the site soon after its charter was granted. Both the National Temperance League and the National Temperance Society opposed this request without success.[43] The ban on alcohol was consequently softened in December 1855 when the Crystal Palace Company was allowed to sell 'any wines and fermented liquors, other than spiritous liquors'.[44] Though Charles Gilpin warned shareholders that 'the People's Palace should no longer be polluted by the people's curse', the directors of the company managed to get the prohibition on spirits lifted soon after. Despite these changes, the financial problems that dogged the company grew worse and this led to serious depreciation in the value of the company's shares by the mid-1850s. One of the original shareholders, H. G. Bohm, blamed mismanagement for the financial crisis which loomed in 1856: 'Eyes and ears were shut out against the common principles of mercantile speculation, till it was too late to apply them', Bohm explained, and this had caused 'discerning shareholders' to sell their shares as fast as they possibly could.[45]

The complex struggles which occurred over what could be consumed, when, where and by whom, had shifted their focus from Sydenham Hill to Hyde Park by this time. This space, which not long before had been employed to stage an event symbolising in part the possibility of class-harmony, was now the scene of such violent and threatening episodes of class conflict that one eyewitness, Karl Marx, declared that, 'the English Revolution began yesterday in Hyde Park'.[46] The Sunday Trading Riots which took place in the summer of 1855 were provoked by the attempt by Lord Grosvenor to introduce a Sunday Trading Bill, which aimed to close shops on Sundays and thereby encourage religious observance amongst working people.[47] This was seen as an explicitly class-based piece of legislation, and out of the agitation that it generated emerged the National Sunday League which contested the closure of the Crystal Palace throughout the later years of the decade.[48] Eventually in 1860, by means of a legal subterfuge, the Crystal Palace was at last opened to the public on Sundays and over the next decade it became a 'People's Palace' in more than name only.[49]

'A palace for the people': the Crystal Palace and the working classes

During the 1860s the Crystal Palace Company expanded the many attractions on offer at Sydenham. The Palace had its own orchestra from the beginning, and musical festivals were an impressive feature, especially the great Handel Festivals. Many theatrical productions, especially melodramas which enjoyed widespread popularity in Victorian England, were also staged. The popular taste for the spectacular was increasingly catered for: elaborate firework displays and balloon ascents drew great crowds, as did the remarkable feats performed by Blondin on the high wire.[50] As we have noted, the Crystal Palace can be interpreted as a proto-type for the department store in the nineteenth century, but it simultaneously furnished a model for the amusement park in the twentieth.[51] The intention was to provide a packed programme with cross-class appeal, though it seems likely that admission prices separated the Crystal Palace crowd: working people were much more likely to attend on shilling days than pay the usual charge of 2s. 6d.[52] Populist forms of provision would repay detailed study, though my focus in the remainder of this chapter is more particular: this commercialised recreational space was also increasingly utilised by various working-class associations to mark their collective achievements, and it is with the extent and meaning of that usage that I am primarily concerned here.

In early April 1860, for example, the Operative Builders met at the Crystal Palace to celebrate the termination of a strike in the building trade. The company itself was keen to promote these links and drew attention to the event in its official monthly publication, *The Crystal Palace News and Magazine of Literature, Science and Art*. According to this periodical, the 'fairy-like edifice' – built by 'the labour of free hands, receiving a remuneration agreed upon between the master and the labourer' – was itself symbolic of a new relationship between capital and labour. At the builders' meeting, the article noted, 'thousands of well-dressed, well-conducted, and intelligent artisans' listened attentively to speeches by G. W. M. Reynolds, George Potter and Mr Ayrton MP'.[53] All kinds of voluntary associations used the Crystal Palace from this time and the magazine enthusiastically reported meetings organised by the Volunteer Force and the Manchester Unity of Oddfellows later that year. The latter body held its fifth annual fête at the Crystal Palace in early August 1860 and the subsequent notice praised friendly societies in general for encouraging thrift amongst the working classes.[54] *Reynold's Newspaper* covered the annual festival of the Society of Foresters soon after which was attended by nearly 68,000 visitors. The editor contrasted the case of a cavalry officer who had been convicted for cowardly assault on the same day as 'nearly seventy thousand working men were rationally, peaceably, and innocently amusing themselves at the Crystal Palace'.[55]

It was the temperance movement, however, that really made the Crystal Palace its own during the 1860s, with regular annual fêtes that became ever larger and more elaborate as the decade wore on. The links with temperance went back to the Great Exhibition itself: Thomas Cook, who had organised excursion trains in 1851, was himself a keen temperance reformer.[56] The Crystal Palace was popular from the start because it was seen as an appropriate space for 'the people's' pleasures and celebrations. Joseph Livesey, the self-made cheesemonger from Preston and editor of *The Weekly Record of the Temperance Movement*, argued for this appropriation most explicitly in 1860: 'We are not talking of Buckingham or St. James's, they are not holiday places; nor of Windsor, nor Hampton Court, though they are. It is with our Palace just now we have to do – yours and mine, and everybody's, who can muster 1s. 6d. to take him or her to Sydenham and back, and from 10 am till dusk the Palace is theirs.'[57] For Livesey, the building itself gave access to a completely novel, almost utopian experience and was therefore the key attraction at the 'Sydenham fairyland':

> A dream comes the nearest to it … We defy you to do anything for the first half hour, but give yourself up to the willing enchantment, the most delicious bewilderment, the fullness of gratification … The light, the space, the sound, the knowledge of vastness, the consciousness of height and breadth and room and variety, are in themselves a joy. You may walk on and on, turn here and there, up and down, right and left; still something new, never the same; all bright, all excellent, all chiefest of its kind – all yours, ours, to look at, to admire, to feast the eyes and minister to the sense – what can the possessive 'mine' give more?[58]

Livesey also fully recognised that the Crystal Palace was a kind of department store, 'where you may purchase anything (from a paper of pins to a curricle)'. The first major temperance gathering took place the following year when about 10,000 members of temperance societies, drawn mainly from the London area, attended a demonstration at the Crystal Palace. The National Temperance League that organised the event attempted to broaden participation in 1864 and at least one society arranged for the payment of tickets in instalments so that poorer members could attend. A second class rail ticket from London plus admission cost two shillings and special excursion trains ran from the Midlands and the south of England. The programme included speeches by temperance leaders like George Cruikshank, a concert by a choir made up of 1,500 Band of Hope children, a fountain display and a large procession.[59] In 1865 an exhibition of skilled craftsmanship produced by the 'working-classes' in England and France was a major feature, along with Cruikshank's monumental engraving 'The Worship of Bacchus', which was displayed to the public for the first time. Well over 32,000 people attended the fête.[60] By 1868 the Band of Hope choir consisted of 5,000 vocalists and attendance stood at nearly 43,000; three years later this figure had increased to over 63,000.[61] The editor of *The British Temperance Advocate*, which was published in Bolton, described the festival with 'especial pleasure' in 1873, 'because it has become so thoroughly national'.[62]

Though temperance organisations made determined efforts to secure a ban on the sale of alcoholic beverages every year on the day of the fête, they often failed – and this caused continuous friction with the Crystal Palace Company.[63] *The Weekly Record* made light of these difficulties in 1865: 'A few non-abstaining visitors treated themselves during the day to occasional glasses of beer or ale, but in so doing they had to put up with a very large amount of ridicule and chaff, which they attempted to return, but with poor success', observed its reporter.[64] In 1875 the National Temperance League decided to shift the fête to the Alexandra Palace because it could not stop the sale of alcohol which the League had by this time come to insist upon. Other venues, including the Horticultural Gardens and the Royal Albert Hall, were also tried but attendance fell off dramatically.[65] In 1878, however, the United Kingdom Band of Hope once again managed to organise a very successful and alcohol-free fête at the Crystal Palace, though they had to compensate vendors for their loss of trade.[66] Although a record number of nearly 67,000 participated in the 1883 event, this proved to be a kind of swan song and by the end of the decade the *Temperance Record* could note that, 'it has long been clear to onlookers that the days of great fêtes of this description have practically passed'.[67] Temperance fêtes continued to be held at the Crystal Palace during the early 1890s, though their popularity had peaked some twenty years before. This accords well with Brian Harrison's work, which demonstrated that the temperance movement reached its zenith in the early 1870s and thereafter 'began to acquire the conservative outlook which signalled its long-term decline'.[68] By 1895 the event had assumed 'more of the character of a Choral Festival than of a popular fête' and it limped on in this form into the next century.[69]

In 1888, as the great temperance fêtes were in full decline, the first National Co-operative Festival was organised at the Crystal Palace. With nearly one million members, the Co-operative movement was by this time a central institution of working-class life, particularly in the industrial north. At least 140 local societies subscribed to the festival in 1889 and funds of £1,300 were raised. Festival day commenced at 9 a.m. on Saturday 24 August with the opening of an exhibition of goods produced in profit-sharing workshops. The rest of the day's activities included a demonstration of Edison's phonograph, a testimonial to Mrs Lawrenson of the Women's Co-operative Guild, members' arts and crafts exhibitions, a gigantic flower show, athletics, and a balloon ascent. The Handel Orchestra and a choir consisting of 5,000 voices gave a concert between 4 and 6 p.m.; the festival hymn was entitled 'The Triumph of Labour'. Performing elephants accompanied by a brass band entertained in the gardens, followed by a spectacular fountain display. A didactic play was performed in the theatre at 7 p.m., while the Christian Socialist E. V. Neale delivered the presidential address in the great concert hall. As dusk fell the gardens were illuminated and at 8.30 a floral ballet entitled 'A Golden Dream' was performed outdoors. The day ended with a great fireworks display, the crowning attraction of which was a flaming co-operative wheatsheaf. Over 32,000 people attended.[70]

The festival had been the brain-child of the co-operative propagandist, Edward Owen Greening, who had conceived it as a stimulus to co-operative growth in London and the south. Moreover, it served to advertise the important role of the movement in Victorian England and was a great success in this respect: the London press coverage of the festivals was exhaustive, in contrast to the relatively muted response of Northern newspapers where co-operation was already an integral part of community life. Determined efforts were made to make the festival accessible and cost was kept down: in the 1890s the rail fare from London was 1s. 6d. including admission; for children it was half price. Arrangements were made with railway companies to secure reduced rates for parties from the provinces. In 1893 the festival was extended from one to five days, Tuesday to Saturday. The following year an article in the *Bolton Co-operative Record* proudly declared that the demonstration at the Crystal Palace proved decisively 'that working-class Co-operation is now a power in the land'.[71] By 1895 it could be described as 'the great object lesson in co-operation. The tens of thousands of co-operators − perhaps themselves the greatest sight of all − the exhibitions of productions, the gigantic choir, the flowers and fruits from workmen's gardens, the speaking, the sports, make up a day not to be forgotten. Nothing else helps one to realise the movement as a great living organism'.[72] The attendance in 1896 reached almost 42,000 for 'Festival Saturday' alone. New features were continually introduced; children's sports, musical drill and choir contests especially, grew in size and importance. By the late 1890s over 5,000 exhibits were sent to the flower show. The senior choir grew as local societies were prompted to establish choirs to send to the festival; the United Choir numbered 10,000 in 1897. Cricket matches were arranged between societies; photographic displays began to appear.[73] It was almost as if the dream of the editor of the *Northern Star* in 1851 had been partially realised: the Crystal Palace was now appropriated, at least temporarily, by the organised working class and used to proclaim the superiority of democratic and co-operative forms of manufacture and pleasure (see figure 4.2).

June, 1897.] LABOUR CO-PARTNERSHIP. 103

TENTH GREAT NATIONAL

CO-OPERATIVE FESTIVAL,

Crystal Palace, SATURDAY, 21st August, 1897.

F I R E W O R K S

F I R E W O R K S

Upwards of £400 in Prizes, and Gold, Silver and Bronze Medals.

THE

TWELFTH NATIONAL "ONE & ALL" FLOWER SHOW

(Under the Auspices of the Agricultural and Horticultural Association Limited.)

COMPRISES CLASSES FOR

Flowers, Fruit and Vegetables

PRODUCED BY MEMBERS OF CO-OPERATIVE SOCIETIES.

Grand Concert of 6,000 Voices.   Choral Contests for Adult Choirs. for Junior Choirs.

MUSICAL DRILL COMPETITION.

THE IMPERIAL VICTORIAN EXHIBITION. Illustrated by most valuable Relics and Mementoes of Her Majesty, the Royal Family, and the leading personages of the Victorian Era. Naval and Military Section ; Telegraph Section ; Railway Section ; Docks ; Weights and Measures of the Victorian Era ; Sanitary Section ; Photography ; Indian and Colonial Sections ; Arts and Crafts of the British Nation ; Sports and Pastimes Section ; Pictures and Sculpture.

Co-operative Productive Exhibition,
Under the auspices of the Labour Association for Promoting Co-partnership Workshops.

An Athletic Meeting,
The Competition being restricted to Members and Employees of Co-operative Societies.

CHILDREN'S SPORTS AND GAMES, all day long in the Palace Grounds.   CHILDREN'S FLORAL FETE.

EXCURSIONS from all parts (see Railway Announcements).   Fare from London, including Admission, 1s. 6d. ;   Children Half-price.

All Particulars on application to the NATIONAL CO-OPERATIVE FESTIVAL SOCIETY LIMITED, 15, SOUTHAMPTON ROW, W.C.

4.2 'The Tenth Great National Co-operative Festival'

Unfortunately the festival was soon to be undermined by what looked like a boycott by railway companies which commenced a few years later. Cheap excursions to the Crystal Palace and discounts for large parties made the expansion of the festival possible throughout the 1890s. Special excursion trains were laid on for the great northern societies and choir singers and exhibitors were permitted to make the return journey to London for the price of a single ticket. Exhibits and displays were also usually transported at low rates, but in 1900 all these concessions were abruptly discontinued and fares rose on average by 25 per cent. The privilege of half fares for singers and exhibitors was stopped completely. This meant that for a workman, his wife and two children, travelling from Lancashire or Yorkshire, the cost of the journey rose from 30s. to £2 10s. Moreover, Saturday excursions were cut out altogether from some towns; thirty-eight societies which had sent singers to the United Choir in 1899 were absent in 1900. The railway companies argued that these price rises were due to the increased cost of coal and labour and to the congestion of traffic. The effect on the festival was devastating.[74] Other working-class organisations that used the Crystal Palace – such as the Non-conformist Union, for example – were also adversely affected.[75]

Reaction inside the Co-operative movement was prompt and highly critical – a motion condemning the railway companies was passed unanimously at the annual Congress in 1900.[76] The general secretary of the Co-operative Union, J. C. Gray, reported to Congress the following year that letters of complaint, incorporating the resolution, had been sent to the companies concerned, but little had been achieved.[77] The old Owenite G. J. Holyoake, making an effort to be optimistic, wrote after the 1901 festival: 'though the paralysing hand of the railway was laid upon its excursionists and visitors it was a great Festival'.[78] However, the fact remained that attendance was reduced to less than 29,000 and these came mostly from the London area. The choir was a mere shadow of its former self, made up of 3,000 singers. The culture of the Co-operative movement drew its strength from organising and including in its ambit working-class families, not just the male breadwinner at the point of production or the male citizen in the 'public' sphere. But this strategy could also pose problems, as small increases in cost could easily undermine a recreational activity that was designed to involve women and children besides men: 'None know better than the wives and mothers what the increased charges mean', wrote Holyoake's daughter, Mrs Emilie Holyoake-Marsh, in an angry article in 1904.[79] Although the festival survived until 1910 attendance never rose to more than 25,000 throughout the 1900s. There had been no love lost between

the movement and the railway companies for a long time –
individual employees were often victimised for their co-operative
involvement and boycotts had been unsuccessfully attempted in
some areas – but this concerted offensive raised the temperature
considerably. Whether or not this was a deliberate policy
designed to hamstring co-operative culture, it was certainly
perceived as such by the leaders of the movement who voted in
favour of the nationalisation of the railways at the Co-operative
Congress in 1901. Moving the motion, Ben Jones spoke for many
when he declared that the movement was 'powerless to stem the
tide of rampant injustice in the railway world, which was taxing
co-operators severely'.[80]

Regardless of this set-back, however, the long-term success of
the festival was never secure owing to the internal conflicts
which marked the movement in the late nineteenth century.
Briefly, the festival was primarily conceived as a propaganda
vehicle for advocates of profit-sharing and co-partnership, many
of whom like Greening came from middle-class backgrounds.
Individuals like Greening and E. V. Neale tended to regard co-
operation primarily as an antidote for class struggle and anathe-
matised the more class-conscious, combative tone adopted by
many other advocates, particularly those connected to the Co-
operative Wholesale Society (CWS). Thus goods produced in workshops and factories owned by the CWS – which had abandoned
profit-sharing in the mid 1870s – were always marginalised if not
totally excluded from the showpiece exhibition. This generated
much acrimony and convinced many that it was necessary to wrest
control away from these distinguished patrons; from about 1896
alternative regional festivals were held in the North and the
Midlands and these expanded as the cost of travelling to London
increased. The Oldham co-operator Frank Hardern visited the
National Co-operative Festival in 1896 and questioned whether it
could be properly described as co-operative at all; the exhibition
of co-operative productions 'was not near so good a show as we
had at our Oldham Co-operative Exhibition two or three years
ago'. The Crystal Palace – a 'time-worn institution' – also failed to
impress.[81]

One of the largest regional festivals was organised by the
Manchester and Salford Society four years later and took place in

the Botanical Gardens at Old Trafford. A correspondent in the *Wheatsheaf* explained that it 'seemed only fitting' that such a festival should be held in the north of England, 'because it is the home of the mass of the working people of this country and co-operation is ideally a movement of the working-classes'.[82] The Manchester festival lasted four days and was attended by about 60,000 people. Northern societies rallied support – the Pendleton Society alone sent 5,000 members. The cost was 4d. for children and 1s. for adults and almost thirty concerts were held over the four days. Friday was 'Children's Day' and several schools in the area were forced to close as over 15,000 children enjoyed the free entertainment and refreshment provided.[83] The aim of the large exhibition was to present a 'thoroughly representative' display of co-operative productions and consequently CWS goods were highlighted. At the opening ceremony John Shillito, chairman of the English CWS, emphasised that this democratically controlled body was an integral part of the movement. As a sign of unanimity J. C. Gray lent his support and dismissed the National Festival as a gathering 'of irresponsible nobodies in London'.[84]

Conclusion: the limits to appropriation

Working-class consumers in Victorian and Edwardian England have frequently been represented as either seduced by the showy delights of consumer capitalism, rendered 'open-mouthed' and depoliticised by an increasingly commercialised culture; or else divided amongst themselves in a competitive scramble over the world of goods.[85] In these accounts consumer culture is necessarily corrosive of class-consciousness and solidarity, and although a gross over-simplification, based often on very thin evidence, this interpretative framework continues to command support.[86] It makes more sense perhaps to situate the developing world of working-class association in the late nineteenth and early twentieth centuries within the context of an emergent and evolving consumer culture, in order to reveal the kinds of connection, as well as the moments of conflict, that existed between these historical alternatives.[87] An expansive network of voluntary associations – including trade unions, friendly and co-operative societies, as well as recreational forms such as working men's clubs – constituted an impressive working-class public sphere before World War One.[88] This associational culture placed a premium on the principles of autonomy and independence, but was never completely separated from commercialised forms of popular culture embodied in the music hall, the mass-circulation newspaper, or the Crystal Palace itself. The latter was a key site where these different cultures – the consumer culture and the associational culture – intersected in the second half of the nineteenth century. The apparently minor strand in the history of popular leisure discussed in this chapter brings out very well the complex links and contradictions that existed between these interpenetrating worlds.

Despite the fact that the Crystal Palace attracted millions of visitors and secured a key place in the popular imagination, the enterprise was continually beset by financial difficulties throughout its existence. When crisis threatened, those advocates of rational recreation associated with the project took the opportunity to launch a moralistic offensive against more commercially driven interests within the company. The original managing director Francis Fuller, for example, tried to convince shareholders to dissolve the company and set up a new association based on the original principles from the summer of 1874 onwards. Though he was unsuccessful, other important shareholders agreed with Fuller, J. Scott Russell arguing that management had made 'a great blunder' over the preceding decade, 'by lowering the tone of its amusements, to please the uneducated and unrefined portion of the visitors', in an attempt to boost revenue.[89] Russell went on to recommend 'elevating, instructing, and refining' forms of recreation, as did William Gibbs in a pamphlet addressed to fellow shareholders in 1876. Gibbs maintained that the degeneration of the Crystal Palace crowd had caused the value of ordinary shares to plummet and histrionically asserted that the situation was now so bad that respectable newspapers, 'not unfriendly but the contrary, have unmistakably hinted that it is an objectionable place for ladies.'[90] Despite these serious problems the company managed to remain afloat throughout the late nineteenth century, which would have been highly unlikely had the directors taken the advice of Fuller and his supporters and excluded 'low' elements entirely from Sydenham Hill.

The financial instability of the Crystal Palace Company became more apparent during the early 1900s and the accelerating decline of the venture was not halted by the largest event ever held at Sydenham, the 'Festival of Empire', staged over six months in 1911 to mark the coronation of George V. A scale model of the British Empire was constructed in the grounds and visitors could tour a South African diamond mine, an Indian tea plantation complete with natives and a Canadian logging camp, on a miniature railway named the 'All red route'. Thousands of people witnessed this 'Social gathering of the British family', as it was called in the official souvenir, and at the end of June nearly 6,000 teachers herded approximately 100,000 children to the Palace on special trains for a coronation fête. The sugary commemorative account published soon after, entitled *The King's Day With the Children*, failed to conceal how London schoolboys and girls had been marshalled in military fashion and used as props for this royal pageant; no smiling faces can be discerned amongst the copious photographs that accompanied the text.[91] According to some historians the majority of the working class was relatively unmoved by imperialism and it seems unlikely that there was much authentic popular enthusiasm for the 'Festival of Empire'.[92] The event failed to save the company from bankruptcy; two years later the Crystal Palace was purchased by the state and rapidly became dilapidated.

It is very difficult indeed for the social historian to recover the experience of those working people who claimed the Crystal Palace as their own in the second half of the nineteenth century. The many spectacles and entertainments, as well as the frequent demonstrations of collective achievement, would surely have contrasted vividly with the monotony and hardship of everyday life. In this way perhaps the space of the Crystal Palace contained a utopian potential; for some it allowed access to a qualitatively different or alternative future. A co-operator from the Midlands who visited in the mid-1890s provided the following description:

> The Co-operative Festival, with its flowers, fruit and music, is the brightest hope of Co-operation. 6,000 young voices swelling in rhythmic harmony ... is a grand and glorious sound, speaking of the future of Co-operation, voicing the first notes of that triumphal chorus which shall increase and swell until it destroys all sound of

discord and strife, uniting all families, peoples and nations in everlasting peace.[93]

We may agree with the French sociologist Henri Lefebvre here, who suggested that the 'space of leisure' attempts to bridge the existing gap between work and pleasure and therefore ought to be regarded as 'contradictory space ... where the existing mode of production produces both its worst and its best – parasitic outgrowths on the one hand and exuberant new branches on the other – as prodigal of monstrosities as of promises (that it cannot keep).' Such spaces thus contain a utopian potential according to Lefebvre and make it possible, however briefly, for use value to 'gain the upper hand over exchange value: appropriation, turning the world upon its head, may (virtually) achieve dominion over domination, as the imaginary and the utopian incorporate (or are incorporated into) the real'.[94]

However, this potential was and is always circumscribed by commercial imperatives and the wider capitalist context; such spaces may appear to be truly 'deviant' at first glance but they cannot escape 'the control of the established order'; workers never owned the Crystal Palace after all, even if the company was run almost as a charity throughout much of its history.[95] The higher cost of railway excursions only served to exacerbate factors which threatened to undermine the possibility of working-class appropriation from the beginning; for some associationists the sticking-point was the sale of alcohol, whilst for many others the heritage of rational recreation and middle-class patronage meant that relations were always likely to be fraught. Quite simply, working-class people were demanding more control across the field of politics and culture from the late nineteenth century onwards; they were increasingly going to seaside resorts on trips organised by their own associations, for example, as well as building locally. Connections and contests between the consumer culture and the associational culture continued, but the Crystal Palace had been largely abandoned by the organised working class – if not by all of 'the people' – to the monarchy and the state, long before November 1936 when it was razed to the ground by a mysterious fire.[96]

Notes

1 Cook explained her project in the first issue. See *Eliza Cook's Journal* 1, 5 January 1849, p. 1.

2 *Ibid.* 116, 19 July 1851, pp. 1–2. See T. Travers, 'The problem of identification of articles: Samuel Smiles and *Eliza Cook's Journal*, 1849–1854', *Victorian Periodicals Newsletter* 20, June 1973, pp. 41–5. Cook later published many of her contributions (though not 'The Cheap Tripper') in *Jottings From My Journal* (London: Warne & Routledge, 1860). For the intellectual context see K. Gleadle, *The Early Feminists. Radical Unitarians and the Emergence of the Women's Rights Movement* (London: Macmillan, 1995).

3 P. Bailey, *Leisure and Class in Victorian England: Rational Recreation and the Contest for Control, 1830–1885* (London: Croom Helm, 1978), p. 113; H. Cunningham, *Leisure in the Industrial Revolution 1780–1880* (London: Croom Helm, 1980), p. 140; F. M. L. Thompson, *The Rise of Respectable Society. A Social History of Victorian Britain 1830–1900* (London: Fontana, 1988), p. 261.

4 H. Mayhew and G. Cruikshank, *1851: or, the Adventures of Mr. and Mrs. Sandboys and Family, who came up to London to 'Enjoy Themselves' and to see the Great Exhibition* (London: George Newbold, 1851), pp. 129, 132. Cruikshank provided the illustrations for the volume.

5 See A. Short, 'Workers under glass in 1851', *Victorian Studies* 10 (1966), pp. 193–202; G. Best, *Mid-Victorian Britain 1851–75* (London: Weidenfeld & Nicolson, 1971), p. 253; François Bédarida, *A Social History of England, 1851–1971* (London: Methuen & Co., 1979), p. 8. A number of labour historians have more recently stressed that relations between the classes continued to be marked by suspicion and hostility. See especially J. Saville, *1848: The British State and the Chartist Movement* (Cambridge: Cambridge University Press, 1987); N. Kirk, *Change, Continuity and Class: Labour in British Society, 1850–1920* (Manchester: Manchester University Press, 1998).

6 This sanguine view has been rehearsed by many historians including Bédarida, *A Social History*, p. 7; A. Briggs, *Victorian Things* (London: Penguin, 1988), p. 78; T. Richards, *The Commodity Culture of Victorian England. Advertising and Spectacle, 1851–1914* (London: Verso, 1991), p. 37.

7 A. Briggs, *Victorian People* (London: Pelican, 1965), p. 48.

8 *Ibid.*, p. 28.

9 See T. Kusamitsu, 'Great Exhibitions before 1851', *History Workshop Journal* 9 (1980), pp. 70–89.

10 *Northern Star*, 3 May 1851, p. 4. For working-class enthusiasm for the Crystal Palace itself see M. Berman, *All That Is Solid Melts Into Air. The Experience of Modernity* (London: Verso, 1983), p. 238.

11 *Reynold's Newspaper*, 9 March 1851, p. 7. My thanks to Rohan McWilliam for identifying 'Gracchus'.

12 *Ibid.*, 16 March 1851, p. 8.

13 *Northern Star,* 19 April 1851, p. 4.

14 *Reynold's Newspaper,* 20 April 1851, p. 8.

15 *Ibid.*, 4 May 1851, p. 8.

16 *Northern Star,* 3 May 1851, p. 4.

17 *Northern Star,* 31 May 1851, p. 6.

18 Mayhew and Cruikshank, *1851*, p. 153.

19 *Northern Star,* 18 Oct 1851, p. 1. On organised trips for workers from provinces patronised by local employers see R. J. Morris, 'Leeds and the Crystal Palace', *Victorian Studies* 13 (1970), pp. 283–300.

20 *Reynold's Newspaper,* 25 May 1851, p. 7.

21 *Ibid.*, 3 June 1851, p. 7. For the political context in 1851 see Asa Briggs' well-known essay, 'The Crystal Palace and the Men of 1851', in *Victorian People*, pp. 23–59.

22 See J. Epstein, 'Feargus O'Connor and the Northern Star', *International Review of Social History* 21/1 (1976), p. 82.

23 *Northern Star,* 14 June 1851, p. 4.

24 *Ibid.*, 21 June 1851, p. 1.

25 *Reynold's Newspaper,* 24 August 1851, p. 7.

26 The importance of populism as an explanatory concept has been the subject of much controversy amongst social historians at the end of the twentieth century. Patrick Joyce's *Visions of the People. Industrial England and the Question of Class 1848–1914* (Cambridge: Cambridge University Press, 1991) has been most influential here. For a judicious summary of the ensuing debate see R. McWilliam, *Popular Politics in Nineteenth Century England* (London: Routledge, 1998). For an account and analysis of the popular figure who claimed to be disappeared aristocrat Sir Roger Tichborne, see R. McWilliam, 'Radicalism and popular culture: The Tichborne case and the politics of "fair play"', in E. F. Biagini and A. J. Reid (eds), *Currents of Radicalism* (Cambridge: Cambridge University Press, 1991). pp. 44–64.

27 *Reynold's Newspaper,* 19 October 1851, p. 8.

28 P. Beaver, *The Crystal Palace, 1851–1936. A Portrait of Victorian Enterprise* (London: Hugh Evelyn, 1970), pp. 79, 105; C. Hobhouse, *1851 and the Crystal Palace* (London: John Murray, 1950), pp. 153–61; H. Cunningham, *Leisure in the Industrial Revolution*, pp. 156–7; *The Illustrated London News*, 17 June 1854, pp. 580–4.

29 *The Crystal Palace Company. Deed of Settlement, Royal Charters and List of Shareholders* (London: H. G. Bohn, 1856), pp. 5, 64.

30 See *Royal Crystal Palace Almanack for 1857* (London: Arthur Hall, Virtue and Co., 1857). This publication featured advertisements for fish tanks, corsets, specialised mirrors and a host of other consumer goods which were on sale at the Palace.

31 P. Greenhalgh, *Ephemeral Vistas. The 'Expositions Universelles', Great Exhibitions and World's Fairs, 1851–1939* (Manchester: Manchester University Press, 1988); A. Briggs, *Victorian Things*.

32 H. W. Bellows, *The Moral Significance of the Crystal Palace* (New York: G. Putnam & Co., 1853) pp. 17–18.

33 *Reynold's Newspaper*, 6 February 1853, p. 8. For reports of other protest meetings see *ibid.*, 13 March 1853, p. 9.

34 See B. Harrison, 'Religion and recreation in nineteenth century England', *Past and Present* 38, December 1967, pp. 108–11.

35 G. Cruikshank, *The Glass and the New Crystal Palace* (London: John Cassell, 1853), pp. 17–18.

36 J. R. Butlin, *The Sabbath Made for Man, or, Defence of the Crystal Palace* (London: Saunders and Otley, 1853), p. 13.

37 J. B. Brown, *The Sabbath, the Crystal Palace and the People* (London: Arthur Hall, Virtue and Co., 1853), pp. 21–2.

38 J. Dacres Devlin, *The Sydenham Sunday; its good promise, and why so needful: and shewing the vagueness and thorough impracticability of the Rev. Dr. Cumming's proposal to supersede the necessity, as regards the working classes, of opening the New Crystal Palace on Sundays* (London: Saunders & Stanford, 1853), pp. 2, 13.

39 *The Crystal Palace in 1853. A Dialogue* (London: John Henry Parker, 1853), p. 23. This pamphlet took the form of a dialogue between Lady Fanny Seymour (upper-class, philanthropic, pro-Sunday opening) and Miss Caroline Howard (independent, lower-middle-class sabbatarian).

40 J. Hall, *The Sons of Toil and the Crystal Palace: in reply to Mr Mayhew* (London: John Snow, 1853), pp. 26, 33. Hall was also concerned about the immoral proclivities of 'a gaping crowd' that would require 'vigorous control' by the police.

41 *A Correspondence Between Edward Baines, Esq. and B. Oliveira, Esq. MP on the Sunday Opening of the Crystal Palace* (London: Seeleys, 1854), p. 8.

42 B. Bouchier, *The Poor Man's Palace and the Poor Man's Day. A Letter to the Directors and Shareholders of the Crystal Palace Company* (London: John Farquhar Shaw, 1854), p. 7.

43 D. Burns, *Temperance History. A Consecutive Narrative of the Rise, Development, and Extension of the Temperance Reform* (London: National Temperance Publication Department, 1889), Vol. II, p. 370.

44 *The Crystal Palace Company. Deed of Settlement*, p. 75.

45 *Ibid.*, preface, p. iii.

46 K. Marx and F. Engels, *Articles On Britain* (Moscow: Progress Publishers, 1971), p. 238.

47 See B. Harrison, 'The Sunday Trading Riots of 1855', *The Historical Journal* 8/2 (1965), pp. 219–45.

48 See *The Sabbatarian Clergy and the Crystal Palace, issued by the National Sunday League* (London: National Sunday League, 1858).

49 E. Royle, *Modern Britain. A Social History 1750–1997* (London: Edward Arnold, 1997), p. 257.

50 See *Dean's Moveable Book of Blondin's Astounding Exploits at the Crystal Palace & elsewhere, showing all his most wonderful feats in large moveable pictures* (London: Dean & Son, 1862).

51 T. Bennett in *The Birth of the Museum* (London: Routledge, 1995) argues for the link between international exhibitions and amusement parks.

52 Social mixing sometimes caused complaint from upper-class patrons. Note the diary entry by Sir William Hardman from 1862 in S. M. Ellis (ed.), *A Mid-Victorian Pepys* (London: Cecil Palmer, 1923), p. 151.

53 *The Crystal Palace News and Magazine of Literature, Science and Art* 15, 1860, p. 129.

54 *Ibid.* 10, 1860; 31, 1860, p. 274.

55 *Reynold's Newspaper*, 26 August 1860, pp. 8, 12.

56 At the 1882 temperance festival Cook maintained that he had thought of organising temperance trips to London from this time. See *Temperance Record*, 7 September 1882, p. 562; Burns, *Temperance History*, Vol. I, pp. 337–8. An interesting account of Cook's career can be found in *Temperance Record*, 5 July 1888, p. 420.

57 *The Weekly Record of the Temperance Movement*, 11 August 1860, p. 357.

58 *Ibid.*, p. 357–8.

59 *Ibid.*, 22 June 1861, p. 258; 23 July 1864, p. 472; 30 July 1864, p. 496.

60 *Ibid.*, 26 August 1865, p. 446; 2 September 1865, p. 492.

61 *Ibid.*, 5 September 1868, p. 422; 5 August 1871, pp. 361–2.

62 *The British Temperance Advocate. The Organ of the British Temperance League*, June 1873.

63 The early historians of the movement complained bitterly about this; see Burns, *Temperance History*, Vol. II, p. 371; P. T. Winskill, *The Temperance Movement and Its Workers* (London: Blackie & Son, 1892), Vol. III, p. 54. According to Winskill the directors 'made the Crystal Palace a gigantic public-house'.

64 *The Weekly Record of the Temperance Movement*, 26 August 1865, p. 454.

65 *Temperance Record*, 10 July 1875, p. 349.

66 *Ibid.*, 12 July 1877, p. 441; 18 July 1878, p. 450. Trade depression was also blamed for falling attendance.

67 *Ibid.*, 12 July 1883, p. 434; 11 July 1889, p. 437.

68 B. Harrison, *Drink and the Victorians: The Temperance Question in England, 1815–1872* (Keele: Keele University Press, 2nd edn 1994), p. 22.

69 *Temperance Record*, 12 July 1894, p. 438. A history of the National

Temperance Festivals appeared in this journal the year after. See 4 July 1895, pp. 425–6.

70 *Co-operative News*, 3 August 1889, p. 830; 17 August 1889, pp. 877–9.

71 *Bolton Co-operative Record*, September 1894, p. 17.

72 *Labour Co-partnership*, August 1895, p. 164.

73 *Ibid.*, September 1897, pp. 152–3.

74 A brief history of the festival can be found in E. O. Greening's article in the *Economic Review*, January 1902, pp. 87–90.

75 *Manchester and Salford Co-operative Record*, August 1900, p. 121.

76 *Co-operative Congress Report*, 1900, pp. 157–8.

77 *Ibid.*, 1901, pp. 38, 185.

78 *Labour Co-partnership*, September 1901, p. 134.

79 *Ibid.*, September 1904, p. 139. For an analysis of the movement culture see my monograph, *Co-operative Culture and the Politics of Consumption in England, 1870–1930* (Manchester: Manchester University Press, 1996), pp. 29–140.

80 *Co-operative Congress Report*, 1901, p. 190.

81 *Oldham Industrial Co-operative Society Record*, October 1896, p. 64.

82 *Wheatsheaf*, September 1900, p. 39.

83 *Co-operative News*, 1 September 1900, pp. 974–6; *Manchester Co-operative Record*, October 1900, pp. 165–6.

84 *Wheatsheaf*, September 1900, p. 42; *Manchester Co-operative Record*, October 1900, pp. 159–60.

85 G. S. Jones, 'Working-class culture and working-class politics in London, 1870–1900: Notes on the remaking of a working class', *Journal of Social History* 7:4 (1974), pp. 460–508; P. Johnson, 'Conspicuous consumption and working-class culture in late-Victorian and Edwardian Britain', *Transactions of the Royal Historical Society* 38 (1988), pp. 27–42.

86 J. Benson, *The Rise of Consumer Society in Britain, 1880–1980* (London: Longmans, 1994).

87 For a useful theoretical treatment of the concept of consumer culture see D. Slater, *Consumer Culture and Modernity* (Oxford: Polity Press, 1997).

88 For brief assessments of the centrality of this culture see J. Harris, *Private Lives, Public Spirit: Britain 1870–1914* (London: Penguin, 1993), p. 193; M. Savage and A. Miles, *The Remaking of the British Working Class 1840–1940* (London: Routledge, 1994), pp. 66–8. For the working-class public sphere in an earlier phase see G. Eley, 'Edward Thompson, Social history and political culture: The making of a working-class public, 1780–1850', in H. J. Kaye and K. McClelland (eds), *E. P. Thompson: Critical perspectives* (Oxford: Polity Press, 1990), pp. 12–49.

89 *Crystal Palace: Evidence Given Before the Court of Inquiry, 24 February, 1875* (London: Alfred Boot, 1875), p. 13.

90 W. Gibbs, *The Misfortunes of the Crystal Palace and How to Retrieve Them* (London: Effingham Wilson, 1876), pp. 4–5.

91 Beaver, *The Crystal Palace*, p. 132; *Souvenir of the Royal Visit to the Festival of Empire, Imperial Exhibition and Pageant of London. Crystal Palace, Coronation Year 1911* (London: Bemrose & Sons, 1911); E. I. Husey, *The King's Day With the Children* (London: Simpkin & Co., 1911).

92 H. Pelling, 'British labour and British imperialism', in H. Pelling (ed.), *Popular Politics and Society in late-Victorian Britain* (London: Macmillan, 1968), pp. 82–100; R. Price, *An Imperial War and the British Working Class: Working-Class Attitudes and Reactions to the Boer War, 1899–1902* (London: Croom Helm, 1972); H. Cunningham, *The Volunteer Force: A Social and Political History 1859–1908* (London: Croom Helm, 1975). The debate provoked by these studies has proved inconclusive. For an alternative view see J. M. Mackenzie, *Propaganda and Empire: The Manipulation of British Public Opinion* (Manchester: Manchester University Press, 1984). On imperial exhibitions generally see A. Coombes, *Reinventing Africa* (New Haven: Yale, 1994).

93 *Co-operative Record of the Birmingham District*, July 1896, pp. 14–15.

94 H. Lefebvre, *The Production of Space* (Oxford: Blackwell, 1991), pp. 385, 348.

95 *Ibid.*, p. 383.

96 The Co-operative movement made a belated return to the Palace in 1934 with an exhibition and children's gala organised as part of an International Co-operative Congress. For details see *Co-operative News*, 15 September 1934, p. 1.

5

Narrating the subcontinent in 1851: India at the Crystal Palace

LARA KRIEGEL

> India, the glorious glowing land, the gorgeous and the beautiful;
> India, the golden prize contended for by Alexander of old, and
> acknowledged in our day as the brightest jewel in Victoria's crown;
> India, the romantic, the fervid, the dreamy country of the rising
> sun; India the far-off, the strange, the wonderful, the original, the
> true, the brave, the conquered; India, how nobly does she show in
> the Palace devoted to the industrial products of the world![1]

With this rhapsodic reverie, John Cassell introduced the readers
of his *Illustrated Exhibitor* to the Great Exhibition's Indian Court
(see figure 5.1). A newspaper for England's artisanal classes, *The
Illustrated Exhibitor* led its audience from the Crystal Palace's
'main avenue' into the collections of its empire in the East, which
evoked a land of lush fertility and Oriental fantasy. Inside the
Indian Courts, rich displays of jewels, shawls, agricultural
produce, arms, and elephant trappings transported visitors from
the metropole to an imaginary, colonised subcontinent. As *The
Illustrated Exhibitor* pointed to these pieces, it rhetorically
embraced its readers as members of an imperial nation – real and
metaphorical consumers of the subcontinent as it was displayed
in Hyde Park. All the while, it offered them narratives of splendour
and conquest which gave meaning to the Oriental assemblage. 'We
gaze upon the myriad objects, rare and beautiful, which [India]
contributes, and our thoughts wander back to the day when she

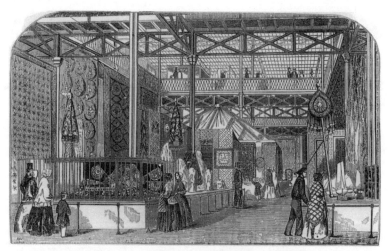

5.1 'General view of the Indian Court'

was free and powerful', Cassell remarked. He prompted his readers to reflect upon the former greatness of the subcontinent, and reminded them that this 'glorious' and 'brave' land was now conquered – a condition that was reinforced visually and symbolically by the empty throne that occupied the centre of the page on which *The Illustrated Exhibitor* introduced the Indian Courts (see figure 5.2).[2] As it continued, the periodical directed its readers' attention to 'curiously executed carvings', musical instruments, and carpets that would satisfy English imaginations of an Oriental bazaar. 'How suggestive they are', wrote Cassell, 'and what stories they tell'.[3]

When he presented the Indian Court to his readers, Cassell suggested that the commodities it held actually contained and expressed narratives. Inanimate objects, the displays in the Crystal Palace could not tell stories of their own accord. Instead, a variety of cultural techniques of display and textualisation rendered them legible, narrating them for the British producing, consuming and reading public.[4] Historians, literary critics and nineteenth-century observers have all understood the Great Exhibition to be the culmination of early nineteenth-century practices of visual display and spectacle.[5] At the same time, the Exhibition inspired and compelled the production of numerous narrative and cataloguing texts such as Cassell's. This literature

No. 18.]   OCTOBER 4, 1851.   [Price 2d.

India and Indian Contributions to the Industrial Bazaar.

India, the glorious glowing land, the gorgeous and the beautiful; India, the golden prize contended for by Alexander of old, and acknowledged in our day as the brightest jewel in Victoria's crown; India the romantic, the fervid, the dreamy country of the rising sun; India the far-off, the strange, the wonderful, the original, the true, the brave, the

IVORY CHAIR.—INDIAN ROOM, NORTHERN DEPARTMENT.

conquered; India, how nobly does she show in the Palace devoted to the industrial products of the world! We gaze upon the myriad objects, rare and beautiful, which she contributes, and our thoughts wander back to the day when she was free and powerful; we examine the rich stuffs which cover her walls—velvet, and silk, and muslin, and cloth

5.2 Title page from *The Illustrated Exhibitor*

ordered the event, gave meanings to its displays, and commemorated the Great Exhibition for posterity.[6] The set of texts produced around the Exhibition employed a number of common strategies – including storytelling, classification, mapping and illustration – to make the objects, and the nations that they metonomyically represented, audible. Using narratives of the gigantic and miniature, as well as the practice of gendering objects on display, these texts simultaneously gave voice to the displays in the Crystal Palace and domesticated them for consumption in the metropole.[7]

In this chapter, I am interested in the ways in which Exhibition texts animated the objects held inside the Crystal Palace, and the work these stories performed in defining Britain's imperial project, particularly with regard to India, the colony that the Great Exhibition helped to enshrine as the 'Jewel in the Crown'.[8] At the Exhibition, the East India Company, the body that was nominally responsible for governing the subcontinent in 1851 and the organisation that assembled the Indian Courts, endeavoured to represent India and the imperial project favourably to British and cosmopolitan visitors. As they discussed the East India Company's displays, texts such as Cassell's and other Exhibition literature participated in this effort, portraying the subcontinent as a fertile land, an Oriental treasure trove of ornate manufactures, and, finally, the colonised and feminised 'Jewel in the Crown'. These texts both aided and interrupted the East India Company's programme. By narrating India for the British public, the Exhibition's texts domesticated the subcontinent. At the same time, this literature, written by multiple authors and intended for different audiences, complicated the project of representing the subcontinent for the purposes of governance and consumption.[9] Even as they animated the objects on display with stories of productivity, oriental splendour, and conquest, these texts also produced surprising and unintended narratives – narratives that destabilised the relationship between colony and metropole, criticised Britain's history of rule on the subcontinent, and ultimately questioned the ideals of progress, industry, and capitalism that the Exhibition celebrated.[10]

India on display in 1851

The Great Exhibition opened following the 1849 annexation of
the Punjab, just as the focus of rule on the subcontinent was
shifting from trade to military domination. In the years preceding
the Great Exhibition, the East India Company struggled to redefine
its role. Having lost its trading and monopoly privileges in a series
of charter renewals between 1788 and 1833, the Company seemed
to be a 'bureaucratic shell' of its former self, directed largely by
the Indian army, which belonged to the Company only in name.
The civil and military personnel involved in its running wished to
make India a profitable endeavour at a moment when many
doubted the Company's efficacy, and some went so far as to question
the very desirability of England's maintaining an empire at all.[11]

In 1851 the East India Company emerged as one of the earliest
and most ardent supporters of the Exhibition, which offered an
opportunity to 'dazzle' and 'astound' visitors to the Crystal Palace
by displaying the riches of Britain's empire in the East. By
assembling a rich and thorough exhibit, the East India Company
hoped to convince the nation that Britain's engagement with
India was indeed beneficial.[12] To use the words of historian Paul
Greenhalgh, the East India Company aimed simultaneously to
'glorify and domesticate' the subcontinent by displaying its
material culture in Hyde Park.[13] In 1849 medical doctor John
Forbes Royle spearheaded the Company's efforts, which were co-
ordinated through the three presidencies of Bengal, Madras and
Bombay. His task was an onerous one, since it involved over-
seeing a wide expanse of territory on the subcontinent, working
in several languages, and shipping the displays from India to
Britain.[14] Ultimately, the Company assembled an exhaustive display of raw materials that attested to the financial benefits of
empire, a splendid array of artisanal manufactures that catered to
contemporary fantasies of Oriental splendour, and exhibits of
jewels and models that represented a domesticated India. As it
celebrated, commodified and classified India, the East India
Company was assisted by the Commissioners for the Exhibition,
who gave the subcontinent a 'place of honour' in the Crystal
Palace. Located near the main entrance and the Queen's retiring
room, the subcontinent's collections filled the west side of the

Palace's north–south transept. Space was at a premium in the Crystal Palace, and the Commissioners provided India with an area of 30,000 square feet – more than any other 'Colony', 'Possession', or 'Dependency' (as the *Official, Descriptive and Illustrated Catalogue of the Great Exhibition of 1851* alternatively referred to the points on Britain's imperial landscape) received by far.[15]

When the Great Exhibition opened, the Company received numerous accolades. Extensively collected and painstakingly indexed, India's collections stood out among the 'most complete, splendid, and interesting', enticing the British and cosmopolitan public alike.[16] *Tallis' History and Description of the Crystal Palace*, which appealed to a select audience through its rich narrative descriptions and engravings, advertised the appeal of the Indian Courts by including remarks by the French political economist Jerome Adolph Blanqui within its text. Tantalised by the Indian Collection, Blanqui found himself compelled to return to gaze at its holdings repeatedly. He revelled in its completeness, which exemplified the Exhibition's aim of ordering and governing through the practice of collecting. In Hyde Park, Blanqui claimed, Exhibition-goers could find an encyclopaedic representation of India, where the climate was the only thing missing (see figure 5.3).[17] For Tallis, refracting the East Indian Courts through the eye

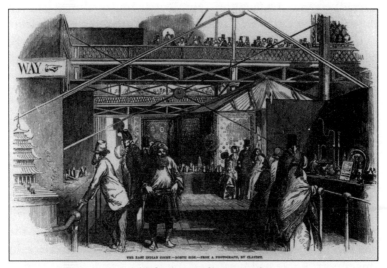

5.3 'The East Indian Court'

and pen of Blanqui – a native of Britain's most formidable rival, France – offered an effective strategy for conveying the desirability of empire to English readers and for encouraging Britons to identify proudly as members of the premiere imperial nation of the day.

As Blanqui's praise of the installation suggested, the Great Exhibition showcased the most comprehensive display of Indian material culture exhibited in London to date. Before the Exhibition, India had appeared in 'piecemeal' fashion in the metropolis.[18] Techniques of pleasure and discipline such as panoramas, dioramas and museums literally rendered India visible. In 1851, London's pleasure seekers could visit the Diorama of the Taj Mahal and the Overland Mail at Regent Street's Gallery of Illustration, as well as the Diorama of Hindoostan at the Baker-Street Bazaar. Literature for a growing reading public – whether in the form of periodical publications, novels or orientalist tales – also circulated multiple representations of India.[19] As the Exhibition approached, journalists sought to penetrate the abundant accounts of Oriental despotism and sensuality, and to define a 'real' India – or, to use the language of visuality, to render a 'faithful picture' of the subcontinent. These images themselves were varied, ranging from a fruitful 'farm' to a 'great camp' to a land of squalid poverty.[20] At mid-century, an accrual of images, narratives and commodities represented India, constituting an imperial culture that was available for consumption by members of the artisanal and middle classes. Together, such texts materialised the subcontinent, and provided a 'map of prior meanings' upon which the East India Company presented its display of raw materials, manufactures and jewels.[21]

The most 'valuable appendage': cultivating the subcontinent

The *Official Catalogue* prefaced its lengthy discussion of India by reprinting John Forbes Royle's 1849 report to the East India Company, *On the Exhibition of Raw Products and Manufactured Articles from India*, which had offered a blueprint for forming the collection of goods from the subcontinent at the Crystal Palace. In this report, Royle had portrayed India as a grand, fertile plantation, ripe for the production of raw materials. 'INDIA, vast in extent and diversified in surface', Royle rhapsodised. He maintained that the subcontinent could produce 'the useful products of every other quarter of the globe'. A microcosm of the world, India held several uncultivated riches within its seemingly infinite borders. According to Royle, the natives' inability to develop their natural resources, the lack of knowledge about Indian natural products on the part of British manufacturers and scientists, and cumbersome commercial tariffs that had only recently been abolished had all provided barriers to commercial progress.[22]

In order for its productive capacities to be harnessed, India – and by extension, the collection of raw and finished commodities that represented the subcontinent at the Exhibition – required organisation. The *Official Catalogue* aided this process by subsuming the commodities gathered by the East India Company into the four sections and thirty classes devised by Scottish scientist Lyon Playfair. At the Exhibition India's was the only collection other than the United Kingdom's that employed (or was subjected to) Playfair's system of categorisation. A foil to finite and developed Britain, vast and fertile India held resources that could render the metropole complete. The *Catalogue* also ordered India's raw materials through the use of Latin nomenclature. For instance, it gave so-called 'scientific' names to such staples as dhal (*cytisus cajan*) and muttar (*pisum sativum*). In the words of Robert Ellis, the editor of the *Official Catalogue*, this taxonomic exercise represented an attempt to 'convert the changing and inaccurate terms of trade' to 'the precise and enduring expressions of science'. The practice of applying Latin terminology to Indian produce – down to the last pea and lentil – provides one of the most striking examples of the Commissioners' understanding that, by classifying the earth's commodities and the habits of its consumers, they could know, order and colonise the subcontinent and, ultimately, the globe.[23]

Through such practices of classification and display, Royle hoped to harness and domesticate a feminised India characterised by 'natural fertility'.[24] In the minds of Royle, Robert Ellis and several Exhibition commentators, the production of imperial knowledge would enable Britain to intervene in the cultivation and manufacture of such commodities as tobacco, tea, silk and sugar, staples for Britain's domestic and export trades. They understood this endeavour to be a mutually beneficial one for the metropole and its colonies. This project would free the 'natives' of the subcontinent from the poverty so evident on their lean bodies, and from the stasis that their 'singularly rude' ploughs belied. At the same time, harnessing Indian agriculture would enable the British to procure commodities in demand at home, but cultivated elsewhere, mostly outside of the Empire. This was a timely concern. The Exhibition publicised itself as a celebration of free trade among nations, but it coincided with an intensi-fication in the concern over Britain's inability to produce its own raw materials. At the moment of the Exhibition, commentators expressed misgivings about Britain's dependence on other lands in a number of ways. They voiced concern about the slave labour that fuelled the production of cotton in the southern United States; they complained about the impurity of commodities such as tobacco, tea and opium cultivated in China and the Americas, where the British could not oversee production; and they worried about the disorder of recently emancipated slaves in the British West Indies, who grew and harvested sugar cane.[25]

The case of cotton was the most highly charged, in part because the cotton manufacture employed so many operatives in the north of England's textile industry and because cotton production was synonymous with the plantation slavery of the American South at the moment of the Exhibition.[26] Britain's reliance on this important foreign staple produced a number of reactions. When he visited the Crystal Palace, Blanqui noted that, for their livelihoods, the English depended more on American-grown cotton than upon their own domestic iron. According to the French political economist, who celebrated the ever-increasing 'mutual dependence of nations', this fact attested to civilisation's progress.[27] Many British commentators did not regard this pheno-menon as the litmus test of progress. For instance, a contributor to The Illustrated London News, which marketed the Exhibition to its middle-class readers through its weekly supplements, expressed grave concern about Britain's dependence on goods grown by people in slavery, 'the worst institution of modern times'. Whether this writer's objection to slavery was a moral or rhetorical one remains a question. Regardless, the journalist argued that Britain should supply its 'own wants' by cultivating cotton in India, just as France did by importing cotton from its colony, Algiers.[28]

Effecting this arrangement required reforming Indian habits of cultivation – a formidable task, since the natural resources of the subcontinent had experienced only 'a very slight degree of development'.[29] In the minds of Exhibition commentators, the agricultural arts of the subcontinent had remained stationary for 'centuries'. From 'time immemorial', the people of the subcontinent had used rough handmills and bows to remove seeds, dirt and knots from raw cotton. Commentators held that this practice was ineffective, particularly when it was juxtaposed to the facility, precision and speed of the mechanised cotton gin and mill. Frequently, they claimed, Indian cotton reached Britain in 'so dirty and adulterated a state' that it was 'troublesome' to 'work up'. It was unnecessarily expensive to import Indian cotton into Britain. When they did so, merchants and manufacturers incurred the cost of the 'carriage and freight of the dirt'. Not only was Indian cotton dirty; in comparison to the American product, it was considered to be short and coarse. These qualities did not present a problem to the 'Hindoos', who spun their goods by hand, but Indian cotton fibres were not long enough for use by a good deal of Western machinery in the early nineteenth century. However, a writer to *The Illustrated London News* forecasted that, with proper cultivation, India could one day provide enough cotton, wool and silk of a suitable grade to employ 'all the steam looms of Great Britain'.[30]

For several contributors to Exhibition texts, India represented an attractive – if not wholly ideal – solution to Britain's dependence on 'foreign' products, ungovernable markets and American plantation slavery. At the Crystal Palace, the subcontinent emerged as an 'immense region', a 'rich and gigantic territory', and the closest approximation of infinity on Earth. It contained the 'productions of every kingdom of nature' within its 'great diversities of climate' and offered 'every possible kind of soil and cultivation'. According to several commentators, India's 'endless fields and valleys' would one day produce everything that the 'civilized nations' of the earth required.[31]

The Great Exhibition's catalogues and classificatory methods offered an opportunity for the East India Company to order the subcontinent and assert a future economic programme that would provide a map for imperial governance. In a forceful endorsement of the colonising project as it was displayed in Hyde Park, *The Illustrated London News* claimed that India held 'more future' for British commerce than any other place on the globe. The subcontinent provided one feasible solution to the problems of British manufacture in 1851, but its displays of raw materials at the Crystal Palace also invited questions about the material relationship between England and India at mid-century. As it multiplied and complicated the ways of configuring the connections between metropole and colony, the Exhibition provided an opportunity for meditating on the ambiguities of the colonial project. The *Official Catalogue* referred to Britain's possessions as 'colonial dependencies'. However, the Exhibition ultimately revealed the relationship between metropole and colony to be one of intense interdependence. John Forbes Royle had exposed the complexity of this relationship when he referred to India as a 'valuable appendage' in 1849. By calling India a 'valuable appendage', Royle suggested several ways of configuring metropole and colony. His description was both a gesture of incorporation and an act of sublimation. It provided an imperial extension to the practice of imagining Victorian society as an anatomical body, whose components most frequently included the middle-class male head and female heart, as well as the working-class hands.[32] By designating India as a 'valuable appendage' – at once necessary and subsidiary to the metropole – Royle ensured that India was integral to the composition of Greater Britain, while also subordinate, or peripheral, to its centre.[33] His designation of India as an 'appendage' is interesting, furthermore, in light of the contemporary practice of portraying the subcontinent as gigantic. Compared to India, with its vast expanse of territory as well as its multitude of languages, climates and religions, Britain was only a 'petty island', in the words of *Bentley's Miscellany*. By deploying such a characterisation, *Bentley's* suggested that colonised India dwarfed colonising Britain – and perhaps that the metropole could be subsumed by the seemingly infinite colony.[34]

Rudeness and refinement: Indian art manufactures in 1851

Exhibition commentators maintained that the collection of raw materials from the subcontinent was the most important part of the collection in economic terms. However, it was the 'gorgeous manufactures' of India that produced the greatest 'sensation' in 1851. Hyde Park's 'fairyland' of howdahs, hookahs, shawls, carpets, arms and jewels made visitors 'pause to gaze in wonder' (see figure 5.4). The lavish displays seemed to confirm, and sometimes even to surpass, the 'Oriental magnificence' conveyed in the tales of the *Arabian Nights* that circulated in the metropole at the moment of the Exhibition and nurtured imaginations of a luxurious, sexualised and homogenised East. Following Cassell's example, several commentators began their discussions of India's art manufactures by professing their awe. Ultimately, however,

5.4 'State howdah – exhibited by the East India Company'

they almost all moved beyond the rhetoric of rapture and wonder and studied India's artisanal traditions more analytically. Their investigations materialised an India that was not simply a land of 'Oriental magnificence', but a much more complicated, contradictory culture.[35] In these discussions, India emerged as a sort of museum, an archive which held the unchanging originals of civilisation, and a land of inspiring craft traditions that had guided Britain in its own industrialisation.[36] The Exhibition also materialised the subcontinent as an economic and a military rival – a colony that was not as tractable as the Exhibition made it appear on first glance. Finally, when they meditated on artisanal India, British writers questioned and critiqued the benefits of industry and progress that the Exhibition celebrated.

Cassell's *Illustrated Exhibitor* maintained that visiting the Indian courts had the effect of carrying visitors 'back to the infancy of time'. Other commentators also portrayed the subcontinent as a veritable 'cradle of civilization'. Such trades as cloth- and pottery-making were 'remarkable' for their combination of antiquity and constancy. According to Royle, an essential and unchanging artistic sensibility – an 'unerring taste' – had guided Indian craftsmen throughout history. In 1851, the subcontinent seemed to be a living museum which showcased 'industrial habits' preserved in their ancient form. 'From age to age', the 'natives' of the subcontinent had passed on traditions of making umbrellas, gold cloth and bejewelled robes. This continuity separated ageless India not only from the industrialised nations of Europe, but also from ancient societies such as Egypt and Assyria that only had 'ruins' to offer modernity. It also distinguished India from the 'aboriginal' colonised nations of West Africa and Ceylon, which represented themselves at the Crystal Palace through displays of simple painted baskets and rude cloths and weapons.[37] A civilisation that was simultaneously ancient and flourishing and a guide for contemporary European manufacturers, India seemed to defy history.[38]

If India's art manufactures inspired admiration, the rough tools that produced them aroused a sort of ethnographic curiosity. Numerous Exhibition commentators paused to note the marked disparity between the 'primitive' tools on display in the Crystal Palace and the ornate, delicate and intricate results they produced.[39] This was a subject that fascinated Matthew Digby Wyatt, who compiled *The Industrial Arts of the Nineteenth Century* from displays at the Exhibition. His two-volume work included chromolithographs of treasures displayed by several nations at the Crystal Palace. Wyatt used his illustrations as points of departure for his lively meditations on artisanal culture. Quite frequently, he professed his intrigue at the seeming incongruity between the rude tools of the subcontinent and the ornate works they produced. For instance, Wyatt proclaimed his 'wonder' at such 'admirable and elaborate' productions as the crystal vases pictured here, which had been wrought by steel chisels and iron mallets (see figure 5.5). Illustrations of Dacca embroidery prompted him to celebrate the 'marvellous sensibility of touch' and the 'delicate fingers' of the 'Hindoos'. In a similar vein, *The Illustrated Exhibitor* proclaimed the Indian artisan's ability to produce ornate fabrics from rude implements to be 'one of the marvels of the Exhibition'.[40]

Matthew Digby Wyatt's illustrative strategy extracted the showcased objects both from their sites of production and from their locations of display in the Crystal Palace. Though Wyatt discussed habits of manufacture in the texts that accompanied his illustrations, his chromolithographs never pictured the actual tools of production. In the Crystal Palace itself, on the other hand, machinery and manufacturing implements were prominently showcased. This practice of display collapsed the distance between civilisations, ultimately intensifying the seeming 'rudeness' of India's methods of manufacture. Next to the looms of Lancashire, the jaw-bone of the boalee fish and the iron spinning roller – two implements used in the production of cotton on the subcontinent – appeared particularly primitive. This striking practice prompted commentators to reflect upon the ideals of progress and mechanisation that the Exhibition celebrated. One contributor to *Tallis' History and Description* was astonished by the disparity between models of Bengal blacksmiths with their anvils and the replication of Nasmyth's steam hammer. This writer also celebrated the speed with which the United Kingdom's locomotives delivered mail on the subcontinent in comparison to the primitive Indian 'Dawk-runners', which performed the same function, only at an exponentially slower pace.[41]

5.5 'Group of crystal vases and Indian jewellery'

Together, the Great Exhibition's texts and techniques of display produced an image of India as an antiquated, and even barbaric, civilisation. At the same time, the subcontinent seemed to resist consignment to the past. Despite the apparent simplicity of their tools, Indian artisans produced wares that British manufacturers failed to 'rival', even with the triple advantages of mechanisation, steam power and the division of labour. There were some commentators who cast doom on India's arts, as they envisioned that Western innovation would soon threaten the livelihood of the subcontinent's artisans, and others who noted the economic reality that such Indian goods as calicoes had been 'nearly driven out' of the European market by 'cheap and successful imitations' produced in Britain and on the continent.[42] At the moment of the Exhibition, however, numerous observers employed a rhetoric of competition as they contemplated India's muslins, calicoes and chintzes. All of these commodities continued to 'surpass' Britain's in execution and aesthetic merit, it seemed. This widely held opinion posed a problem for the project of colonial representation in 1851. Even as the Exhibition's texts heaped praise on the artisanal wares from India, they also tried to contain the subcontinent's productions. To this end, they consigned these goods alternatively to the realms of the past or the mythological. Spun by the distaff and spindle, Dacca's muslins were so exquisite that they seemed to resemble the 'woven wind'. India's celebrated cashmere shawls, 'designed for eternity in the unchanging East, copied from patterns which are the heirloom of a caste, and woven by fatalists', remained unapproachable in colouring and execution.[43] With such exultations, Exhibition writers constructed India as a museum – its crafts consigned to the past and their merits unattainable by modern, Western habits of production.

Afficionados of the arts such as Matthew Digby Wyatt held these museumised productions in high esteem, but other Exhibition-goers dismissed the ornate and fine products of India as evidence of Oriental savagery, barbarity, backwardness, wastefulness, and even filth.[44] In the apparent disparity between the utilitarian British wares in the Crystal Palace and the ornate productions of the East, Cambridge scientist William Whewell found a material-isation of the differences between liberty and despotism. Aided by their 'million fingers', Britain's machines made consumer goods available to 'millions of purchasers'. In the backward East, on the other hand, 'tens of thousands' performed manual labour for a handful of tyrants. According to Whewell and many of his contemporaries, production systems that used the labour of the masses in the service of a privileged few perpetuated social inequality; they squandered the efforts of the population on wasteful labour.[45] This tendency – and its effects of reinforcing barbarity and despotism – was particularly evident in the production of weapons and arms. *The Illustrated Exhibitor* noted that the artisans of the subcontinent tended to decorate 'warlike weapon[s]' in the 'most elaborate style'. However, they manufactured useful implements such as scissors in a rude manner 'worthy of the South Sea Islanders'. For a contributor to the liberal *Westminster Review* who wrote under the pseudonym of 'Helix', the ornate daggers, arrows and guns in the Indian collection appeared to be the work of an 'idle people' who 'indulged in cruel and morbid fancies'. Frequently reproduced in engravings such as figure 5.6, taken from the *Official Catalogue*, these ornamented instruments of war and 'barbaric pomp' interrupted the notion that the subcontinent was a tractable, knowable entity that could be controlled through practices of categorisation and display.[46]

As they meditated on the objects from the subcontinent that comprised the Indian collection, contributors to Exhibition texts vacillated between sentiments of reverence, disdain and fear. Often, they were able to contain their reactions as ethnographic reflections on a foreign, colonised society. At times, however, the exercise of studying the foreign displays at the Crystal Palace – or anticipating the reactions of overseas visitors to the United Kingdom's exhibits – prompted metropolitan writers to question the notions of civilisation and progress that the Crystal Palace commemorated with such vigour. William Henry Smith, a contributor to *Blackwood's Edinburgh Magazine* – which represented the landed, rural Tory interest – wrote 'Voltaire at the Crystal Palace' with the intention of critiquing the Exhibition's celebration of mechanisation. Here Smith speculated about what the renowned Enlightenment *Philosophe* might say if he returned from the grave to visit the Great Exhibition. In Smith's account,

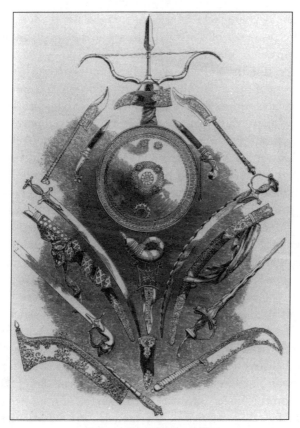

5.6 'Trophy of arms. India'

'Voltaire' reached London by train, where he arrived at King's Cross Station. There, the *Philosophe* noticed an 'industrious mortal' greasing the wheels of a locomotive. This labourer greased wheels 'from morning to night'; he seemed to work 'eternally'. As he considered the merits of the steam engine, 'Voltaire' cautioned British readers that mechanisation did not expunge the need for human labour, but merely altered its character: 'Your iron slave wants many other slaves, unfortunately not of iron, to attend on it; on this condition only will it serve you', he warned. 'No despot travels with so obsequious a train, and so subservient, as this quiet-looking engine.' By invoking slavery and despotism, two institutions antithetical to the notion of the free-born Englishman as it had been constructed in contrast to Continental despotism

and Oriental profligacy, Smith encouraged his readers to scru-
tinise the promises of the age of iron and steam that the Great
Exhibition celebrated so confidently.[47]

By creating the Voltaire-character, Smith wittingly or unwit-
tingly compensated for an important, if ironic, erasure in the
Crystal Palace. Although the Exhibition billed itself as a celebration
of industry, its classificatory system rendered labourers themselves virtually invisible. The division of objects into Playfair's
categories of Raw Materials, Machinery, Manufactures and Fine
Arts offered no self-evident place for displaying labour, and the
Exhibition did not showcase the living villages representing
Britain's internal and external colonies that were to figure at later
world's fairs.[48] In 1851, the Indian Court offered one exception to
this practice of effacing workers from the Exhibition. Its
collection of 'Ethnographic Models' depicted over 150 miniature
figures representing various Indian trades: among these, cotton
spinners, blacksmiths, cooks, ayahs, snake-charmers, and the
potter pictured here (see figure 5.7). These representations of thin
Indian labourers, both male and female, inspired a wide range of
responses, from awe to disgust. Exhibition writers often portrayed their experiences of gazing at the models or seeing South
Asian bodies at work in terms of 'repulsion' or 'laughter'. The
Exhibition chronicler Edward Concannen found himself sickened
by the 'distorted' bodies of the models, and Cassell described
Indian labourers as 'a lean, starved-out regiment of squalid

5.7 'The potter'

beggars, half naked, or with scanty folds of coarsest cotton flung around their wasted limbs.'[49]

As they emphasised the strangeness, poverty and effeminacy of Indian workers, such descriptions often facilitated the celebration of disciplined labour performed by healthy English bodies.[50] At other moments, however, meditations on imagined Indian artisans produced an altogether different effect that destabilised the project of celebrating English progress. Many evocations of Indian labour displayed a longing for a sort of work that was antithetical to the disciplined and mechanised toil of modern Britain. Repeatedly, Exhibition literature conjured scenes of unregulated, natural and embodied labour: weavers sat cross-legged in the dirt; silk-winders used their teeth, tongues and fingers as they toiled. In particular, the female Hindu spinner emerged as the living repository of the artisanal, the natural and the pre-industrial. Nature, rather than the clock, regulated her workday. This labourer rose before the sun had 'dissipate[d] the dew on the grass' so that she could spin her 'finest thread' before dawn. As she toiled in the open air under a pine or mango tree, she relied on rough tools, including the boalee fish-jaw, a small iron roller and a bow. This invented female labourer lived in a world apart from the mechanised, regulated toil performed by political economy's archetypical English factory worker – an idealised figure who existed only in limited numbers in 1851.[51] In moments such as these, India as embodied in its artisanal labourers – 'ignorant in the world's estimate, yet wise in all that is necessary to life', to use the words of *The Illustrated Exhibitor* – provided a spiritual and material foil to Britain's industrial modernity.[52]

The 'koh-i-noor in the British crown': commodifying India

It was not the East India Company but Queen Victoria who was the official exhibitor of the most celebrated display that was associated with the subcontinent in 1851, the coveted diamond 'koh-i-noor', or 'mountain of light'. In the Crystal Palace, the gem's 'worshippers' made a 'spectacle of themselves' as they gazed. The jewel's appeal transcended gender and social station, enticing the 'sturdy labourer', 'his wondering wife', and the 'millionaire' alike. Dubbed the 'loadstone of the fair sex', the jewel was particularly attractive to ladies, who reportedly swarmed it with particular enthusiasm. Men allegedly tried to resist the diamond's charms through exercises in reason. A 'Lady Contributor' to *The Illustrated London News* maintained, however, that even the most rational men were not inured to the jewel's allure. She argued that, among the male Exhibition-goers, the 'most learned of *savants*, the coldest of utilitarians, the political economist, the bishop and the Quaker' all found themselves seduced by the koh-i-noor.[53]

During the Exhibition, the koh-i-noor resided in what *The Illustrated London News* referred to as 'a golden cage or a prison' – elsewhere a 'great parrot-cage with gilded bars' – so that it would remain secure against any threat of theft or desecration from the swarming crowds. On shilling days it sat in its cage, 'ornamented' by a policeman on watch nearby. Over the weekends, the jewel appeared for the more privileged Exhibition-goers in its 'best dress', a 'tent of red cloth'. Such characterisations feminised the jewel. Exhibition writers ultimately framed the gem as the single object in the Crystal Palace that most intensely represented India itself. Domesticated through the rhetorical and visual strategies of feminisation, the koh-i-noor was a miniature crystallisation of the subcontinent enclosed in a cage. It is striking that, in 1849, John Forbes Royle had referred to India not simply as the 'Jewel in the Crown', but as the 'Koh-i-Noor of the British Crown'. The display of the koh-i-noor behind bars in 1851 provided British and foreign visitors with a material reminder of Britain's hold over the subcontinent.[54] 'Hindoo legends' told that this diamond had been the emblem of 'dominion', 'prosperity', and 'dominance' on the subcontinent for centuries, its 5,000-year history filled with 'various acts of rapine and fraud'. Before the East India Company won the diamond, it had been in the possession of the Mughal Runjeet Singh. While the ruler was on his deathbed 'Hindoo Jesuits' had attempted to persuade him to offer it to 'the great Indian idol Juggernaut'. With Runjeet Singh 'too far gone' to convey this desire, the East India Company took hold of the gem and presented it to the Queen following the ruler's death and Britain's annexation of the

Punjab. The koh-i-noor thus sat in the Crystal Palace as a reminder of Britain's colonial successes – 'the forfeit of Oriental faithlessness, and the prize of Saxon valour'.[55]

In 1851 a variety of accounts conflated the koh-i-noor and India to such a degree that even the jewel's shortcomings seemed to mirror those of the subcontinent. The diamond was poorly cut, and therefore unable to display its true 'purity and lustre'.[56] In its uncut condition, the diamond resembled the same India replete with raw materials that the *Official Catalogue* had attempted to organise. Like India, the diamond was 'gigantic' and 'rough' in its original state. In order for the diamond to reach its full potential, it would have to be freed of the Oriental proclivity for extravagance and show. *The Illustrated London News* maintained that Indian rulers, partial to 'rich and lavish magnificence', had only been able to appreciate the diamond because of its striking 'magnitude'. Nothing short of a reduction in size would render its 'beauty' fully visible. If cut by a European jeweller, the gem, while smaller, would increase in value. *The Illustrated London News'* saturation of the jewel with Indian-ness is telling. It provides yet another example of the Exhibition texts' practice of overdetermining the relationship between material goods and imagined national cultures. The gem was not actually cut by an 'Indian', but by the Venetian lapidary, Hortensio Borgis. Having performed his task in an 'unartist-like manner', Borgis was fined 10,000 rupees, and subsequently ordered executed.[57]

Whether in visual, narrative or material terms, these strategies of feminisation and miniaturisation domesticated India in 1851, rendering the infinite and gigantic land manageable and available for consumption. A letter printed in the 1851 Christmas issue of *The Illustrated London News* suggests that the reproduction of the gem further enabled the project of domestication in which the koh-i-noor was implicated. In this letter, Arthur Lamb, a 'simple' – and perhaps, a fictional – Englishman, wrote of his experiences in Hyde Park to his wife, Dorothy. The provincial Lamb had previously understood the world as a dangerous place, but his travels in the Crystal Palace seemed to render the globe safe. 'I have seen the world', Lamb reported to Dorothy after he visited its condensed representation in Hyde Park. 'The upshot is this; I love the world, and all that's in it.' As he professed his adoration for his wife, Arthur Lamb promised her he would return with a souvenir, a trinket of his affection. This souvenir was the literal commodification of India. It rendered the subcontinent available to the provincial English household in a strikingly tangible fashion. 'I shall bring you home the koh-i-noor in glass; which is no other than the diamond adapted to the lowest capacity of pocket', Lamb vowed to Dorothy. 'Quite as good – judges tell me – as the real stone, with the superior advantage of cheapness.'[58]

The koh-i-noor offers the most striking instance of the practice of miniaturising the 'vast' subcontinent for the purposes of entertainment, consumption and rule at mid-century, but other contemporary metropolitan displays produced similar effects. Dioramas such as the one at the Baker Street Bazaar familiarised Londoners with Britain's 'little territory' in India, as they depicted scenes of Bengali women, elephants and the Moorshedabad Mosque.[59] The Ethnographic Models in the Indian Courts provide another example of the strategy of miniaturisation at work inside the Crystal Palace. Alongside the displays of labourers, the collection included a number of colonial scenes in miniature. 'The Encampment of a Collector of Revenue Settling with the Cultivators' inspired the most copious reflection in Exhibition literature. This display, which included 300 figures, depicted the English collector receiving payments from natives within a lush landscape filled with elephants. A visual gesture of colonisation, it reassured viewers that the vast subcontinent was indeed knowable and governable through practices of bureaucracy and spectacle.[60]

Even as it domesticated the subcontinent, the display of the koh-i-noor in Hyde Park invited critiques of colonial rule. One visitor to the Crystal Palace copied a piece entitled 'Who are the Wealth Producers?', credited to 'Expositor', into a scrapbook commemorating the Great Exhibition. 'Your diamond-finders add nothing to the world's wealth', this writer charged. According to 'Expositor', the 'grower of corn and cotton', the 'breeder of cattle', or the 'weaver of wool' truly enriched the earth. The 'diamond-finder', on the other hand, contributed nothing to the prosperity of the globe. 'Richer we might be a hundred-fold the value of that world-wonder of a diamond', 'Expositor' had claimed, 'if instead of the sword, we had carried to India honour, justice, and industry'.[61] The very production of a personal Exhibition scrapbook – a collage of printed texts and auto-biographical remembrances of the Crystal Palace – testifies once again that the organisers of the Exhibition could not contain or circumscribe the meanings produced around its displays and, furthermore, that the writers of Exhibition texts could not control the consumption of their productions. The multiple cultural texts that materialised India in 1851 – not to mention the ungovernable practices of consuming them – produced several versions of the story of conquest, ranging from valiant victory to self-serving bravado.

Conclusion: imperial representation in 1851

The Great Exhibition's texts animated the objects on display in the Crystal Palace with stories of productivity, oriental splendour and acquisition. They portrayed the subcontinent alternately as a fertile land, an Oriental bazaar, a military threat and a colonised possession. Exhibition commentators referred to the Crystal Palace as a great dictionary, an encyclopaedia, a museum and even a latter-day Tower of Babel.[62] Though the Exhibition was lauded as the greatest collection to date, the Crystal Palace could not contain the meanings produced around its exhibits within its 'great glass case'. In Hyde Park, India surfaced as a civilisation that was at once miniature, gigantic, governable, unruly and uncontainable.

The contradictions that emerged in the project of narrating the subcontinent are suggestive of the conflicting demands both on imperial rule and on imperial representation in its textual, pictorial and material forms. They also indicate the slipperiness of such categories as the 'feminine' and the 'domestic', which Exhibition commentators mobilised in their efforts to portray India. As they endowed the displays with narratives that told real and imagined stories of production, trade, consumption and national culture, the Exhibition and its texts endeavoured to produce a set of stable relationships between Britain and India. Ultimately, however, these texts exposed contemporary anxieties about the imperial project, industrial modernity, and the nation's pre-eminence in a global capitalist order. An exercise in cataloguing, collecting and representation, the Exhibition kindled imperial sentiment in Britain, but it did not render the subcontinent wholly manageable and governable, as the challenge to British rule posed by the 1857 uprisings in Northern India would fatefully demonstrate. Instead, as they engaged in the project of imperial governance, the Great Exhibition and its texts produced a grammar of spectacular representation. During the age of international exhibitions and world's fairs, this grammar would provide a bulwark for practices of imperial display as they developed in increasingly spectacular, animated and embodied directions alongside the project of empire.[63]

Notes

I would like to thank Louise Purbrick for her guidance on this chapter. Thanks also to my friends and colleagues in British History, Imperial Culture and Women's Studies at Johns Hopkins University, especially Charles Barker, Antoinette Burton, Nadja Durbach, Karen Fang, Rachel Karol-Ablow, Mary Catherine Moran, Kathy Trevenen and Judith Walkowitz. Generous grants from the Winterthur Museum, Library and Gardens in Winterthur, Delaware, and from the Huntington Museum, Library, and Gardens in San Marino, California, made research for this project possible.

1 'India and Indian Contributions to the Industrial Bazaar', *The Illustrated Exhibitor. A Tribute to the World's Industrial Jubilee, comprising Sketches, by Pen and Pencil, of the Principal Objects in the Great Exhibition, of the Exhibition of the Industry of All Nations* 18, 4 October 1851, p. 317.

2 Perhaps this piece was the intricate and ornate ivory throne that Queen Victoria possessed, but that had belonged formerly to the Raja of Travancore. This was the very chair in which Prince Albert sat at the Great Exhibition's closing ceremony. *Official Descriptive and Illustrated Catalogue of the Great Exhibition of 1851* II (London: William Clowes and Sons, 1851), p. 929. On the collection and display of thrones and other 'signs of rulership' at British Exhibitions and in museums, see C. Clunas, 'Oriental Antiquities/Far Eastern Art', *Positions* II:1 (1994), pp. 318–55, particularly pp. 318–19, 336–8.

3 *The Illustrated Exhibitor*, 4 October 1851, pp. 317–18.

4 For one discussion of the representational power of commodities in 1851, see T. Richards, *The Commodity Culture of Victorian England: Advertising and Spectacle, 1851–1914* (Palo Alto: Stanford University Press, 1990), Introduction and Chapter 1, particularly pp. 3, 4, 59, 69. Although I disagree with Richards' privileging of the Great Exhibition as the singular event that focused the nation's attention on commodities, his discussions of

the representational capacities of commodities have been helpful. Richards suggests that commodities were vehicles for the representation of capitalism; at the same time, he argues, they required representation themselves.

5 See R. Altick, *The Shows of London* (Cambridge: Harvard University Press, 1978), Chapters 32–3, Epilogue; J. Crary, *Techniques of the Observer: On Vision and Modernity in the Nineteenth Century* (Cambridge: MIT Press, 1990); Richards, *Commodity Culture*, Introduction and Chapter 1; 'Speaking to the eye', *The Illustrated London News*, 4 May 1851, pp. 451–2.

6 See the following texts, for example: 'Memorabilia of the exhibition season', *Fraser's Magazine* XLIV:260 (August 1851), pp. 119–32, particularly 120–1; *The Exhibition in 1851 of the Products and Industry of All Nations. Its Probable Influence upon Labour and Commerce* (London: Arthur Hall, 1851), pp. 5, 8; W. Whewell, 'The general bearing of the Great Exhibition on the progress of art and science', *Lectures on the Results of the Great Exhibition of 1851, Delivered Before the Society of Arts, Manufactures and Commerce* (London: David Bogue, 1852), pp. 6, 13; R. Ellis, 'Preface', *Official Catalogue* I, pp. v–viii. On the 'market-driven conflation of text and image' in the art and publishing world at this moment, see G. Curtis, 'Dickens in the visual market', in J. O. Jordan and R. L. Patten (eds) *Literature in the Marketplace: Nineteenth-Century British Publishing and Reading Practices* (Cambridge: Cambridge University Press, 1995), p. 226.

7 C. Breckenridge, 'The aesthetics and politics of colonial collecting: India at world's fairs', *Comparative Studies of Society and History* 31 (April 1989), pp. 195–216, particularly p. 204. For a discussion of the gendering of exchange and objects, see V. de Grazia, 'Introduction', in V. de Grazia (ed.), *The Sex of Things: Gender and Consumption in Historical Perspective* (Berkeley: University of California Press, 1996), pp. 1–10. On the 'social life' of commodities within capitalism, see A. Appadurai, 'Introduction: commodities and the politics of value', in A. Appadurai (ed.), *The Social Life of Things: Commodities in Cultural Perspective* (Cambridge: Cambridge University Press, 1986), pp. 3–63. For the germinal discussion of the production of narratives around things, see S. Stewart, *On Longing: Narratives of the Miniature, the Gigantic, the Souvenir, and the Collection* (Baltimore: Johns Hopkins University Press, 1984), particularly pp. ix, xi. On the adherence of anxieties in these narratives, see B. Brown, 'How to do things with things (A toy story)', *Critical Inquiry* 24 (Summer 1998): pp. 936–64. See also, A. Brydon, 'Sensible shoes', in A. Brydon and S. Niessen (eds), *Consuming Fashion: Adorning the Transnational Body* (Oxford: Berg, 1998), p. 3.

8 This is a process that has been repeated in the production of the colonial archive and more recently in the scholarship of historians of Britain and its empire.

9 On the authorship of Great Exhibition catalogues, and particularly the *Official Catalogue*, see 'The Records of the Great Exhibition', *The Builder* 460, 29 November 1851, p. 754; 'The Catalogue's account of itself', *Household Words* II, pp. 519–23; R. Ellis, 'Scientific revision and preparation of the Catalogue', *Official Catalogue* I, pp. 82–7.

10 On the subversive possibilities contained within texts that discuss the
    nation, see A. Appadurai and C. A. Breckenridge, 'Public modernity in
    India', in C. A. Breckenridge (ed.), *Consuming Modernity: Public Culture in
    a South Asian World* (London: University of Minnesota Press, 1995), p. 4.
    Although he does not investigate the status of India at the Crystal Palace in
    depth, Jeffrey Auerbach's characterisation of the Exhibition as a 'protean
    event with numerous meanings' is particularly helpful here. See J. A.
    Auerbach, *Exhibiting the Nation: British National Identity and the Great
    Exhibition of 1851*, (Ph.D. Dissertation, Yale University, 1995), pp. ii, 4.

11 See P. Lawson, *The East India Company: A History* (New York: Longman,
    1993), Chapters 6–8, particularly pp. 145, 159, 162; T. Metcalf, *Ideologies of
    the Raj* (New York: Cambridge University Press, 1994), Chapter 2,
    particularly pp. 28–43, 49; J. Walvin, *Fruits of Empire: Exotic Produce and
    British Taste, 1660–1800* (London: Macmillan, 1997), p. 31. For mid-
    nineteenth-century critiques of India's governability, see 'The peasants of
    British India', *Household Words* IV:95 (17 January 1852), pp. 389–93;
    'Modern India', *Bentley's Miscellany* 31 (1852), pp. 465–73; 'Shall we retain
    our colonies?' *Edinburgh Review* 93:190 (April 1851), pp. 475–98. See also
    Official Catalogue II, pp. 858–60.

12 The words 'dazzle' and 'astound' come from 'Modern India', *Bentley's
    Miscellany* 31 (1852), p. 470. On the challenge of representing empires at
    Exhibitions for political ends, see P. Kramer, 'Making concessions: race and
    empire revisited at the Philippine Exposition, St. Louis, 1901–1905', *Radical
    History Review* 73 (Winter 1999), pp. 74–114; on the work that the
    exhibition form plays in promoting the projects of empire and Orientalism,
    see T. Mitchell, 'Orientalism and the exhibitionary order', in N. Dirks (ed.),
    Colonialism and Culture (Ann Arbor: University of Michigan Press, 1992),
    pp. 289–318.

13 P. Greenhalgh, *Ephemeral Vistas: The Expositions Universelles, Great
    Exhibitions, and World's Fairs, 1851–1939* (New York: St. Martin's Press,
    1988), p. 54.

14 The Agra presidency worked alongside the Bengal presidency. The son of
    an East India Company officer and a student of botany and natural history,
    Royle served in the Bengal Army as a doctor. On Royle's role in the
    Exhibition, see A. Desmond, *The India Museum, 1801–1879* (London: HMSO,
    1982), Chapter 5, 'Royle and international exhibitions'.

15 See Breckenridge, 'The aesthetics and politics of colonial collecting', pp.
    202–3. Of Britain's remaining colonial possessions, the Canadian territories
    came in second with regard to floor space, and they filled only 4,000 feet:
    Official Catalogue I, p. 17.

16 *The Times*, 2 October 1851, as cited in Desmond, *The India Museum, 1801–
    1879*, p. 73. See also *Tallis' History and Description of the Crystal Palace, and
    the Exhibition of the World's Industry in 1851* (London: John Tallis, 1851–
    52), I, pp. 31, 238–40; II, pp. 67–71; III, pp. 39–44.

17 *Tallis' History and Description of the Crystal Palace* I, pp. 31, 201, 238–40;
    see also *Official Catalogue* II, pp. 858–60. For a discussion of French

reactions to the displays in the Crystal Palace, see W. Walton, *France at the Crystal Palace: Bourgeois Taste and Artisanal Manufacture in the Nineteenth Century* (Berkeley: University of California Press, 1992).

18 See Breckenridge, 'The aesthetics and politics of colonial collecting', p. 205.

19 A. Burton, *At the Heart of the Empire: Indians and the Colonial Encounter in Late-Victorian Britain* (Berkeley: University of California Press, 1998), Chapter 1, particularly pp. 28–32, 44–6. On panoramas and dioramas, see *The Illustrated London News*, 24 May 1851, p. 469; 'Diorama of the Holy Land', *The Builder* 421 (8 March 1851), p. 148; 'Diorama of Hindostan', *The Builder* 462 (13 December 1851), p. 783; Altick, *Shows of London*, Chapters 10–15, 21.

20 'Society in India', *Bentley's Miscellany* 31 (1852), pp. 242–9. 'The overland mail bag', *Household Words* IV:88 (29 November 1851), pp. 229–34, particularly p. 229. See also 'Pearls from the east', *Household Words* IV:93 (3 January 1852), pp. 336–41; 'The peasants of British India', *Household Words* IV:95 (17 January 1852), pp. 389–93; 'An Indian wedding', *Household Words* IV:100 (21 February 1852), pp. 505–10; *The Illustrated London News*, 10 May 1851, 392.

21 This phrase is Tim Burke's. See *Lifebuoy Men, Lux Women: Commodification, Consumption, and Cleanliness in Modern Zimbabwe* (Durham: Duke University Press, 1996), p. 3. On the production of meaning through a variety of cultural texts, see Appadurai and Breckenridge, 'Public modernity in India', pp. 12–13; J. R. Ryan, *Picturing Empire: Photography and the Visualization of the British Empire* (London: Reaktion, 1997), p. 20.

22 J. F. Royle, *On the Exhibition of Raw Products and Manufactured Articles from India* (1849), Henry Cole Miscellanies III, National Art Library, Victoria and Albert Museum, London; see also *Official Catalogue* II, pp. 857–60.

23 R. Ellis, 'Scientific revision and preparation of the Catalogue', *Official Catalogue* I, p. 86; *Official Catalogue* II, pp. 870–1; 'The records of the Great Exhibition', *The Builder* 460 (29 November 1851), p. 754.

24 For an example of this in the colonial Algerian context, see, Y. S. Fletcher, 'Irresistible seductions: gendered representations of Colonial Algeria around 1930', in J. Clancy-Smith and F. Gouda (eds), *Domesticating the Empire: Race, Gender, and Family Life in French and Dutch Colonialism* (Charlottesville: University of Virginia, 1998), pp. 194–9, 209. On India's vastness and fertility, see *India and the Hindoos* (London: William Collins, 1853), Chapter 2. For a discussion of the treatment and display of India's raw materials at later exhibitions in the empire, see P. H. Hoffenberg, *To Create a Commonwealth: Empire and Nation at English, Australian, and Indian Exhibitions, 1851–1914* (Ph.D. Dissertation, University of California at Berkeley, 1993), pp. 171–81.

25 *Official Catalogue* II, pp. 874–5, 929–30; 'British India', *The Illustrated London News*, 2 August 1851, p. 163; *Tallis' History and Description of the Crystal Palace* II, p. 84; 'An opium factory', *Household Words* V:134 (16

October 1852), pp. 118–20; 'Justice to chicory', *Household Words* V:138 (13 November 1852), pp. 208–10; Walvin, *Fruits of Empire*, pp. 31, 135, 174.

26 It is striking that, while meditations on materials at the Exhibition often obscured the labour process, many discussions of cotton displayed an acute awareness of Britain's dependence on American slave labour, which was responsible for cultivating 85 per cent of the cotton imported into Britain at mid-century. At mid-century Britain imported over 700 million pounds of raw cotton. *Official Catalogue* II, p. 509; 'British cotton', *Household Words* V:106 (3 April 1852), pp. 51–4. For a visual indictment of slavery, see G. A. Sala, *The House that Paxton Built* (London: Ironbrace, Woodenhead and Co., 1851). Sala cites among the contributions from the 'Western world' an 'American Planter's Arm Chair made of ebony – a very free and easy invention supported by slavery.'

27 *Tallis' History and Description of the Crystal Palace* II, p. 17.

28 'The East Indian Courts', *The Illustrated London News*, 14 June 1851, p. 563.

29 *Ibid.*

30 'Cotton Manufactures', *The Illustrated London News*, 31 May 1851, pp. 487–8; 'The East Indian Courts', *The Illustrated London News*, 14 June 1851, p. 563; 'British India', *The Illustrated London News*, 2 August 1851, p. 163. See also *Official Catalogue* II, 881–3. For impressions of the quality and length of Indian cotton from the early nineteenth to the twentieth centuries, see A. W. Silver, *Manchester Men and Indian Cotton, 1847–1872* (Manchester: Manchester University Press, 1966), pp. 32–7; Government of India, *India's Raw Materials* (Bombay: Times of India Press, n.d.), p. 13; A. Redford, *Manchester Merchants and Foreign Trade, 1794–1858* (Manchester: Manchester University Press, 1934), pp. 219–23.

31 'Foreign minerals and metals', *The Illustrated London News*, 25 May 1851, p. 456; 'The East Indian courts', *The Illustrated London News*, 14 June 1851, p. 563; 'British India', *The Illustrated London News*, 2 August 1851, p. 163; *Official Catalogue* II, p. 60. The catalogue framed the African, Australian and American colonies similarly, as markets for finished goods and plantations for cultivating raw materials. *Official Catalogue* II, pp. 949, 952, 960, 976.

32 For a discussion of Victorian society in the anatomical terms described here, see L. Davidoff, 'Class and gender in Victorian England: the diaries of Arthur J. Munby and Hannah Cullwick', *Feminist Studies* 5 (Spring 1979), pp. 87–141.

33 *Tallis' History and Description of the Crystal Palace* I, p. 239; *The Illustrated London News*, 10 May 1851, p. 392. For a discussion of 'implication' and interdependence, see 'The overland mail bag', *Household Words* IV:88 (29 November 1851), pp. 229–34.

34 'Modern India', *Bentley's Miscellany* 31 (1852), pp. 465–73.

35 *Tallis' History and Description of the Crystal Palace* I, pp. 23, 33, 158, 239–40; 'The Great Exhibition', *The Illustrated London News*, 3 May 1851, p. 359; 'East Indian courts', *The Illustrated London News*, 14 June 1851, p. 563;

'A lady's glance at the Great Exhibition', *The Illustrated London News*, 4 October 1851, p. 43; 'India and the Indian courts, *The Illustrated Exhibitor* 18, 4 October 1851, pp. 317–18. On the production and circulation of the *Arabian Nights* (a set of tales that emerged from the oral folkloric tradition central to India, Persia, Iraq, Syria and Egypt) in the West during the nineteenth century, see R. Kabbani, *Europe's Myths of Orient: Devise and Rule* (London: Macmillan, 1986), Introduction, Chapters 2 and 3.

36 After the Exhibition, the founders of the Museum of Manufactures – the collection that would become the South Kensington Museum and eventually the Victoria and Albert Museum – portrayed the artisanal wares of India in this light, and ultimately institutionalised this incarnation of the subcontinent for posterity. However, treatment of Indian artisanal wares at the Exhibition was far more complex. On the relationship between the Exhibition and this museum, see T. Barringer, 'The South Kensington Museum and the Colonial Project', in T. Barringer and T. Flynn (eds), *Colonialism and the Object: Empire, Material Culture, and the Museum* (London: Routledge, 1998), pp. 12–13.

37 'India and the Indian courts', *The Illustrated Exhibitor* 18 (4 October 1851), pp. 317–18; J. F. Royle, 'The arts and manufactures of India', in *Lectures on the Results of the Great Exhibition*, pp. 333–400, particularly pp. 334–35, 340; *The Illustrated London News*, 10 May 1851, p. 392; *Official Catalogue* I–II, pp. 483, 917, 929–30, 936. See also *Tallis' History and Description of the Crystal Palace* I, pp. 238–9; II, p. 128.

38 On the way in which representing India as a non-historical entity has served as a tool of colonialism, see N. Dirks, 'Introduction', in N. Dirks (ed.), *Colonialism and Culture* (Ann Arbor: University of Michigan Press, 1992), pp. 8–9.

39 'India and the Indian courts', *The Illustrated Exhibitor*, 4 October 1851, pp. 317–18; *Official Catalogue* II, 932–3; *Tallis' History and Description of the Crystal Palace* I, pp. 33–4; 'Indian ivory carvings for the Great Exhibition', *The Illustrated London News*, 26 April 1851. For a discussion of Indian machinery and industrial arts at later exhibitions, see Hoffenberg, 'To Create a Commonwealth', Chapter 4, pp. 218–29.

40 M. D. Wyatt, *The Industrial Arts of the Nineteenth Century: A Series of Illustrations of the Choicest Specimens Produced by Every Nation at the Great Exhibition of Works of Industry, 1851* I, Plate 24, 'Indian kincob patterns woven at Ahmedabad and Benares' and Plate 40, 'Group of crystal vases and Indian jewellery'; *The Illustrated Exhibitor* 18, 4 October 1851, p. 319.

41 *Tallis' History and Description of the Crystal Palace* I, p. 193. This author suggests that the displays of machinery at the Great Exhibition were legible and transparent to the visitors to Hyde Park. For a refutation of this point and a discussion of the display of machinery at exhibitions and through illustrative practices, see L. Purbrick, 'Ideologically technical: illustration, automation and spinning cotton around the middle of the nineteenth century', *Journal of Design History* 11:4 (1998), pp. 275–93, particularly pp. 283–8, 293. On the Exhibition's ability to collapse the distance between

civilisations, see Royle, 'Arts and manufactures of India', *Lectures on the Results of the Great Exhibition*, pp. 366–7, 394–6; 'Textile fabrics', *The Illustrated London News*, 3 May 1851, p. 369; 'India', *The Illustrated London News*, 10 May 1851, p. 392.

42 On the language of rivalry in manufactures, see 'The duty of our manufacturers at the present crisis', *Art-Journal* (October 1850), pp. 304–6.

43 'Shawls', *Household Words* V:127 (28 August 1852), pp. 552–6; 'British India', *The Illustrated London News*, 2 August 1851, p. 163; *Official Catalogue* II, pp. 479, 483–4, 881, 933–5; Wyatt, *Industrial Arts of the Nineteenth Century* I, Plate 44.

44 *The Illustrated London News*, 10 May 1851, p. 392; 'Wanderings in the Crystal Palace', *Art-Journal* (July 1851), p. 196.

45 Whewell, 'The general bearing of the Great Exhibition on the progress of art and science', pp. 18–19. Similarly, in his Exhibition travelogue, the American visitor William A. Drew had argued that the appearance and availability of manufactures provided an index to the 'freedom and independence' of the nation where they were produced. W. A. Drew, *Glimpses and Gatherings during a Voyage and Visit to London and the Great Exhibition in the Summer of 1851* (Augusta, ME: Homan and Manley, 1852), p. 357. See also *Official Catalogue* III, p. 1,430; *Tallis' History and Description of the Crystal Palace* I, p. 127; 'The Exhibition – A Gossip', *The Builder* 453 (11 October 1851), p. 637.

46 *The Illustrated Exhibitor* 18 (4 October 1851), pp. 317–18; W. B. Adams (pseudonym 'Helix'), 'The Great Exhibition' *Westminster Review* LV:109 (July 1851), p. 200; *Tallis' History and Description of the Crystal Palace* I, p. 238; see also M. D. Wyatt, *Industrial Arts of the Nineteenth Century* II, Plate 123, 'Specimens of enamelling from Indian arms'; Royle, 'Arts and manufactures of India', in *Lectures on the Results of the Great Exhibition*, p. 352; *The Illustrated London News*, 31 May 1851, p. 491; 'The East India courts', *The Illustrated London News*, 14 June 1851, p. 563.

47 W. H. Smith, 'Voltaire in the Crystal Palace', *Blackwood's Edinburgh Magazine* 430, pp. 142–53, particularly p. 143. Henry Sunderland Edwards' *An Authentic Account of the Chinese Commission, Which was Sent to Report on the Great Exhibition; wherein the Opinion of China is Shown as Not Corresponding at All with Our Own* (London: Vizetelly, 1852) provides another instance of the construction of a foreign visitor to the Great Exhibition to perform the work of reconfiguring the ethnographic gaze and returning it to Britain. For a discussion of how colonial subjects, and Indian male travellers in particular, 'refigured' the ethnographic gaze themselves to examine the metropolis later in the century, at the time of the Colonial and Indian Exhibition, see A. Burton, 'Making a spectacle of Empire: Indian travelers in fin-de-siècle London', *History Workshop Journal* 42 (1996), pp. 127–46, particularly pp. 128, 137–43.

48 See A. Coombes, *Reinventing Africa: Museums, Material Culture, and Popular Imagination in Late Victorian and Edwardian England* (New Haven: Yale University Press, 1997), Chapters 5 and 9.

49 *Tallis' History and Description of the Crystal Palace* I, p. 240; II, pp. 72–3; E. Concannen, *Remembrances of the Great Exhibition, complete in Twenty Views, Beautifully Engraved on Steel, from Drawings Made on the Spot, including a General History of its Origin, Progress, and Close, and a Pleasing Description of Each Department Illustrated* (London: Ackerman and Co., 1852); 'Indian Handicrafts', *The Builder* 440 (12 July 1851); *Official Catalogue* II, pp. 930–3; 'A cinnamon garden', *Household Words* II:49 (1 March 1851), p. 566.

5 0 The foundational discussion of the production of the categories of the 'manly Englishman' and the 'effeminate Bengali' as a strategy of rule is Mrinalini Sinha's. See her *Colonial Masculinity: The 'Manly Englishman' and the 'Effeminate Bengali' in the Late Nineteenth Century* (Manchester: Manchester University Press, 1995), Introduction.

51 On the uneven development of mechanisation, see R. Samuel, 'The workshop of the world', *History Workshop Journal* 3 (Spring 1977), pp. 6–72. Madhavi Kale argues that the colonial encounter played a constitutive role in the construction of the 'category of labor'. See *Fragments of Empire: Capital, Slavery, and Indian Indentured Labor Migration in the British Caribbean* (Philadelphia: University of Pennsylvania Press, 1998), p. 3.

52 *Tallis' History and Description of the Crystal Palace* I, p. 201; II, pp. 67–71; III, pp. 39–44; 'Shawls', *Household Words* V:127 (28 August 1852), pp. 552–6; 'Silk from the Punjab', *Household Words* V:146 (8 January 1853), pp. 388–90; Royle, 'Arts and manufactures of India', pp. 366–7; Wyatt, *Industrial Arts of the Nineteenth Century*, Plates 28 and 48; *Official Catalogue* II, p. 933. *The Illustrated Exhibitor*, pp. 317–18.

53 *Tallis' History and Description of the Crystal Palace* I, pp. 36, 158, 240; 'A lady's glance at the Great Exhibition', *The Illustrated London News*, 23 August 1851, p. 242; W. B. Jerrold, *How to See the Exhibition in Four Visits* (London: Bradbury and Evans, 1851), p. 24; 'The gems', *The Illustrated London News*, 17 May 1851, p. 486. For another discussion of English-women and Indian jewellery, see N. Chaudhuri, 'Shawls, jewelry, curry, and rice in Victorian Britain', in N. Chaudhuri and M. Strobel (eds), *Western Women and Imperialism: Complicity and Resistance* (Bloomington: Indiana University Press, 1992), pp. 231–46.

54 *The Illustrated London News*, 3 May 1851, p. 359; *Official Catalogue* I, p. 111; see also S. Warren, *The Lily and the Bee: An Apologue of the Crystal Palace of 1851* (London: Blackwood, 1854), p. 19.

55 *Tallis' History and Description of the Crystal Palace* I, pp. 36, 150.

56 'A lady's glance at the Great Exhibition', *The Illustrated London News*, 23 August 1851, p. 242.

57 'The gems', *The Illustrated London News*, 17 May 1851, p. 426; *Tallis' History and Description of the Crystal Palace* I, p. 36; see also 'A Chapter on Diamonds', *New Monthly Magazine and Humourist* LXXXIX (1850), pp. 427–39, particularly pp. 432 and 439.

58 'Christmas Thoughts of the Crystal Palace by Douglas Jerrold', *The*

Illustrated London News, 20 December 1851, p. 738. For another discussion
of the ways in which Exhibitions commodified Empire, see P. Greenhalgh,
Ephemeral Vistas, p. 54. On the miniature and its narrative effects, and on
the souvenir and metonymy, see Stewart, *On Longing*, p. xii, Chapter 2
(particularly p. 68), Chapter 5. For a contemporary discussion of the Rosetta
Stone as a 'loaded talisman' which has been reproduced as a souvenir at the
British Museum, see M. Beard, 'Souvenirs of Culture: Deciphering (in) the
Museum', *Art History* XV:4 (December 1992), pp. 504–31.

59 'Diorama of Hindostan at the Baker-Street Bazaar', *The Builder* 462 (13
December 1851), p. 783.

60 'Models', *The Illustrated London News*, 5 July 1851, p. 19; *Tallis' History
and Description of the Crystal Palace* II, pp. 192–3.

61 Winterthur Manuscripts, FOL 240, Great Exhibition Scrapbook, hand-
written entry. Winterthur Museum, Library, and Gardens, Winterthur,
Delaware, USA.

62 See 'The proposed Exhibition of 1851', *Blackwood's Edinburgh Magazine*
LXVIII:419 (September 1850), pp. 278–90, particularly p. 281; 'Iron and
glass buildings', *The Builder* 409 (7 December 1850), p. 585; 'The Great
Exhibition', *The Builder* 431 (10 May 1851), p. 293; F. Lush, 'Teachings of
the Exhibition', *The Builder* 440 (12 July 1851), p. 432; *Tallis' History and
Description of the Crystal Palace* I, pp. 100, 207, 258; 'Three May days in
London', *Household Words* III:53 (3 May 1851), pp. 122–4.

63 See, for instance, A. Coombes, *Reinventing Africa*, Chapters 4–5, 9;
P. Greenhalgh, *Ephemeral Vistas*. By using the word 'alongside', I mean to
suggest that empire and exhibitions developed contemporaneously, yet
never in an uncomplicated union. For a discussion of the historiographical
tendency to equate the projects of exhibition and empire as unproblematic
expressions of one another and the limits of this practice, see Kramer,
'Making Concessions', pp. 75–81, 107–8.

6

Thackeray and *Punch* at the Great Exhibition: authority and ambivalence in verbal and visual caricatures

RICHARD PEARSON

This chapter will explore the reporting on the Exhibition in *Punch*, the journal that coined the term 'the Crystal Palace'.[1] *Punch* produced a series of both satirical and laudatory articles and visual caricatures based on the Exhibition, and seems to have been uncertain of its own editorial stance on the event. Its version of the Crystal Palace is ambivalent and contradictory, comical and yet still 'John Bullish'. Founded in 1841 and well established by 1851, *Punch* had become a magazine institution appealing to the mildly iconoclastic sense of humour of the expanding middle-classes. Its irreverence for British institutions was probably its main attribute, and it provided a weekly satirical glance at the week's news events. Like its other news, *Punch's* version of the Great Exhibition found its inspiration in parodying contemporary newspaper reports and in creating an alternative or comic burlesque of the festivities. One of the magazine team, however, William Makepeace Thackeray, found the corporate response to the Exhibition, and other items of current affairs, distasteful. The radicalism of the 'savage little Robespierre', Douglas Jerrold, for instance, made the humanist in Thackeray increasingly uncomfortable, particularly where it targeted personalities, such as Louis Napoleon, and fuelled international tensions.[2] Thackeray wrote several satirical analyses of the Exhibition for *Punch*, inscribing the ambivalence of his attitude into the articles and challenging the English orientation of *Punch*'s point of view. In 1851 Thackeray resigned from the *Punch* team, and one of his reasons for the departure was cited as the *Punch* Exhibition reporting. Remembering this event in 1855, he wrote:

> I had some serious public differences with the conduct of Punch – about the abuse of Prince Albert and the Crystal Palace on wh. I very nearly resigned, about the abuse of Lord Palmerston, about the abuse finally of L. Napoleon – in all wh. Punch followed the Times, wh. I think and thought was writing unjustly at the time, and dangerously for the welfare and peace of the country.[3]

Thackeray's different approach to the general run of articles in *Punch* at the time, different too from the run of reporting generally, intimates a more modern perception of the Exhibition and its relationship to racial and class tensions of the time. Thackeray insists on the need to see the Exhibition from other perspectives, or, rather, from the perspective of the Other. In literary studies of colonial discourse, the concept of Otherness has become a means of examining the methods by which a dominant culture comes to establish itself in relation to its perceptions of the colonised. An imperial culture thus affirms its hegemony over

6.1 'Specimens from Mr. Punch's Industrial Exhibition of 1850'

other cultures by placing its values and mores in opposition to those of the Other. Such a dialectical relationship suggests the necessity of and the central defining of these colonised cultures; as Chris Bongie maintains: '[t]his barbaric Other will have a double status: it is both that which is doomed to disappear in the progressive light of a liberalizing modernity and that which must be represented as having not yet been surpassed'. He continues, 'this dialectical revelation of the liberal State thus simultaneously anticipates and forestalls the Other's complete disappearance'.[4] I shall argue here that the *Punch* version of world relationships in the Great Exhibition largely conforms to this notion of the simultaneous need for and rejection of the alien foreigner. However, whilst the Exhibition might be seen to assert cultural hierarchies through production, Thackeray's satirical ambivalence destabilises the assurance of such.

Whilst many newspapers offered object-by-object commentaries on the Great Exhibition, *Punch's* focus is very much on the people who visit or occupy other relationships to the Exhibition (cabbies, shopkeepers, the police).[5] Virtually the only objects to be represented in *Punch* during the period of the Exhibition were the koh-i-noor diamond and the statue of an Amazon, both of which were used to signify racial, social and gendered meanings

6.2 'The shipwrecked ministers saved by the Great Exhibition steamer'

(women visitors, for instance, are accused of making a bee-line for the diamond!). It is a central concept in their political cartoons of 1850 and 1851 that exhibition objects are replaced by people (see figure 6.1).[6] For example, in 'Specimens from Mr. Punch's Industrial Exhibition of 1850', caricatures of sweated labour are presented for inspection under bell-jars by a corpulent and grim Mr Punch to Prince Albert. The images are a stark reminder of the post-1848 class tensions in society, and of *Punch*'s radicalism; the figure of Albert (never caricatured as a grotesque by the magazine) contrasts in his solid thoughtfulness the frozen and emaciated figures of industry. In addition, *Punch* uses as a visual emblem, the Exhibition building itself, and not its contents, as a carrier of significance (see figure 6.2).[7] In John Leech's 'The shipwrecked ministers', the style is more that of an eighteenth-century political caricature, using words within the cartoon to convey the meaning directly, as government policies and bills are seen washed away by the sea. The cabinet ship has sunk and the picture shows Lord John Russell frantically waving to a passing ship for rescue – the Exhibition 'steamer', which will raise the popularity of a defeated and helpless government. From its outset, *Punch*'s reporting dwelt on the ideologies of the Exhibition. However, its discussion of these was not consistent.

Punch's nineteenth-century visual caricatures are less vindictive and personal than those of the preceding century. As Thackeray commented, 'How savage the satire was … But we have washed, combed, clothed, and taught the rogue good manners'.[8] The cartoons were visually immediate, focused on small central groups of figures and 'quickly comprehensible topical or literary tropes'. They were 'designed for the man who was accustomed to reading on the run.'[9] As David Kunzle points out, caricature in the Victorian period, led by *Punch* which came to dominate the cartoon industry in the 1840s, became 'domesticated' and more genteel or middle class. 'Caricature became broader and flatter;' he writes, 'the new political cartoon sought to admonish and reform, not to injure; and the graphics of social comedy tended to apoliticism and the elision of social conflict'.[10] I would argue that *Punch*, as a corporate magazine, was more market driven than earlier free-standing graphic prints, and the tendency towards 'elision' was necessary in a periodical aimed at a broad market of readers.

The early political satire against the Exhibition was not sustained as May arrived and the popular public success of the event was assured. M. H. Spielmann offered a cynical view of this development. *Punch* 'scoffed at first, at the GE of 1851, and seriously retarded its progress', but '*Punch* had made a dead set against the exhibition in Hyde Park (until his friend Paxton was appointed its architect)'.[11] Justin McCarthy notes how *Punch* 'was hardly ever weary of making fun of it … and nothing short of complete success could save it from falling under a mountain of ridicule…'[12] It was that very success which ensured that a popular journal like *Punch* could not afford to wholly denounce public opinion. Negative images were replaced by positive ones. Take, for example, a poem, illustrated by John Tenniel, describing nostalgically the close of the Exhibition, entitled 'The Last Night in the Crystal Palace':

'Twas in this awful silence I stood within the place,
And thought of all this toiling and triumph of my race;
Of the weary stretch of ocean, the weary waste of shore,
That for this wondrous gathering must have been travelled o'er;
What toiling hands and thinking heads; what wealth and want
    and woe;
What hopes and fears, and joys and griefs, have joined to make
    the show.
…
How, not recking creed or colour, her summons she sent forth
From African saharas, to the snow-fields of the North.
…
She folded in her great embrace the whole world for a guest –
And my heart swell'd high with thankful pride that I was
    England's son.[13]

This paean to English 'pride' and 'triumph', which, in its illustration, sees 'The spirit of my own England – a spirit of peace and power' stand high above all other nations in a processional jumble of goods and people, offers the curious ideological assertion that England can 'summons' the world and yet remain beyond issues of race ('not reckoning creed or colour'). Here, the Exhibition is viewed purely in terms of the Englishman's response to its effect. The signification is Anglo-centric and self-satisfying. Whilst engendering debate around the class and gender issues raised by the

Exhibition, *Punch* almost entirely maintains the proud English point of view. The famous Leech drawing of Mr. Punch at the head of the Derby Day race for 1851 (see figure 6.3)[14] clearly expresses this meaning. Joseph Paxton and John Bull lead the chase over their foreign rivals, even though Mr Punch steals a head to look back cheekily at the whole pack. This illustration might also be read as a representation of the monologic authority asserted by *Punch*. The satirical commentator's eye observes itself at the head of the race gazing backwards at a series of racial caricatures, an enlightened press authority on the divisions in mid-Victorian (multicultural) society.

Nevertheless, *Punch* certainly saw that home-grown responses to the Exhibition would be varied. In its 'Morals of the Great Exhibition', it predicts the oppositional meanings which commentators would evolve. *Punch* searches for a 'moral' in the Exhibition:

> So it is with the Industry of all Nations. All sorts of morals grow out of it, or are tacked on to it. You overhear them in the Crystal Palace; you pick them up in the Park; they obtrude themselves upon you in leading articles; they oust the weather in casual street encounters; they beguile the pauses of a quadrille, and set conversation a-going in the railway-carriage.[15]

Punch demonstrates how the semiotics of the Exhibition can be interpreted to fulfil the interests of both sides of the free-trade question (free trade was often seen as the main economic ideology of the Exhibition), followed by a series of 'fashionable', 'marital', and class-orientated remarks. Finally, *Punch* declares his own understanding of the enigma: 'That the different nations of the world, and the different classes of society, might meet oftener, with much advantage to each other.'[16] In the issue of race, however, it is only Thackeray who is prepared to expose the British privileging of meaning. *Punch*, despite its attempts to narrate the Englishness of 1851, centralises racial and class issues in the final sentence here, and, indeed, in most of its reporting. But the voice of *Punch* remains ambivalent: simultaneously revelling in the diversity produced, and maintaining the English monocle; wanting to stress its Radical political stance, but also aware of the nation's generally positive reception of the Exhibition.[17]

6.3 'The great Derby race for eighteen hundred and fifty-one'

The Exhibition made itself available to sections of the working classes by the advent of shilling days; at other times, entrance cost 5s or 1 guinea. In close proximity to the last throws of the Chartist agitation and the European revolutions of 1848, this apparent levelling of class privilege was bound to stir the emotions and the intellect. John Leech's drawing of class confrontation of family generations, 'The Pound and the Shilling',[18] shows a peaceful, dignified, and yet rather hesitant meeting (see figure 1.1). Only the children seem able to cross the divide, and only then through the coy vehicle of comical romance. The paper caps of the mechanics contrast with the bonnets, military headwear, and top hats of the middle and wealthy classes, and indeed that of Mr Punch, watching wryly from the balcony.[19] If the illustration seeks largely to play down tensions and the benign smiles of the faces to smooth over difference, in the verbal reports on the shilling days, at least initially, *Punch* was more cutting. The middle classes expected trouble; their prejudices imagined the social balloon was about to be pricked (as John Tenniel's small initial drawing to the article suggests). The first day was the most tense and uncertain.

> On reaching the doors of the Exhibition, we found massive barriers intended to contain the multitude; but the multitude consisted of so few that they could scarcely contain themselves, for they kept

bursting with laughter at the ponderous preparations for resisting
their expected violence.[20]

Clearly, the idea of visiting the Exhibition took a while to catch on
with the working classes.

Punch makes much of the superficiality of the middle-class
reasons for attending the Exhibition. While they were expostu-
lating in fear of 'Communism' and 'Socialism' – the working
classes invading their palace and removing their 'precious assets'
with the goal of 'an equal distribution of property', which
demanded that 'the koh-i-noor was guarded by an extra policeman' – the working classes visiting the Exhibition actually attended
to improve their education. *Punch* commented, '[t]he koh-i-noor
is safe; indeed, the intelligence of the shilling visitors caused them
to pass with indifference the rather uninteresting object, which
attracted the vulgar and stupid gaze of the guinea and five
shilling visitors at the opening of the Exhibition'. *Punch* surmises
how '[t]he high-paying portion of the public go to look at each
other, and to be looked at, while the shilling visitors go to gain
instruction from what they see'.[21] The drawing for the 1851
Almanack, 'The Looking-Glass Department of the Great Exhibition'
(see figure 6.4)[22] both caricatures the middle-class self-absorption
at the Exhibition, and is analogous to the whole ethos of the glass

6.4 'The Looking-Glass Department of the Great Exhibition'

palace. Here, crowds of round-faced and wide-eyed females, joined by two top-hatted dandies, gaze at themselves in a series of ornate mirrors in one of the Exhibition salons. Naked cupids carry the looking-glasses, one of whom has a globe on his shoulders supporting the glass, a clever emblem of how the English see themselves in relation to the world, and how their self-image is thus propped up by the Exhibition. The artificial poses demonstrate the shallowness of English fashionable society, while a little girl to the left, eager to see her reflection, is learning the craft for the future. Ironically, perhaps, *Punch* often plays into this very same middle-class attitude; as a magazine, its primary intention is to report on the people at the Exhibition and to place itself, as in the Leech drawings, visibly observing in the scene.

A few weeks later, in 'The Front Row of the Shilling Gallery', it is the shilling classes who covet a glimpse of the diamond.[23] The illustration depicts the crowd surrounding the koh-i-noor diamond, and suggests that there is more of a genteel appearance to these shilling crowds. The article is fraught with contradictions. *Punch* sits high in the gallery, enjoying 'all the little incidents that are being quietly exhibited below', and 'peeping at the audience' from a vantage point of some secrecy.[24] Down below is '[t]he great mob', now a mixture of class signifiers: 'a sunny corn-field of bonnets', 'a sullen acre of black hats', 'an immense plantation of popular-looking boys', and 'sturdy men of the circumference of oaks'. This canvas of natural humanity is contrasted with the almost ineffectual attempts by the Exhibition organisers to brighten up the koh-i-noor by artificial gas-lighting shining underneath. *Punch* takes the opportunity for a pointed Radical joke: diamonds and gas are both from coal, and thus, 'this is not the first time, by many, that the koh-i-noors of society only shine with the borrowed light of those working beneath them in station!'[25] However, the Radical intention is undermined by a general inseparability of the 'great mob'. No longer stand-offish and separate as in the earlier illustration, the classes have combined more thoroughly, and it is at an absent group contained within a metonymic diamond that *Punch* has to aim his stick. Although the crowd is figured satirically in the caricatures, within the letter-press *Punch* has to step beyond its own public. The shilling days were a popular success.

In its reporting on the Great Exhibition, *Punch* becomes less and less certain of its targets and more and more ambiguous. In the earlier days of its publishing history, *Punch* frequently mocked its own class, and itself. It was a kind of anti-newspaper, established as a direct parody of the daily press reporting on events largely relevant to a middle-class male audience. By the 1850s, things were clearly changing. Now most targets stand outside of its own class of readers, and, where it does poke fun at its own audience, it does so with more good nature and less malicious bite. In fact, it retreats from such an interpretation. During the Exhibition, the 'foreigners' became a useful comic target. For all of its gesturing towards the ideal of a universal cameraderie and 'the peace and goodwill of all nations',[26] it can never really rid itself of the accusation that its great shaking of hands was becoming a great shaking of fists. For *Punch*, the Exhibition was most definitely for *us*. Again, however, there is a slight tension between visual and verbal content. The Exhibition did not live up to its own grandiose claims to bridge cultural divides. Like the China-man, mistakenly thought to be a foreigner of importance at the opening ceremony, but later discovered to be a local man in costume who forced his way through to the front of the crowd, the Exhibition is not quite as real as it seems.[27] It is a construct, a simulacrum, self-contained and meaningless except as political capital. Leech's drawing of the departing Amazon at the end of the Exhibition represents this theme (see figure 6.5).[28] Two of the most reproduced images from the Exhibition, frequently referred to in *Punch*, were, firstly, a statue of a half-naked Amazon warrior-ess on horseback, her horse rearing as a lioness attacks its neck, and she defends it with a thrusting spear. Secondly, a half-naked Greek slave girl pouring water at a well. In this drawing, both Greek slave girl and Amazon warrior have dressed in more modern clothes, indicating that the posturing or 'attitude' of the Exhibition is over, and they can return to polite and conventional society. The terrifying energy of Africa (and the sensuality of antiquity) is present only through representation, and dissipates at the end of the event. Two assistants tidy up the horse which is now standing calmly. The Greek girl, no longer a slave, is modestly dressed. The Amazon's spear is propped aside, and even the ferocious wild cat is now seen as a domestic pet; the foreign is made English.

CLOSING OF THE EXHIBITION.
The Amazon Putting on her Bonnet and Shawl.

6.5 'Closing of the Exhibition'

The letter-press of the articles on racial subjects are, however, less penetrating or probing. 'Where are the Foreigners?' remarks on the absence of the Other in the streets of London during the opening of the Exhibition. Promised an influx of aliens to whom England could demonstrate her progress, *Punch* is bemused by the lack of arrivals: 'We have looked for them everywhere – in the streets – in the theatres – even in the Exhibition – but we have not seen them yet.'[29] The Exhibition organisers were at fault; they created a marketable image for England but no one was yet buying. *Punch* noted,

> If it were not for a feeling of shame, we should confess that we are disappointed. We had expected to have seen foreigners every- where – foreigners in thousands ... The innumerable prints of the

Exhibition had cherished this fond expectation. They had represented groups of foreigners hob-nobbing, elbowing, all together,
as at a Masquerade, only looking much happier ... These gorgeous
visions have not yet been realised. We made sure of being knocked
over by a Laplander, or of seeing the traffic of the City interrupted
by an unwieldy elephant, who, from his enormous size, had stuck
in the narrow aperture of Temple Bar ... As it is, London is nearly
the same as at any other season.[30]

As there is no one to look, to promote the promised Lacanian
'dialectic of recognition' (we learn of ourselves from how others
see us), *Punch* can only speculate on these comic 'visions' of Otherness being observed. There is an obvious train of caricature in the
portraits presented here. Foreigners have 'gold-embroidered legs',
'turbaned heads', and 'long, raven, greasy locks', ride 'elephants',
'sledges' and 'camels', carry giant 'parasols', and knock you over.
Punch envisages a theatrical and burlesque version of the happy
inter-racial groups of the Exhibition prints. In fact, the only alien
presence detected so far by the *Punch* writer is the growth of beards
and moustaches in 'a foreign air' that Englishmen are cultivating.[31] This leads *Punch* to an assertion of Bullish superiority.
Once more, the Other remains outside of the readerly appeal:

> We suppose the foreigners will come – and we hope they will; but
> if not, we have the consolation of knowing that our countrymen
> are making themselves up to look like foreigners more and more
> every day; so that we shall soon have the foreign and native
> gentleman both combined in one. Decidedly a great saving, only
> we are doubtful whether the Englishman gains anything by it![32]

Although *Punch* appears to desire some form of positive relationship with the foreign visitor (yet this remains at a level which
more generally contains the distant caricatured alien, rather than,
say, the French), the magazine remains cynical towards the English
public response and the 'official' intentions behind the Exhibition. In 'The Cosmopolitan before and after the Exhibition', a
wife, Sarah Veal, writes a letter to *Punch* complaining of the bad
influence the foreign visitors are having on her husband: 'from
continually reading about peace and friendship with all mankind,
and cultivating good feeling between ourselves and foreigners,
he has become a regular POLLY [i.e. cosmopolitan]'.[33] She describes the degenerative transformation in his dress and manners,

from his beard and tight-fitting clothes, to his 'flower-pot' hat
and endless smoking. The 'letter' carries no editorial comment
but stands simply as an ambiguous satire on the effects of the
Exhibition and the narrow-mindedness of the English, whilst
retaining the sense of the un-Englishness of the Other. Sarah Veal
is both the object of ridicule and the carrier of comment; the focus
of the joke is the clash of cultures which again suggests that,
beneath the hand-shaking, there remains a distaste for the ways
of the visitor. Sarah observes:

> he generally brings two or three of those foreigners with him that
> he has picked up at the Exhibition ... He calls this cementing the
> bonds of universal brotherhood ... After they are gone, I always
> sprinkle the floors with vinegar, and I am thankful to say that we
> have caught nothing yet, and – that I will admit – they have not
> taken anything.[34]

Punch's most significant inability to offer international friendship
comes in its articles on America. In 'America in Crystal', *Punch*
comments on the early absence of the Americans from the Exhibition halls (their products were late in arriving) and so wonders
why their nation did not simply send an American Eagle, 'with
the treasures of America gathered below its hovering wings'.
These would be 'some choice specimens of slaves? We have the
Greek captive in dead stone – why not the Virginian slave in living
ebony?'[35] The small accompanying illustration (see figure 6.6)[36] is
a sharp reminder of continuing differences between England and
America over the slave question, which was to be fought out over
Harriet Beecher Stowe's *Uncle Tom's Cabin* of the following year,
and in actuality in the American Civil War ten years later.

6.6 'Sample of American manufacture'

Punch's line of argument, then, partakes of that plurality of meaning which it discovered in the interpretations of the overall message of the Exhibition. It shifts, it cannot be fixed. *Punch* consists of several writers – including Mark Lemon, Douglas Jerrold and others – and illustrators – including John Leech, John Tenniel and Richard Doyle. But all of its items are published under the authoritative eye of Mr Punch himself – he stamps both the jibes at America (its anti-slavery line), the Bullish British morality, and the universal shaking of hands. In some ways, *Punch* sees itself as offering a similar ambivalence as the Exhibition: in its Preface to volume 20 (January–June, 1851), it draws parallels between its own aims and those of the Exhibition. The magazine is aware of a comedy indicative of the potential failure of both to deliver these aims; *Punch* IS the Exhibition, offering 'his own Collection – the accumulation of vast Intellectual Wealth, and the produce of the richest Mines of Wit, brought together by the combined resources of Art and Industry'.[37] The Crystal Palace in the Tenniel illustration for the Preface is a vast beehive, making the analogy that, in *Punch*, 'there may be a little taste of the sting, [but] there is no lack of the honey'. [38] The satirical goals have their parallel too in the Exhibition's aims: '[*Punch's*] exhibition has the same object in view as that now collected in the Crystal Palace … the advancement and happiness of mankind, with the peace and goodwill of all nations'. In the end, rather than opposing the Exhibition, *Punch* comes to occupy the same space.

W. M. Thackeray wrote part of the *Punch* response to the 1851 Exhibition, although his contributions were not extensive.[39] He wrote a comic poem and two comic sketches in May 1851, and three further satirical items in September, October and November. He also possibly drew an illustration for another writer's Exhibition item. But Thackeray's *Punch* pieces are somewhat different from the bulk of the magazine's reporting. Most significantly, he unsettles the relationship between Self and Other, between English and foreign, highlighted by the Exhibition. He focuses his work on what might be described as the anthropological design of the Exhibition: that doubleness of response that the Exhibition provoked between the desire to establish a standard of Englishness based upon how others will view us AND the enabling of the English public to view the Otherness of nations, establishing an anthropology of the English as well as of the foreign. The former is, as I have suggested, an attempt to control what Lacan called the 'dialectic of recognition', to expect that the Other will view the Self with favour. For *Punch*, this was often a hearty back-slapping by middle-class England, which saw the Exhibition as a great project of imperial and cultural transference. As *Punch* put it, succumbing to Anglo-centrism himself, the Other nations were 'observing the advantages of British order', and might be seen 'shaking hands together, with JOHN BULL in their midst, instructing them in that only genuine mode of fraternising'.[40]

The attitudes of Thackeray and *Punch* towards the Great Exhibition were characterised by ambivalence. However, Thackeray consciously inscribes ambivalence, where *Punch* tends towards inconsistency and a jest for the moment. Thackeray avoided the political jibes used by *Punch*, to adopt a more humanistic response that hinted at the folly of any attempt to fix and stabilise the meanings of one's own culture for an alien audience. Most of Thackeray's *Punch* articles on the Great Exhibition (and many others) are written from the perspective of an alien Other, a foreign reporter or visitor who focuses on and interprets aspects of the Exhibition which satirise English pretensions. However, the comic voices he uses are also distinctly English stereotypes (caricatures of the Irish, French and Arab-Israeli), which further displaces the reader's reaction. This use of the double voice, in Bakhtinian terms an inscribing of both utterance and reception, of both Other and Self, in a dialogic form, is in contrast to the main *Punch* satire. Thackeray's work is self-reflexive and conscious of its own medium; the normative *Punch* voice is direct, unmediated discourse and obtains the authority of the *Punch* corporate voice.

It is probably the reputation of *The Times* that is responsible for Thackeray's most frequently remembered response to the Great Exhibition. The 'May-Day Ode' appeared in *The Times* for 1 May 1851 as an official Laureate-like offering to celebrate the opening of the Exhibition.[41] The language is enthusiastic and eulogistic, tinged with a moral deference towards higher powers of authority who sanction and make possible the event.

A peaceful place it was but now,
And lo! within its shining streets
A multitude of nations meets;
   A countless throng
I see beneath the crystal bow,
A Gaul and German, Russ and Turk,
Each with his native handiwork
   And busy tongue.
 ...

People and prince a silence keep!
Bow coronet and kingly crown,
Helmet and plume, bow lowly down,
   The while a priest,
Before the splendid portal step
(While still the wondrous banquet stays),
From Heaven supreme a blessing prays
   Upon the feast.
 ...

From Mississippi and from Nile –
From Baltic, Ganges, Bosphorus,
In England's ark assembled thus
   Are friend and guest.
Look down the mighty sunlit aisle,
And see the sumptuous banquet set,
The brotherhood of nations met
   Around the feast!
 ...

Swell, organ, swell your trumpet blast,
March, Queen and Royal pageant, march
By splendid aisle and springing arch
   Of this fair Hall:
And see! above the fabric vast,
God's boundless heaven is bending blue,
God's peaceful sunlight beaming through,
   And shines o'er all.[42]

The 'brotherhood of nations' message in Thackeray's poem is more typical of *Punch* and popular political rhetoric such as was to be found in *The Times*. One might suggest that Thackeray held out great hopes for the Exhibition, which were to alter and turn more critical as the year progressed. One might be unkind to him and suggest that he wrote such a piece merely for this particular newspaper market, if indeed there is anything immoral in writing for money as Thackeray was simultaneously denying in 'The Dignity of Literature' (12 January 1850) and 'Thunder and Small Beer' (5 January 1851). Furthermore, in his letters, Thackeray suggests that he was more intrigued by the popular effect of the Exhibition than by the collection itself: a typically Thackerayan reaction, placing the human response above the object observed.

> ... and as for the Exhibition wh. don't interest me at all so much, it was a noble awful great love inspiring goose flesh bringing sight ... of wh. no particular item is wonderful but the general effect the multitude the riches the peace the splendour the security the sunshine great to see – much grander than a coronation – the vastest & sublimest popular festival that the world has ever witnessed – What can one say about it but commonplaces?[43]

However, in the canon of Thackeray's works, the *Times*, poem perhaps ought to be read alongside the comic *Punch* verse, published a week earlier, entitled 'Mr. Molony's Account of the Crystal Palace', and also subsequently anthologised as simply 'The Crystal Palace'.[44]

> With ganial foire
> Thransfuse me loyre,
> Ye sacred nympths of Pindus,
> The whiole I sing
> That wondthrous thing,
> The Palace made o' windows!
> ...
> O would before
> That Thomas Moore,
> Likewoise the late Lord Boyron,
> Thim aigles sthrong
> Of godlike song,
> Cast oi on that cast oiron!
> ...
> There's statues bright
> Of marble white,
> Of silver, and of copper;
> And some in zinc,
> And some, I think,
> That isn't over proper.

There's staym ingynes,
That stands in lines,
Enormous and amazing,
That squeal and snort
Like whales in sport,
Or elephants a-grazing.

This is a more irreverent view of the Great Exhibition spoken from the perspective of an Irish observer–reporter (Molony was Thackeray's persona-author of several verses in *Punch*, but also of other pieces of journalism, such as 'Mr. Molony on the position of the Bar and Attorneys', *Punch* 21, 15 November 1851). In some ways, the poem is a clever parody of *The Times* verse, demonstrating an inherent ambivalence in Thackeray's view of the Crystal Palace as at one and the same time a place of awe and a place of absurdity. The verse technique of the Molony poem is similar to that of the 'May-Day Ode' and of other responses to the spectacle – a list of the artefacts, suggestive of the beholder's inability to comprehend the totality of the experience. A catalogue is the only means of holding together this diverse and visually overwhelming display.[45] The language invoked by Molony, beginning with a phonetic Classical parlance, burlesques the popular current encomiums in the press including Thackeray's own. I disagree with Christopher Morash's disparagement of the poem in which he comments that Thackeray 'could think of few things more humorous than an Irishman marvelling at the sights of the Crystal Palace'.[46] The disjunction of Anglo/Irish perspectives in the poem is not an accidental one between the 1851 Exhibition and the Irish Famine, but a deliberate rending of the line between the English/Subject's control of symbolic meaning, and the Irish/Other's unexpected reaction. Thackeray's poem is a sophisticated one because, in the context of its reception, it forces the predominantly English readers to reassess their position in relation to it. Do we stand along with the Irishman in awe and confusion? Or pretend to some fuller comprehension? The very technique of the poem, the comic list of miscellaneous objects and fragments of erudition (whales, elephants, various metals, Pindar, and, elsewhere, holy saints, pigs, toys, wheelbarrows, cabs, waggons, fans, shawls, Byron and Thomas Moore, and so on), provides both an actual and alternative collection which is recognisably the Exhibition itself.

It is this difference of response, this uncertainty of signification, that lies behind Thackeray's later recollection of the Exhibition in *The Four Georges* (written 1855–56, but published in 1860).
In 'George I', he asks:

> Any of you who were present, as myriads were, at that splendid
> pageant, the opening of our Crystal Palace in London, must have
> seen two noble lords, great officers of the household, with ancient
> pedigrees, with embroidered coats, and stars on their breasts and
> wands in their hands, walking backwards for near the space of a
> mile, while the royal procession made its progress. Shall we wonder
> – shall we be angry – shall we laugh at these old-world ceremonies?
> View them as you will, according to your mood; and with scorn or
> with respect, or with anger and sorrow, as your temper leads you. [47]

The reader's 'mood' will be varied, the response oppositional,
'with scorn or with respect'. For Thackeray, authority cannot fix
its own meaning or eradicate subversive receptions. Pageantry
can also be carnival in the Bahktinian sense (*The Four Georges*
rests upon such a view). Cultural assumptions differ, and hence
meanings will always proliferate.

Two of Thackeray's three main *Punch* articles on the Great
Exhibition appeared in the edition of 10 May 1851. 'What I
remarked at the Exhibition' (an unsigned first-person account)
and 'M. Gobemouche's Authentic Account of the Grand Exhibition' (purporting to be by a French reporter) offer two different
perspectives on the event, and demonstrate further this notion
that Thackeray was investing his reports with a conscious deconstruction of the grand narratives that the Exhibition generated
elsewhere. A passage from the first, describing the koh-i-noor
diamond, undercuts the significant symbolism surrounding this
particular object, one of the most talked about in the whole
Exhibition. For Thackeray's persona, the diamond is not what it
seems; indeed, it is not invested with its own visibility, but has to
be induced in its appearance/meaning.

> I remarked in the gold cage, to which the ladies would go the first
> thing, and in which the Koh-i-noor reposes, a shining thing like a
> lambent oyster, which I admired greatly, and took to be the famous
> jewel. But on a second visit I was told that that was not the jewel –
> that was only the case, and the real stone was that above, which I
> had taken to be an imitation in crystal.

> I remarked on this, that there are many sham diamonds in this
> life which pass for real, and, vice versa, many real diamonds which
> go unvalued. This accounts for the non-success of those real
> mountains of light, my 'Sonnets on Various Occasions'.[48]

For Thackeray, the diamond appears as a symbol of the whole
Exhibition, but the meaning it generates is one of the falseness or
fakery of the show. The 'imitation in crystal', which invokes the
Crystal Palace itself, promotes an ambivalence towards the object
viewed; it is apprehended as fake, but subsequently recognised as
genuine. The crystal is both sham and real simultaneously.
Furthermore, value is discovered not in the sham/real diamond,
but in the 'lambent oyster' case: perhaps again metaphorically to
stand for the building encasing the collections. Thackeray seems
to be questioning whether the Great Exhibition is actually the
palace or the contents. The moral of his observation ironically
asserts the subjective interpretation of the onlooker: the persona
is more concerned about finding an analogy that gives hope (and
advertisement) to his own ambitions (the 'Sonnets on Various
Occasions' also being of a type that was frequently published on
the 'occasion' of the Exhibition, including, of course, Thackeray's
own). No one escapes in Thackeray's satire. The Exhibition is
paired with the onlooker/persona's own self-aggrandisement,
and both are absurd but human. There is no stable position from
which to judge here; the sham and the real occupy the same space
because both carry equal authority and truth. This dialectical
relationship can never be resolved.

In his second piece, a report by the fictional French journalist,
M. Gobemouche, Thackeray again inscribes the opposition of
affirmation and critique. The florid style of the article acts as
parodic mimicry of the caricatured Frenchman's emotional
babble. Gobemouche's artistic pretensions emerge from his insistence on seeing design in even the poorest of representational
executions. However, the panoply of images and their allegorical
suggestiveness also mimics the designers of the Exhibition itself.
'What do I see around me?' Gobemouche asks on entering the
vestibule of the Exhibition, 'another magnificent allegory. The
cities of the world are giving each other hand ... a great idea this
– greatly worked out, in an art purposely naïve, in a design
expressly confused.'[49] The French reporter's uncritical eye (and

Thackeray's representation of his heightened enthusiasm) serves to satirise the naivety of the aim to represent world harmony and the poor quality of the attempt. The satire is double-edged. It takes the Frenchman as a target (as 'The Crystal Palace' does the Irishman), but it contains within it that deconstruction of the comfortable position of the reader-Englishman that is typical of Thackeray's longer fiction. The confusion of images undercuts the pretension of England to fix its own meanings to the Great Exhibition. Alongside World Harmony, Gobemouche also discovers some animosity: 'In everything the Briton does lies a deep meaning ... fiends, dragons, monsters, curl and writhe through the multitudinous hieroglyphic, and typify the fate that perhaps menaces the venomous enemies that empoison the country.'[50]

The Great Exhibition, then, operates through a kind of inverse anthropology: an attempt to establish English greatness through the meaning of her products and commodities, her 'gestures'. The meaning predicates the artefacts chosen as representative of Englishness and English industry, rather than, as in anthropology, the artefact being used as the starting point for the defining of racial character. As Foucault said, in *The Order of Things*, 'man's behaviour appears as an attempt to say something; his slightest gestures ... have a meaning; and everything he arranges around him by way of objects, rites, customs, discourse, all the traces he leaves behind him, constitute a coherent whole and a system of signs'.[51] For Thackeray, there is a flaw in the anthropological design – Self and Other have different priorities, different cultural values, and will thus produce different Self-orientated interpretations and meanings. There is a more scathing irony at work in 'M. Gobemouche's Authentic Account of the Grand Exhibition': he is not even at the correct Exhibition! The 'authenticity' is as correct as the appellation 'Grand'. Gobemouche, probably led by his stomach and gormandising lifestyle, has reported on Alexis Soyer's alternative 'Great Exhibition', called the 'Gastronomic Symposium of all Nations', at nearby Gore House, opposite Hyde Park. Thackeray was painted on the wall of Soyer's palace (really a restaurant) amongst various modern-day luminaries, by G. A. Sala.[52] He visited both 'Soyer's Symposium and the Christial Palace' on the same day.[53] The joke is not just on the Frenchman – it is also on us and the real Exhibition designers. Once again,

producing munificent readings of the signs of 1851 is a precarious
business.

There is no stable position to be found. Who is to say what is
absurd? Who escapes critical censure? Not even the critic.
Thackeray's reporting of the Great Exhibition is of the same
journalistic school as the observations in 'The Snobs of England.
By One of Themselves' of the *Punch* of 1846. Thackeray's double
article of 27 September and 4 October 1851 introduced a near-
Eastern context for the Great Exhibition. The first piece, 'Panorama of the Inglese', presents a representation of the West, and
'Lundoon' in particular, constructed by Hadjee Aboo Bosh from
items collected on his travels. The article is purported to be reprinted from the *Beyrout Banner*, *Joppa Intelligencer*, and *Jerusalem
Journal*, a parody of the newspaper format. The description of
London features of course the Great Exhibition, 'the prodigious
Castle of Crystal and pavilion of light'.[54] The misnomer is again
double-edged: the Arab-Israeli traveller is an unreliable commentator, but the Exhibition too has failed to fix its name and its
meaning. The English perspective on the Exhibition is decentred,
and meaning is mediated back to the English public by a voice
that does not partake of the national self-conceit of the English
press. Thackeray is careful to make his fictional reporters praise
the Exhibition. But their overtures work in detriment to the stated
intentions of the event. Here, however, the dialectic also engages
Arab nationalism and Arab self-interest. In a sense, it is sameness
and not Otherness that Thackeray stresses. The reporter's
description is absurd and almost hysterical, the exaggeration of
the traveller, but also a mirror of the exaggerated pride that England
would like to provoke. It also remains, though, an indication of
the Englishman's caricatured view of the Arab. The Palace:

> is many miles long, and in height several furlongs. It is built of rock
> crystal and steel, without putty, wood, bricks, or nails ... This palace
> was built in a single night by an enchanter named Paxtoon. This
> wonderful man possesses all the secrets of nature; he can make a
> melon in ten minutes grow as big as a camel.[55]

Of the interior:

> All the treasures of the world are there, surely. Ten hundred and
> ten thousand persons come thither daily, and they all go first to see

the saddles and embroidery, from Beyrout. What arcades of splendour! What fountains! What images! The tallest trees grow in this palace. The birds cannot fly to the roof: it is so high.[56]

In the second part, the behaviour of a typical English family, 'whom Aboo Bosh has brought with him', is so upsetting to the Arab onlookers that they close the Exhibition and leave in outrage. Thackeray creates a satirical portrait of an English family at breakfast and dressing for dinner, with suitable comments from the Arab reporter in consultation with his Interpreter which reveal their cultural differences (such as the men only having one wife, a shameless display of baldness, reading the newspaper, women's freedoms, and an evening ball). 'All the principles of morality are violated' cries the Governor of Beyrout at the end of the piece, and the Exhibition closes.[57] This final article reverses the expectations of the Exhibition; the English self-revelation innocently causes offence by violating the cultural proprieties of another people. As with the alternative exhibition at Soyer's Symposium, Hadjee Aboo Bosh's exhibition offers another perspective on the Crystal Palace. It entwines the absurdity of the English and the strangeness of the Other, but suggests again that the attempt to stabilise cultural meaning ignores the complexities of cultural difference. The relationship between exhibitor and onlooker, between presentation and interpretation, each deriving meaning from the 'images' on display, is fraught with ambiguity and uncertainty. For Thackeray, the very process of Exhibition exemplifies human vanity and folly.

Although Thackeray's Great Exhibition writings mostly appeared in *Punch* and were thus part of that magazine's collage of perspectives on the festivities, they are sufficiently different from the rest of that reporting to make the drawing of distinctions pertinent. The voices of Douglas Jerrold, Mark Lemon,[58] and others, squarely politicise their arguments around the discourses of class, gender and race. They offer antagonistic responses to the platitudes of the day. But they also find the Exhibition worthwhile, appealing, fascinating and, above all, popular. However, in most if not all of their articles, they cannot avoid positioning England in opposition to the foreignness of international exhibitors and visitors. Thackeray tries to avoid this; indeed, he tries to satirise reporting that falls into this position. His is a dual voice. His satire encompasses journalist and exhibition, authority and subject, self and other. He inscribes ambivalence in the self-reflexivity of his sketches.

The 'human spectacle' and human responses to the Great Exhibition are more significant to Thackeray and *Punch* than the actual objects on display. For both, in many ways, the Exhibition offers a chance to glimpse humanity in microcosm – all races and classes, and both sexes, accommodated under the same transparent roof. They are all observable, all contained, in what *Punch* thinks of as a great zoo. Neither Thackeray nor *Punch* swallowed the government political spin that the Exhibition would smooth over the disharmonies of the 1840s. However, Thackeray is less satirical at the expense of the Exhibition itself and of those behind it. His short articles aim to establish the common faults of humanity in looking at itself. He is looking at both the onlooker and the looked-at: at the Other and at the English. He never leaves himself entirely out of the equation; in part, his comic journalists are comic versions of himself and his colleagues too. His response to the Exhibition is ambivalent, but in a positive way. He wants to celebrate, and yet sees the comedy of celebration. For him, making an exhibition of oneself carries two meanings, and his articles explore both of these. The Great Exhibition is simultaneously a genuine act of human concern (to bring together, to shake hands) and a sham act of self-aggrandisement. Self and Other are always interconnected.

Punch, on the other hand, retains a political agenda in all of its reporting, and uses the exhibition to attack class inequalities, the brutalities of other countries, and the naivety of the symbolic design of the Great Exhibition itself as imagined by its creators. Nevertheless, it cannot forget that popular opinion finds the Exhibition exciting and amazing and *Punch*, in the end, cannot escape the popular nationalist rhetoric of dominant Great Exhibition commentaries.

Notes

1 See R. G. G. Price, *A History of Punch* (London: Collins, 1957), p. 79.

2 Thackeray's comment on Jerrold is cited in Price, *Punch*, p. 50, and see J. Carey, *Thackeray: Prodigal Genius* (London: Faber, 1977), p. 19; R. Altick notes how 'Jerrold railed week after week against corrupt classes, institutions, and doctrines' in his editorial 'Q' papers for *Punch* (R. D. Altick, *Punch: The Lively Youth of a British Institution, 1841–1851* (Columbus: Ohio State University Press, 1997), p. 188); Thackeray's earlier journalism disavowed a focus on politics for the 'lightness' of a satirical humanism.

3 Cited in P. Shillingsburg, *Pegasus in Harness: Victorian Publishing and W. M. Thackeray* (Charlottesville and London: University Press of Virginia, 1992), p. 82; the letter is to his publisher, F. M. Evans, and dated March 1855.

4 See C. Bongie, *Exotic Memories: Literature, Colonialism, and the Fin de Siècle* (Stanford: Stanford University Press, 1991), p. 64.

5 For various recent interpretations of the Great Exhibition, tending to stress the materialist and ideological significance of the event, see S. Johansen, 'The Great Exhibition of 1851: a precipice in time?', *Victorian Review* 22:1 (Summer 1996), pp. 59–64; P. Landon, 'Great Exhibitions: representations of the Crystal Palace in Mayhew, Dickens, and Dostoevsky', *Nineteenth-Century Contexts* 20 (1997), pp. 27–59; A. Miller, *Novels Behind Glass: Commodity Culture and Victorian Narrative* (Cambridge: Cambridge University Press, 1995); T. Richards, *The Commodity Culture of Victorian England: Advertising and Spectacle, 1851–1914* (Stanford: Stanford University Press, 1990).

6 'Specimens from Mr. Punch's Industrial Exhibition of 1850 (to be improved in 1851)', *Punch* 18 (1850), p. 145; see also the illustration entitled 'The Happy Family in Hyde Park', reprinted in Miller, *Novels*, p. 59, from *Punch* 21 (1851), p. 38 (Miller's pagination for this is incorrect).

7 J. Leech, 'The shipwrecked ministers saved by the Great Exhibition steamer', *Punch* 20 (1851), p. 237.

8 Cited in Altick, *Punch*, p. 122; see Altick's chapter on 'Political caricature'.

9 Altick, *Punch*, p. 149.

10 D. Kunzle, 'Between broadsheet caricature and 'Punch'': cheap newspaper cuts for the lower classes in the 1830s', *Art-Journal* (Winter 1983), 'The Issue of Caricature', ed. J. Wechsler, pp. 339, 346. See also D. Donald, *The Age of Caricature: Satirical Prints in the Reign of George III* (New Haven: Yale University Press, 1996), pp. 1–2, 198.

11 M. H. Spielmann, *The History of 'Punch'* (London: Cassell, 1895), p. 111.

12 *Ibid.*, p. 51.

13 'The last night in the Crystal palace', *Punch* 21 (1851), pp. 174–5.

14 J. Leech, 'The great Derby race for eighteen hundred and fifty-one', *Punch* 20 (1851), pp. 214–15.

15 'Morals of the Great Exhibition', *Punch* 20 (1851), p. 233.

16 *Ibid.*

17 *Punch* was 'Radical' in a broad and generally inconsistent sense, and derived much of its anti-authoritarianism in the 1840s from Douglas Jerrold's writings; it remained sympathetic to working-class issues, but was not Chartist. By 1851, the satire had become more mainstream and middle class in tone whilst remaining critical of government policies. Altick suggests that '"radical" meant only that [*Punch*] was in some respects proudly, defiantly, out of step with the orthodox social and political thinking of the time … [it] vehemently expressed dissatisfaction over a few or many aspects of contemporary society', Altick, *Punch*, p. 186.

18 J. Leech, 'The Pound and the Shilling', *Punch* 20 (1851), p. 247; for illustration, see S. Edwards, 'The accumulation of knowledge or, William Whewell's eye' in this volume, pp. 000 000.

19 *Punch* uses the paper cap elsewhere to represent the 'intelligent artisans' of the British workforce: see the illustration of 'The French Socialist Leading the British Lion', *Punch* 20 (1851), p. 159 (and the letterpress on p. 157).

20 'The shilling days at the Crystal Palace', *Punch* 20 (1851), p. 240.

21 *Ibid.*

22 'The Looking-Glass Department of the Great Exhibition', *Punch's Almanack for 1851*, 20 (1851), [p. ix].

23 'The front row of the shilling gallery', *Punch* 21 (1851), pp. 10–12.

24 *Ibid.*, p. 10.

25 *Ibid.*

26 'Preface to the twentieth volume', *Punch* 20 (1851), p. iv.

27 See J. Dodds, *The Age of Paradox: A Biography of England, 1841–1851* (London: Victor Gollancz, 1953), pp. 461–2.

28 J. Leech, 'Closing of the Exhibition', *Punch* 21 (1851), p. 161; Professor A. Kiss's 'Amazon' was sculpted in 1846 and depicted a female warrior on horseback beating off a panther; Hiram Power's 'Greek Slave' was a famous nude statue from the same year; see Dodds, *The Age of Paradox*, pp. 261 and 465.

29 'Where are the foreigners?', *Punch* 20 (1851), p. 207.

30 *Ibid.*

31 Several journals of the day worried over the influx of dangerous foreigners and the potential violence inherent in the visit of working classes from other parts of the country; see R. D. Altick, *The Presence of the Present* (Columbus: Ohio State University Press, 1991), p. 422, and Altick, *Punch*, pp. 622–3.

32 'Where are the foreigners?', *Punch* 20 (1851), p. 207.

33 'The Cosmopolitan before and after the Exhibition', *Punch* 21 (1851), p. 44.

34 *Ibid.*

35   'America in crystal', *Punch* 20 (1851), p. 209.

36   'Sample of American manufacture', *Punch* 20 (1851), p. 209; see also the drawing of 'The Virginian slave', *Punch* 20 (1851), p. 236, which replaces the Greek slave girl with an instance of contemporary slavery.

37   'Preface', *Punch* 20 (1851), p. iii.

38   *Ibid.*, p. iv.

39   Thackeray joined *Punch* in 1843 (though he followed it closely from its founding in 1841), and resigned in 1851; see G. N. Ray, *Thackeray: The Uses of Adversity, 1811–46* and *The Age of Wisdom: 1847–63* (New York: McGraw-Hill, 1955 and 1958).

40   'Visions in the crystal', *Punch* 20 (1851), p. 188; Edgar Harden, *A Checklist of Contributions made by William Makepeace Thackeray to Newspapers, Periodicals, Books, and Serial Part Issues, 1828–1864* (Victoria: University of Victoria, 1996), p. 87, lists the illustration to this article as possibly by Thackeray.

41   Thackeray found the poem difficult to write, and humorously described his obsessive 'tidumtidytidumtidy' rhyme in a letter to Mrs Brookfield, 29 April 1851; G. N. Ray (ed.), *The Letters and Private Papers of W. M. Thackeray*, 4 vols (Cambridge: Harvard University Press, 1945–46), vol. II, p. 767.

42   'May-Day Ode', *The Works of William Makepeace Thackeray*, 26 vols (London: Smith, Elder & Co., 1894), vol. XXI, pp. 43–7.

43   Letter to Mrs Brookfield, 1 May 1851; *Letters*, II, p. 768.

44   'The Crystal Palace', *Punch* 20 (26 April 1851), p. 171.

45   See, for example, Miller, *Novels*, pp. 62–3.

46   C. Morash, *Writing the Irish Famine* (Oxford: Clarendon, 1995), pp. 53–4.

47   'George I', *Works*, XXIII, pp. 13–14.

48   'What I remarked at the Great Exhibition', *Punch* 20 (1851), p. 189.

49   'M. Gobemouche's authentic account of the Grand Exhibition', *Punch* 20 (1851), p. 198.

50   *Ibid.*

51   M. Foucault, *The Order of Things: An Archaeology of the Human Sciences* (New York: Vintage, 1973), p. 357.

52   Dodds, *Paradox*, p. 468.

53   Letter to Mrs Brookfield, 29 April 1851; *Letters*, II, p. 767.

54   'A Panorama of the Inglese', Punch 21 (1851), pp. 138–9.

55   *Ibid.*, p. 139.

56   *Ibid.*

57   'An Ingleez Family', *Punch* 21(1851), pp. 147–8.

58   Altick, *Punch*, p. 197, describes how Lemon's 'invective' could rival that of Jerrold at times.

Notes on contributors

RAFAEL CARDOSO DENIS is Assistant Professor at the Pontifica Universidade Catoloica in Rio de Janerio, Brazil, and Adjunct Professor (visiting) at the Universidade do Estado do Rio de Janerio. He is co-editor of *Art and the Academy in the Nineteeth Century* (Manchester University Press, 2000) and has published numerous articles on Victorian art and design education.

STEVE EDWARDS is Research Lecturer at the Open University. His work examines the relationship between photography, art and industry. He has published in British and American art journals, including *Art History*, *Oxford Art Journal* and *The Art Journal*. He is the editor of *Art and its Histories* (Yale University Press, 1999).

PETER GURNEY took his D.Phil. at the University of Sussex and is presently Lecturer in Social History at the University of Essex. Author of *Co-operative Culture and the Politics of Consumption in England, 1870–1930* (Manchester University Press, 1996), he has also published on a number of other subjects including, '"Intersex" and "Dirty Girls": mass-observation and working-class sexuality in England in the 1930s', *Journal of the History of Sexuality*, Fall 1997. He is currently working on the development of mass consumerism in Britain since World War Two.

LARA KRIEGEL is an Assistant Professor of History at Florida International University. After receiving her Ph.D. from the Johns Hopkins University in 1999, she held a Postdoctoral Fellowship at Brown University for Teaching and Research on Women. She is currently working on a book manuscript entitled *Britain by Design: Industrial Culture, Imperial Display and the Making of South Kensington*.

BRIAN MAIDMENT is Professor of English at the University of Salford. He is author of *The Poorhouse Fugitives* (1987) and *Reading Popular Prints 1790–1870* (Manchester University Press, 1996) as well as many articles on Victorian mass literary production.

RICHARD PEARSON has taught nineteenth-century literature at University College Worcester since 1992. He edited *The W. M. Thackeray Library* (Routledge/ Thoemmes Press, 1996) and has just completed a study of Thackeray, *W.M. Thackeray and the Mediated Text* (Ashgate Press, 2000).

LOUISE PURBRICK is Lecturer in Art and Design History at the University of Brighton. She works on industrial and material culture. She has published articles on patent law and the Great Exhibition of 1851, industrial drawing, the South Kensington Museum, and civic portraiture.

Select bibliography

Allwood, J., *The Great Exhibitions* (London: Studio Vista, 1977)

Altick, R., *The Shows of London* (Cambridge: Harvard University Press, 1978)

Auerbach, J. A., *The Great Exhibition of 1851. A Nation on Display* (New Haven and London: Yale University Press, 1999)

Bailey, P., *Leisure and Class in Victorian England: Rational Recreation and the Contest for Control, 1830-1885* (London: Croom Helm, 1978)

Barringer, T., 'The South Kensington Museum and the colonial project' in T. Barringer and T. Flynn (eds), *Colonialism and the Object. Empire, Material Culture and the Museum* (London: Routledge, 1998), pp. 11–27

Beaver, P., *The Crystal Palace* (London: Hugh Evelyn, 1970)

Bedarida, F., *A Social History of England 1851–1975* (London and New York: Methuen, 1979)

Bennett, T., *The Birth of the Museum* (London: Routledge, 1995)

Berman, M., *All That Is Solid Melts Into Air. The Experience of Modernity* (London: Verso, 1983)

Best, G., *Mid-Victorian Britain. 1851–1875* (London: Weidenfeld and Nicolson, 1971)

Bird, A., *Paxton's Palace* (London: Cassell, 1976)

Bowlby, R., *Just Looking. Consumer Culture in Dreiser, Gissing and Zola* (New York and London: Methuen, 1985)

Breckenridge, C., 'The aesthetics and politics of colonial collecting: India at world's fairs', *Comparative Studies of Society and History*, 31 (April, 1989), pp. 195–216

Briggs, A., *Victorian People. A Reassessment of Persons and Themes 1851–67* (Middlesex: Penguin, 1967)

Briggs, A., *Victorian Things* (London: Penguin, 1990)

Burton, A., *At the Heart of Empire: Indians and the Colonial Encounter in Late Victorian Britain* (Berkeley: University of California Press, 1998)

Coombes, A. E., *Reinventing Africa. Museums, Material Culture and Popular Imagination* (Yale: Yale University Press, 1994)

Coulson, A. J., *A Bibliography of Design in Britain 1851–1970* (London: Design Council, 1979)

Cunningham, H., *Leisure in the Industrial Revolution 1780—1880* (London: Croom Helm, 1980)

Davis, J. R., *The Great Exhibition* (Stroud: Sutton Publishing, 1999)

Debord, G., *Society of the Spectacle* (Detroit: Black and Red, 1983)

Denis, R. Cardoso, 'Teaching by example: education and the formation of the South Kensington Museums', in M. Baker and B. Richardson (eds), *A Grand Design: The Art of the Victoria and Albert Museum* (London: V&A Publications, 1997), pp. 107–16

Fay, C. R., *Palace of Industry, 1851* (Cambridge: Cambridge University Press, 1951)

Ffrench, Y., *The Great Exhibition: 1851* (London: Harvill Press, 1951)

Findling, J. E., *Historical Dictionary of World's Fairs and Expositions, 1851–1988* (New York: Greenwood Press, 1990)

Forty, A., *Objects of Desire* (London: Thames and Hudson, 1986)

Gibbs-Smith, C. H., *The Great Exhibition of 1851* (London: HMSO, 1951)

Golby, J. and S. Meikle, *The Great Exhibition and Re-reading 'Hard Times'* (Milton Keynes: Open University, 1986)

Greenhalgh, P., 'Education, entertainment and politics: lessons from the Great Exhibitions', in P. Vergo (ed.), *New Museology* (London: Reaction Press, 1988), pp. 74–98

Greenhalgh, P., *Ephemeral Vistas. The Expositions Universelles and World Fairs, 1851–1939* (Manchester: Manchester University Press, 1988)

Harvie, C., G. Martin and A. Scharf (eds), *Industrialisation and Culture 1830–1914* (London: Macmillan, 1970)

Hasam, A., 'Portable iron structures and the uncertain colonial spaces at the Sydenham Crystal Palace', in F. Driver and D. Gilbert (eds), *Imperial Cities* (Manchester: Manchester University Press, 1999), pp. 174–93

Hinsley, C. M., 'The world as marketplace: commodification of the exotic at the World's Colombian Exposition, Chicago, 1893', in I. Karp and S. D. Lavine (eds), *Exhibiting Cultures. The Poetics and Politics of Museum Display* (Washington and London: Smithsonian Institute Press, 1991), pp. 344–65

Hix, J., *The Glass House* (Cambridge, Mass: MIT Press, 1974)

Hobhouse, C., *1851 and the Crystal Palace* (London: John Murray, 1950)

Johansen, S., 'The Great Exhibition of 1851: a precipice in time?', *Victorian Review* 22:1 (Summer 1996), pp. 59–64

Klingender, F. D., *Art and the Industrial Revolution* (Chatham: Evelyn, Adams and Mackay, 1968)

Kusamitsu, T., 'Great Exhibitions before 1851', *History Workshop Journal* 9 (1980), pp. 70–89

Landon, P., 'Great Exhibitions: representations of the Crystal Palace in Mayhew, Dickens, and Dostoevsky', *Nineteenth-Century Contexts* 20 (1997), pp. 27–59

Luckhurst, K., *The Great Exhibition of 1851: Three Cantor Lectures by Kenneth Luckhurst Delivered in 1951* (London: Royal Society of Arts, 1951)

Luckhurst, K., *The Story of the Exhibitions* (London: Studio, 1951)

Miller, A. H., *Novels Behind Glass: Commodity Culture and Victorian Narrative* (Cambridge: Cambridge University Press, 1995)

Mitchell, T., 'Orientalism and the exhibitionary Other', in N. Dirks (ed.), *Colonialism and Culture* (Ann Arbor: University of Michigan Press, 1992), pp. 289–318

Morris, R. J., 'Leeds and the Crystal Palace', *Victorian Studies* 13 (1970), pp. 283–300

Nesbitt, M., 'Ready-made originals: the Duchamp model' *October* 37 (summer 1986), pp. 53–75

Nowell-Smith, S., *The House of Cassell 1848–1958* (London: Cassell, 1958)

Pevsner, N., *High Victorian Design. A Study of the Exhibits of 1851* (London: Architectural Press, 1951)

Pevsner, N., *Pioneers of Modern Design* (Middlesex: Penguin, 1960)

Pevsner, N., *The Sources of Modern Architecture and Design* (London: Thames and Hudson, 1968)

Price, R. G. G., *A History of Punch* (London: Collins, 1957)

Purbrick, L., 'South Kensington Museum: the building of the house of Henry Cole', in M. Pointon (ed.), *Art Apart. Art Institutions and Ideology across England and North America* (Manchester: Manchester University Press, 1994), pp. 69–86

Richards, T., *The Commodity Culture of Victorian England. Advertising and Spectacle. 1851–1914* (London: Verso, 1990)

Rifkin, A., 'Success disavowed: the Schools of Design in mid-nineteenth century Britain (an allegory)', *Journal of Design History* 1:2 (1988), pp. 89–102

Scharf, A., *Art and Industry* (Bletchley: Open University Press, 1971)

Short, A., 'Workers under glass in 1851', *Victorian Studies* 10 (1966), pp. 193–202

Slater, D., *Consumer Culture and Modernity* (Cambridge: Polity Press, 1997)

Sparling, T. A., *The Great Exhibition: a Question of Taste* (New Haven: Yale Center for British Art, 1982)

Steegman, J., *Consort of Taste 1830-1870* (London: Sidgwick and Jackson, 1950).

Stewart, S., *On Longing: Narratives of the Miniature, the Gigantic, the Souvenir and the Collection* (Baltimore and London: Johns Hopkins University Press, 1984)

Index